Creative Thinking
FOR
DUMMIES®

by David Cox

WILEY

A John Wiley and Sons, Ltd, Publication

Creative Thinking For Dummies®

Published by:
John Wiley & Sons, Ltd.,
The Atrium,
Southern Gate,
Chichester,
www.wiley.com

This edition first published 2013

© 2013 John Wiley & Sons, Ltd, Chichester, West Sussex.

Registered office

John Wiley & Sons Ltd, The Atrium, Southern Gate, Chichester, West Sussex, PO19 8SQ, United Kingdom

For details of our global editorial offices, for customer services and for information about how to apply for permission to reuse the copyright material in this book please see our website at www.wiley.com.

The right of the author to be identified as the author of this work has been asserted in accordance with the Copyright, Designs and Patents Act 1988.

All rights reserved. No part of this publication may be reproduced, stored in a retrieval system, or transmitted, in any form or by any means, electronic, mechanical, photocopying, recording or otherwise, except as permitted by the UK Copyright, Designs and Patents Act 1988, without the prior permission of the publisher.

Wiley publishes in a variety of print and electronic formats and by print-on-demand. Some material included with standard print versions of this book may not be included in e-books or in print-on-demand. If this book refers to media such as a CD or DVD that is not included in the version you purchased, you may download this material at http://booksupport.wiley.com. For more information about Wiley products, visit www.wiley.com.

Designations used by companies to distinguish their products are often claimed as trademarks. All brand names and product names used in this book are trade names, service marks, trademarks or registered trademarks of their respective owners. The publisher is not associated with any product or vendor mentioned in this book.

LIMIT OF LIABILITY/DISCLAIMER OF WARRANTY: WHILE THE PUBLISHER AND AUTHOR HAVE USED THEIR BEST EFFORTS IN PREPARING THIS BOOK, THEY MAKE NO REPRESENTATIONS OR WARRANTIES WITH THE RESPECT TO THE ACCURACY OR COMPLETENESS OF THE CONTENTS OF THIS BOOK AND SPECIFICALLY DISCLAIM ANY IMPLIED WARRANTIES OF MERCHANTABILITY OR FITNESS FOR A PARTICULAR PURPOSE. IT IS SOLD ON THE UNDERSTANDING THAT THE PUBLISHER IS NOT ENGAGED IN RENDERING PROFESSIONAL SERVICES AND NEITHER THE PUBLISHER NOR THE AUTHOR SHALL BE LIABLE FOR DAMAGES ARISING HEREFROM. IF PROFESSIONAL ADVICE OR OTHER EXPERT ASSISTANCE IS REQUIRED, THE SERVICES OF A COMPETENT PROFESSIONAL SHOULD BE SOUGHT.

For general information on our other products and services, please contact our Customer Care Department within the U.S. at 877-762-2974, outside the U.S. at (001) 317-572-3993, or fax 317-572-4002. For technical support, please visit www.wiley.com/techsupport.

A catalogue record for this book is available from the British Library.

ISBN 978-1-118-38157-1 (pbk), ISBN 978-1-118-38162-5 (ebk), ISBN 978-1-118-38161-8 (ebk), ISBN 978-1-118-38163-2 (ebk)

Printed in Great Britain by Bell and Bain Ltd, Glasgow

WILEY

Creative Thinking

FOR

DUMMIES®

Contents at a Glance

Table of Contents

Part II: Preparing Yourself: Creating Your Creative Mindset 71

Introduction

∙∙

*W*hether you're designing a time-travel machine or experimenting with a new recipe, you're thinking creatively. From the most exotic invention to the most mundane domestic chore, creative thinking is an integral part of the process.

You grew up being creative. Before your earliest memories, you were busy exploring the world and discovering new and ingenious ways to get what you wanted and overcome the problems you encountered.

Creative thinking is hard-wired. If you don't think you're creative, it's only because you've let your creative fires die down. But it's easy to stoke them up again, and that's what this book is for.

Diarist Samuel Pepys said, 'When a man is tired of London, he is tired of life.' Well, creativity is the London of the mind. And creative thinking is the mechanism that gives you the energy to explore it. Children are endlessly curious, and as adults we can all re-kindle our creativity by being curious about the world.

About This Book

The focus of this book is on creative thinking. You already think creatively whenever you face a new challenge, whether that's the need to solve a problem that requires some ingenuity or fresh thinking, or the need to come up with a new idea. You may just want to examine a situation from an original perspective. Each time creative thinking comes into play, you're doing something you haven't done before or going somewhere you haven't been before.

Creative thinking is hard-wired into everyone. It's part of the rich repertoire provided by your marvellous brain. Creative thinking is a journey of discovery that everyone takes to a greater or lesser extent. I intend this book to provide some sign-posts along the way.

The wheel, the axe and the art of making fire were all the result of creative acts, and they confirm that creativity has always been at the heart of human life. Each of those acts was the result of a creative thought.

Did those individuals experience that moment of enlightenment when something magically clicks into place and you get it? Did they each work through a creative process, arriving at the solution through inspirational thought? Or did they work as teams, bouncing ideas around? We shall never know how they did it, but the creative thinking processes that may have contributed to those early inventions are available to everyone today.

Creativity is one of our defining characteristics, along with language. You're already thinking creatively in your day-to-day life, and however creative you are now, you can find ways to further enhance and refine your creative abilities in this book.

This book is full of people. Individuals who have been there and done it are the source of most of the examples. I make no apology for this, because creative thinking is an intensely personal experience. Creativity is about people and what they do.

Conventions Used in This Book

To help you navigate through this book, I've used the following conventions:

- ✔ *Italic* is used for emphasis and to identify new terms or words that are defined.
- ✔ **Boldface** text is used to identify the action part of numbered steps.

What You're Not to Read

I hope you'll want to read everything between the covers, but you can skip a couple of items if you wish:

- ✔ **Text in sidebars:** These are the shaded boxes that appear here and there. They feature a number of stories and observations for your interest, but they're not essential reading.
- ✔ **The copyright page:** I'm afraid there's nothing creative about this page, and it won't contribute to your creative development.
- ✔ **Text marked with technical-stuff icons:** This information is about the nitty-gritty details that you may be interested in . . . but you may not.

Foolish Assumptions

I've made the assumption that you're reading this book because you're a naturally creative human being with an interest in what creative thinking is and how it works. If it's not presumptuous, I've also assumed the following:

- ✔ You know you're already creative, and you'd like to learn more tools and techniques.
- ✔ You're interested in how you can become more creative.
- ✔ You'd like to learn about how other creative individuals think and behave.
- ✔ You're interested in incorporating creative thinking into your work, study and personal life.

How This Book Is Organised

This book is divided into five parts, which include 17 chapters. The table of contents lists all the headings, to help you find all the bits that interest you quickly and easily.

Part 1: Laying the Foundations: Understanding Creativity

You're already living in a creative world, and this is where you explore your own creativity amid creative abundance. You learn how you're hard-wired for music and other kinds of creativity. You take an excursion into politics and creativity. And you get under the surface of how your creative mind works. You also delve into the darker side of creativity.

Part II: Preparing Yourself: Creating Your Creative Mindset

This is where you get into the spirit of creative thinking. Here you discover how to develop a creative mindset and place it centre stage. You also explore the principles for creative living established by Leonardo da Vinci.

Part III: Getting Creative – The Practical Stuff

This part is all about the tools and techniques for facilitating your creative thinking. Here you discover some of the best tools for opening your mind when you want to generate ideas. You have processes for closing in on the solutions to problems. You can change your mind with mapping, language and visualisation techniques. And I explore creative play.

Part IV: Applying Creativity to Your Life

This is where you find the benefits of living the creative life. You see the central role of happiness and humour in creativity. You learn about the natural creativity of children. And you take your creativity to work.

Part V: The Part of Tens

Here you can pick up information on several key topics. You find top tips for getting creative. You discover some examples of acorns that creative thinkers grew into oak trees. I introduce some essential books to help you think creatively. And you also get a glimpse inside ten inspirational creative businesses and individuals.

Icons Used in This Book

The icons in this book help you find particular kinds of information that may be useful to you:

This icon highlights useful information on creative thinking.

This icon indicates a useful reminder for you.

This icon alerts you to jargon and technical stuff you don't necessarily need to read.

This icon warns you not to attempt something in your enthusiasm for thinking or acting creatively.

Where to Go from Here

Creative thinking involves exploring the unknown. You can read this book from cover to cover. Or you may just want to dip into sections that take your fancy and see where they lead you.

Throughout this book, I offer plenty of hints and tips to help you explore your own creative thinking processes.

Part I
Laying the Foundations: Understanding Creativity

The 5th Wave   By Rich Tennant

SINCE INSTALLING PHOTOSHOP, THE POLICE FORCE BECAME NOTED FOR ITS CREATIVE WANTED POSTERS

"Ooo-look! Sgt. Rodriguez has the felon's head floating in a teacup!"

In this part...

1 introduce you to the world of creativity, and you start your journey exploring a world of creative abundance. Find what inspires creativity. Discover how you're hard-wired for music and other kinds of creative activity. Explore how creative thinking is used politically. Get under the surface of how your creative mind works. And catch a glimpse of the darker side of creativity.

Chapter 1

So What Is Creativity?

*C*reativity – a difficult thing to define, but perhaps in its simplest form the act of generating ideas – is at the very heart of human experience. The world is full of creative activity, so wherever you go and whatever you do, you're in reach of it. Creativity takes many forms – from humble products to grand designs, from the simplest crafts to the highest art – and no two people will define it in exactly the same way. There's always something to celebrate.

But creativity is about much more than passive appreciation. You were born creative and you have all the resources you need to partake actively in the abundance of creativity around you.

In some places and situations, creativity is obvious. And sometimes it's under the radar. But it's always there. You're in touch with it daily, whether you notice it at a conscious level or not. As you look around at the products you use and the ideas you work or play with, you're experiencing the flow of creativity that makes modern life possible.

Seeing Creativity Everywhere

Creativity isn't just about 'arty' things. It's manifested in every man-made object. Original works of art and mass-produced products are all the result of creative imagination and an individual's unique ability to turn thoughts into reality. And creativity isn't just about objects, it's also about ideas. Whatever your politics, spiritual beliefs, intellectual preoccupations or personal passions, each object is the result of the creative evolution of original ideas.

Take a moment to consider something you feel passionate about. It may be a sport, a belief or a personal preoccupation. Consider why you feel so strongly about it. Think about how 'real' it feels to you. Now take a step back and recall what first excited your interest here. What was the path that brought you to where you are now? Who first inspired you? Who inspires you now? Those are all elements of the creative thinking that brought this passion into your life.

Spotting obvious signs of creativity

When you watch a film or the television, listen to music or use a computer, you're in direct touch with creative thinking. All those films, songs and software packages began with the germ of an idea. Many people just experience the end product, which is fine because that's what the creator intended.

It can be fascinating to go deeper, though, and consider how the product originated. Some individuals take pleasure in seeking out the processes behind the finished article. Doing so is one way to enhance your own appreciation of the creative process.

Creativity in your hands

This book, whether you're reading a hard copy or an electronic format, is the product of several centuries of creative development.

A few hundred years ago, you may, if you were lucky, have had access to a manuscript or a public proclamation in your village. Unless you were a priest or a member of a small coterie of scholars, you were probably denied the luxury of reading. Gradually, education led to wider familiarity with reading skills, and this in turn created a demand for access to the written word.

By the time Gutenberg came onto the scene, the world was ready. His printing press came about, by his own account, through a flash of inspiration in which he combined the agricultural press with the concept of moveable type. The essential third ingredient was oil-based ink, and together these elements gave the world the printing press. This is a classic illustration of creative thinking, where disparate existing concepts are combined to create something entirely original.

Fast-forward to the present day and modern printing, which is the culmination of countless creative insights and refinements to this original process. It's impossible to imagine a world without printing. The ability to publish came about through generations of creative ingenuity.

Selling High Concept

Hollywood likes originality, but not too much. Many ideas for films are pitched in terms of what's called the *high concept*. This means existing stories or actors are juxtaposed to create a new entity. Examples include *Jurassic Park* (what if you were able to clone prehistoric monsters?), *Groundhog Day* (what if you woke up and every day was the same?) and *Planet of the Apes* (what if apes overtook mankind?). Sometimes the high concept is led by the actors, like Danny DeVito and Arnold Schwarzenegger as *Twins*.

Fleshing out the central idea, the pitch is usually presented in five steps (in descending order of importance):

✔ **Original and unique:** Even if it's based on existing material, there must be a twist that makes it new.

✔ **Mass appeal:** The idea has to attract a large audience.

✔ **Story specific:** There has to be a special factor that drives the story forwards to avoid a 'So what?' response.

✔ **Obvious potential:** The pitch alone should make you want to see the film; that's what the trailer will summarise.

✔ **Short:** Hollywood is overwhelmed with ideas for the next blockbuster, so there's no time for anything superfluous.

 Next time you're really hooked on creative output, whether it's a film, song, programme, work of art, or even a simple wind chime or dream-catcher, track it back to its roots. What was the idea behind it? Where might the inspiration have come from? How did it evolve into the finished article? Can you make another one yourself? If you copied it, how would you start?

Noticing less obvious signs of creativity

Everything man-made has been through a complex series of processes from raw materials to end product. And nowadays almost everything has been through the hands of a designer.

If you choose to look at the world through fresh eyes, you can appreciate the innovation and ingenuity that's gone into many of the most common objects. Even the humblest man-made object is an embodiment of creative thinking. Someone conceived it and then drew a design for it. And if it was manufactured, they drew a blueprint, made the moulds, and assembled it.

A simple disposable modern pen may not appear 'creative' on first inspection, but it's a small masterpiece of creative thinking. For it to exist, someone had to rethink the way pens work. Then the designer had to design an intricate series of components. The manufacturing had to comply with very fine tolerances so the nib and the cap or click mechanism operated as intended. And that's just a cheap pen!

Take a fresh look at a familiar object. Select something you use every day, and examine it as though you were from another planet, experiencing it for the first time. Use all your senses as you study it. How does it feel to the touch? What does it smell or even taste like? What sounds does it make? Don't worry if it's not 'meant' to have a smell or taste – remember, many people like the taste of plastic or the smell of a new car. Now look at it carefully. Examine the materials it's made from, the contours, the shapes, the overall design. Consider the sequence of processes required to arrive at the finished article.

Designers like Sir Jonathan Ive, creator of the range of Apple products, and Sir James Dyson, of innovative vacuum cleaner fame, don't just sit in a studio sketching exciting new products. They spend much of their time exploring materials. They want to know how strong they are, how they feel to the touch, how they look, how they cope with wear and tear. All these considerations inform the design process and contribute directly or indirectly to the end product.

Finding Curious Ways to Fulfil Your Curiosity

Curiosity is an integral feature of creative thinking, and the subject itself is full of curiosities and apparent paradoxes. Many of the tools and techniques used in creative thinking are counterintuitive, and they work precisely because they provide choices that are outside the usual conventions.

Creative thinking encourages you to view the world with fresh eyes and to tolerate ambiguity even when it takes you in unusual, unexpected directions.

Conventional thinking patterns tend to be logical and structured. Creative thinking patterns, on the other hand, tend to be much more fluid. Many of the tools and techniques for creative thinking are designed specifically to encourage detours, leaps of imagination, and reframing of concepts.

Creative thinking encourages you to be curious – seeing the world differently, noticing more. And it also encourages you to tolerate the curious – to be comfortable with ambiguity and to enjoy the paradoxical.

Reconciling paradoxes and juxtapositions

Several creative thinking techniques involve exploring the notion of *paradox*, intentionally upsetting conventions through the use of absurd or apparently self-contradictory observations (like saying 'This true statement is false,' for example). Doing so can be a useful way of opening your mind to fresh possibilities. If you consider the White Queen in *Through the Looking-Glass*, who informed Alice that in her youth she could 'think of six impossible things before breakfast', you have an idea about the possibilities of playing creatively with paradox.

Another of the classic definitions of creativity is *juxtaposition* – the collision of different or contradictory ideas. Much humour – especially the most creative variety – is rooted in juxtaposition, such as: 'A horse walks into a bar and says . . .' Several ideas collide in this brief opening line, even before the punch line. Horses don't usually wander into bars, and they certainly don't talk, but this one does both. Then there's the implication that the barman won't be surprised by this event. And all before we discover what the horse has to say. In the same vein, many creative ideas emerge from this unexpected juxtaposition process.

For another example of juxtaposition (and for evidence that even physicists use creative thinking!), take a look at quantum mechanics – a science full of unlikely and even implausible collisions of ideas. Can an object be a particle and a wave at the same time? Physicists have conducted convincing experiments demonstrating that this is not only theoretically possible, but that it can be observed happening in real time. Black holes and dark matter are just two more examples in this *Alice in Wonderland* world.

Combining the familiar and the strange

Creative thinking is often a matter of combining the familiar and the strange. Indeed, the founder of Synectics, a popular method of creative thinking, described his role with clients as 'making the familiar strange, and the strange familiar'.

Another classic definition of the creative process is 'the association of two different ideas'. Mixing two ideas, especially if they appear entirely unrelated, is one of the more reliable starting points for thinking creatively. Some professionals argue that there are no new ideas, only combinations of existing ones. However, that fails to account for the genuine moments of blinding inspiration – they may be rare, but they do exist.

You can make the familiar strange by pretending to be discovering an object or concept for the first time. Choose something that's part of your everyday life, something you never think twice about. Now imagine it has just appeared out of the blue. One way to do this is to pretend to be the proverbial Martian who has just arrived on earth with no knowledge of earth culture. Ask questions like 'What is this?' 'What does it do?' 'And what else . . .?' Try to surprise yourself.

And you can make the strange familiar by putting yourself in the position of someone who uses that something every day. Say you visit an unfamiliar location – someone's workshop or kitchen, or a new shop for example. You may find yourself encountering an object for the first time. This is a perfect opportunity to play this game and immediately reinvent it as something you use every day (even if your imagined use is not the use you think it was designed for – that makes the game better!).

Familiarity can breed contempt. Until fish farming made salmon affordable, it was considered a luxury on a par with caviar – highly desirable but very rare. However, Queen Victoria's Scottish staff were fed salmon so frequently that they finally rebelled and requested a change of diet.

Entwining the tangible and the elusive

Sometimes, creativity hits you like a bolt of lightning. When this happens, you really know it. It's often reported that a new idea or a solution to a problem can spring into the mind full-grown and vivid, almost touchable. Some creative individuals live for this moment. However, it's also common to find that your creative thinking can leave you 'on the edge' without a clear direction or solution. Don't worry about this, because this book is packed with hints and tips to get you to your creative destination.

Experiencing the seductive and the scary

Many people are irresistibly attracted to creativity. They enjoy experiencing the fruits of creativity, whether in films, music or art, and they actively seek out creative environments. And some of these people also like to roll up their sleeves and participate, whether at work or in their personal lives. If you're in this group, you have a head start, because creativity generates positive energy.

However, the notion of creativity in its various forms makes some people nervous. They find creativity daunting, and don't feel themselves to be part of it. 'I don't know much about art, but I know what I like' is sometimes used as a defence against being exposed to new experiences. This is unfortunate, because opening your mind can be one of the most enriching and rewarding events imaginable.

If you've found yourself rejecting creativity, take a fresh look. Try a different perspective. If you're looking at or listening to the work of an artist, try looking below the surface. Instead of giving up because you feel you don't understand or 'get it', take a little time to see through the artist's eyes or the eyes of someone who likes that particular style. Doing so won't always work, but sometimes you can discover something unexpected and open a new door.

If you feel that you're not particularly creative, this book is packed with material to help change your mind and introduce you to the wealth of creativity that's yours for the taking. After you get a taste for creativity, it can be a bit like chocolate – 'Just one more bite'. Creative thinking is very more-ish.

Adapting Strategies to Help You Survive in the Creative World

Creativity is partly a question of adaptation. When situations change, they require fresh thinking. Persisting with old habits and behaviours in the face of new information can cause frustration and increase stress levels.

External events can instigate the need to act creatively. Sometimes, circumstances demand a rapid shift. Something unexpected happens and you find you need to step up a gear or change your game. In these circumstances, your natural creativity is likely to kick in, providing you with the stimulus necessary to engage in the task. In these situations, having some tools and techniques up your sleeve (such as those covered in Chapters 6–8) to assist the process is always helpful.

You may also have an inner drive to create. This drive can be the result of a period of high pressure or a gradual build-up, like water coming to the boil.

Both external events and internal drives serve the creative spirit well, as higher states of alertness brought on by such events are often all the stimulus needed to trigger creative thinking.

Emulating child's play

Children find it easy to drop old behaviours and beliefs in favour of new ones, which is one reason why they take so readily to technology. Faced with, say, an electronic game, they simply keep trying options until they get the sequences right.

Children don't start from the position that they don't know how to do something – merely that they haven't got there *yet*. They live in a world where many things are unknown quantities, so a new game is just something else to be mastered. As an adult, you're well-advised to take a leaf from that book, as it's a good recipe for creative thinking.

Adults, on the whole, are less adaptable than children and more likely to persist in pursuing routes that aren't working. It's been said that repeatedly doing the same thing and expecting a different result is a path to insanity. And you've probably been in situations where you've seen someone doggedly repeating actions that aren't delivering the required result, and perhaps even commenting on it:

> 'I keep putting this key in the lock but it just won't work!'
>
> 'Perhaps it's the wrong key?' you offer.
>
> 'But I keep trying and it just won't work!'
>
> 'Have you tried turning it the other way?'
>
> Long pause. 'Oh.'

Recognising creativity as a necessity – not a luxury

Despite the resistance of some ultra-rational thinkers, creativity is an integral part of life. In both work and personal situations, problems occur which require more than a purely logical approach:

- ✔ That seems difficult – is there a smarter way of doing it?
- ✔ Something new is required – how do you dream it up?
- ✔ That's a knotty problem – how do you go about cracking it?

Opening the door to your creativity is the first step in dealing with these types of problem.

Brave new world?

Life without creativity would be unimaginably dreary. One of the (many) reasons for the sudden collapse of East Germany in 1989 was the stark contrast between East and West Berlin. On one side of the Berlin Wall was a comfortable consumer society enjoying the benefits of a culture of creative freedom, whereas on the other, shops were permanently starved of products, queues were a daily reality, and the most basic consumer goods were in short supply. Moreover, on the East side of the wall, creativity was actively frowned on and all kinds of artists were considered potential dissidents.

The appalling situation in East Germany gave rise to a stream of jokes about the communists' mistrust of education, one of which is:

'How many Stasi (secret police) does it take to make an arrest?'

'Two. One to write the arrest warrant, and the other to monitor the intellectual.'

Innovate or die

One of the measures of commercial success is sustained innovation. Indeed, many experts regard it as the single greatest determinant of long-term survival in business. Now more than ever, companies that fail to outstrip, or at least keep pace with, their competitors are doomed.

In the past couple of decades, creative thinking has moved closer to centre stage and is no longer regarded as a peripheral benefit. Many leaders recognise that creative thinking isn't a luxury to be added on from time to time, but an integral part of the business process.

Appreciating creativity as your lifeblood

Whether you participate in it or merely enjoy the benefits, creativity enriches your life. Much of life today would be impossible without the stream of innovations that produced the products that make your life and mine more comfortable.

Periodically, television documentaries and magazines review what life was like ten, 20 or 50 years ago. Apart from seeing how quaint and old-fashioned everything appears, it's worth looking a little deeper and observing the pace of change thanks to innovation. Just a few years ago, televisions were big clunky boxes, music was played from vinyl records and programmes were recorded on low-grade videotape. A few years before that, television was black and white and the UK had only a couple of channels and no means of home recording. Tracking the history of consumer products gives an insight into the energy and direction of creative thinking.

Travel back in time and mentally replace your current home or office products with those from a decade or two ago. Consider whether you could live with them, knowing what you know now.

Getting into a Creative Frame of Mind

Do you feel creative? This is a bit like asking 'Do you feel healthy?' Most people do feel healthy, but they just don't think about it, because it's a natural state.

If you're one of those individuals who feels creative, you're fortunate, because you have a head start when it comes to creative thinking. A lot of scientific evidence demonstrates that creativity flourishes most productively in people who already believe themselves to be creative.

However, if you don't recognise yourself in this picture and don't see yourself as creative, don't worry. I've designed this book to show you that you really *are* creative, and to help you develop this resource in your life.

Converging and diverging

Creativity is a natural state, and different people have different 'resting states' where creative thinking is concerned. This difference is largely related to personality. Some temperaments are in a permanent state of high creativity, fizzing and buzzing with ideas, whereas at the other end of the scale, others need time to get revved up. These are known as *divergent* and *convergent* styles of thinking, respectively.

One of the simplest ways to demonstrate the difference between convergent and divergent thinking is to try the exercise of coming up with as many uses as you can for a brick in a limited time. Some individuals find this exercise difficult, thinking that a brick is a brick is a brick, after all. However, some can perceive many ways to use a brick – as a weapon, a paperweight, an ornament, and so on. And at the extreme divergent end of the scale are those who generate a continuous flow of possibilities, playing with all sorts of 'What if . . .?' questions: what if it was made of something else, or as big as a bus, as tiny as an atom, as light as a feather? And so on.

When this experiment is conducted with large groups, a consistent bell-curve pattern emerges, with a few very convergent individuals who can't think of many uses, a few who generate an unending stream of ideas, and the majority bulging in the middle, with maybe eight to 20 uses for a brick.

Thinking divergently

Divergent thinkers find it easy to generate thoughts and can create a stream of ideas, even on unpromising subjects. They tend not to be over concerned with quality or consistency, and don't usually censor their output. They often resent being interrupted while in full flight, even though sometimes their ideas seem bizarre or outrageous to others. The wildness of their flights of fancy isn't usually important, because they'll edit their output after they've concluded their stream of ideas.

If you're naturally a divergent thinker, you're likely to notice what's around you – the little things as well as the big ones. You're inclined to ask a lot of questions, even ones that may seem trivial, obvious or occasionally embarrassing to others. You may also be inclined to see the funny side of things and to enjoy absurdities instead of being over exercised by them.

Thinking convergently

Convergent thinkers tend not to perform so well on idea-generation sessions that involve producing a lot of ideas rapidly. This is because their style of thinking is more evolutionary and their best ideas often come at the end of a considered reflective process. They're not necessarily less creative than their divergent counterparts; they just go about the task differently.

If you're a convergent thinker, you're likely to take a steady approach to tasks, including creative ones. You may get occasional hits of creative inspiration, but in the main you progress toward goals. In tasks like dreaming up uses for a brick, you may not generate a big list in a few minutes, but you're more likely to be coming up with ideas a long time after the task is finished.

Storming ahead

Working individually, everyone finds his or her own right gear for creative thinking, and can learn or be taught the most beneficial techniques and processes for enhancing creative thinking skills.

Problems arise in group situations, such as traditional brainstorming sessions, where everyone is sharing the same task at the same pace. The divergent thinkers usually dominate, because they're the first to come up with ideas, although those ideas may be inferior or off target.

Recent studies have resulted in fresh thinking about idea generation, and the consensus is that traditional brainstorming methods work less well than individual sessions or than alternating structures where individual and group activities are performed successively. I discuss this in detail in Chapter 7.

It's also worth noting that some of the traditional ground rules for brainstorming – and other idea-generation methods, for that matter – were typically based on absence of criticism or negative feedback. But recent research has convincingly demonstrated that a climate of healthy debate – including critical comments – actually works better for creative thinking.

The message here is that, in creative thinking, it's always worth questioning assumptions – even about the nature of creative thinking!

Being physically passive but mentally active

An effective starting point for getting in the mood for creative thinking is total relaxation. In the hurly burly of modern life, it's all too easy to be busy being busy. Even when trying to surmount a creative challenge, many people find that they're inclined to rush the fences and resolve the issue as they would any other kind of task. Unfortunately, the brain isn't wired to do this.

When you take in new information, it's rapidly absorbed and then shifted into the brain's filing cabinets. This cognitive system works beautifully for straightforward, logical tasks: you have a problem, you go to your mental filing cabinet, access the relevant bits of information and hey presto. (This is why so many of the older theories about the brain's workings were based on mechanical and computing analogies.) However, creative thinking requires the deployment of some different cognitive processes, and these aren't so receptive to a file–drawer approach.

Being physically active and mentally alert

As with so many aspects of the creative process, there are completely different ways of getting creative. This is where your tolerance of ambiguity comes into play!

For the actively inclined, instead of relaxing your body (see the nearby sidebar 'Tuning out to tune in'), you can get your creative juices flowing by indulging in physical exercise. Many people find that engaging in physical activity frees the mind from its usual patterns. In fact, many professional athletes describe their exertions as a kind of meditation, so this route can lead to the same destination as meditation.

Tuning out to tune in

An excellent way to put yourself in a receptive state is to fully relax your body. You can do this at any time when you want to access a receptive state quickly and easily. The more you practise relaxing your body, the easier it will become. It's also similar to the method you use for meditating, so it's useful to learn it to apply whenever you want to relax.

Begin by sitting comfortably, hands in your lap, feet on the floor. Close your eyes and let the tips of your thumbs and middle fingers gently touch; keep them that way throughout the session. (You'll discover why in a moment.) Now relax your body from head to toe:

✔ Notice your head, and gently move it on your neck muscles. Feel how comfortably it sits.

✔ Relax your eyes. (You may want to open and close them briefly to ensure you're comfortable.)

✔ Relax your jaw and neck.

✔ Flex and relax your shoulders to make sure the muscles are unstressed.

✔ Move that relaxed feeling down your arms: upper arms, lower arms, hands. Notice your thumbs and middle fingers touching.

✔ Move the relaxation to your chest, and notice your breathing.

✔ Relax your trunk.

✔ Move the relaxation down your legs to your thighs, knees and ankles.

✔ Move your ankles and gently wiggle your toes, and then put your feet back on the floor.

Now you're ready to apply your mind to the task in hand.

Programming Yourself for Creativity with Neuro-linguistic Programming

Several of the concepts you encounter in this book are based on valuable insights originating from *neuro-linguistic programming (NLP)*. (You can read more in *Neuro-linguistic Programming For Dummies* by Romilla Ready and Kate Burton.)

NLP's rather unusual name comes from the amalgamation of its three key elements (one of its founders observed that the choice of name was assisted by generous quantities of fine Californian wine):

✔ **Neuro** describes the neurological component, the part involving the way the human mind works, and the structure of the brain. Sensory channels (the five senses of sight, sound, taste, smell and feeling, as well as some others that are under investigation) handle everything you experience. So 'neuro' deals with the way sensory information is processed, stored and used.

✔ **Linguistic** refers to the fact that, as users of language, humans process raw sensory information linguistically. In practical terms, this means that experience is *encoded* (that is, stored in ways that the brain can handle). As a person's language skills grow, so does the use of metaphors and narrative to make sense of events. So language acts as a filter.

✔ **Programming** is the way the brain encodes the vast amount of sensory information to prevent it becoming overwhelmed. Direct experience is inextricably intertwined with language to give meaning and organisation to events.

While no single definition of NLP exists, it's useful to bear in mind that NLP isn't an 'it' – if anything, it's a 'they'. NLP is a repertoire of tools and techniques for successful living. It's based on a pragmatic model of doing what works. And much of the core material is directly relevant to creative thinking.

NLP is defined in several ways, as befits a system based on a repertoire or toolbox of skills that enable individuals to achieve personal excellence. Here are some of the common definitions:

✔ The science of excellence

✔ The art and science of communication

✔ What makes you and other people tick

✔ A manual for the brain

✔ A toolkit for personal and organisational change

NLP is built on four essential pillars. These are:

✔ **Rapport:** This is your ability to be in tune with others. In creative terms, it's relevant to group activities, and good rapport enables you to understand and be sympathetic to others who work in different ways. Both convergent and divergent thinking skills are valid (I talk about them in the 'Converging and diverging' section earlier in this chapter), and whichever camp you're in, you can appreciate the efforts of others.

✔ **Sensory awareness:** This is the noticing that's so important to a healthy, creative lifestyle. The more you actively use each of your senses in everyday life, the more your acuity grows, and you find yourself becoming more sensitive to events, moods and situations. In short, the more you notice, the more you notice.

✔ **Outcome thinking:** If you fail to plan, you plan to fail. Outcome thinking is the process of asking yourself what you want out of a situation and how you'll know you've achieved it. It empowers you to make the most of the choices available to you. This is very relevant in creative thinking, where you may not always know the answer in advance, but you recognise the choices to take on the path, and you'll recognise the right outcome when you see it.

✔ **Behavioural flexibility:** Behavioural flexibility is doing something different when what you're doing isn't working. Children usually do this much better than adults. Becoming skilled at this kind of adaptation is an important prerequisite for effective creative thinking.

In addition to building on the four pillars, creative thinking at its best makes use of several other contributions from the NLP repertoire:

✔ **Modelling:** One of the core techniques of NLP, it's based on the close observation of the behaviour of peak performers. One of the most efficient ways to learn a new skill is to copy carefully – to model – someone who already does it expertly. In this book, you'll find many examples of the output of creative thinkers – if what they do works for them, you can use it to work for you too.

✔ **Anchoring:** Touching the tips of your middle fingers and thumbs together is an example of anchoring. Anchoring happens when you form an association between a thought and a pattern of behaviour. The brain works on patterning (that's the programming part of the NLP system), and when you link thinking and behaviour in this way, the physical aspect triggers a shift to a new pattern. Then, when the anchor is embedded, repeating the action will evoke that response. So after a while, touching thumb and middle finger alerts your mind to begin the relaxation process.

✔ **Visualisation:** Many creative thinking tools are based on visualisation, which is a core component of NLP. Chapters 6 and 7 explain methods for visualising.

✔ **Curiosity:** Allied to *sensory awareness* – the business of noticing – is the cultivation of what's been called a restless curiosity. A hallmark of many creative individuals is their relentless search for answers to questions ranging from the mundane to the most far-reaching. Children aren't embarrassed to ask, and it's not a bad habit for creative adults to nurture.

✔ **Tolerance of ambiguity:** This is the ability to live with confusion or ambiguity. Many of the tools and techniques for thinking creatively require the suspension of certainty. This usually requires some effort at the outset, but as with any skill, it can be cultivated and becomes easier with experience.

✔ **Resourceful state:** One of the elements of NLP is placing yourself in a state of alertness and awareness. You can describe it colloquially as being bright-eyed and bushy-tailed.

✔ **Timelines:** This is considering events and important moments in the context of when and where they happened. This approach provides many significant, and sometimes surprising, insights.

A useful concept that comes from NLP is the notion of being present or being in the moment. Whatever the term, it boils down to remaining alert to where you are, what's happening and your place in it. Some have described this concept as acuity, or really noticing. In workshops, I use the metaphor of the hawk which hovers still in the sky far above its domain, focusing all its attention on the tiniest movement below that signals the possibility of prey. It economises its own movements, not just because it doesn't want to draw attention, but because it doesn't need distractions where food may be involved.

This subject is full of paradoxes and apparent contradictions, and here it's possible to be both in the moment and out of the moment. Many participants in creative sessions report that just as they achieve that mysterious and compelling sense of really being there, the creative moment has happened somehow without them noticing. Participants in workshops report this phenomenon again and again, and it's echoed in coaching and therapy scenarios, where epiphany (a fancy term for a sudden breakthrough) often occurs when it's least expected. Don't blink or you'll miss it!

Fighting through Uncreative Times

Sometimes, you just can't find your creativity. That solution just won't come. That new idea remains elusive, despite your best efforts. This situation can be very frustrating. Why can inspiration be so hard to attain sometimes? Well, no single, simple answer exists. Stress and anxiety can both be contributors, as can exhaustion after sustained activity. And sometimes, your energy pool is just drained for no apparent reason.

If this happens to you occasionally, remember that you're in good company. Many professionally creative individuals have fallow periods where nothing much happens in the imagination. Through their experience, you can take advantage of some tips and techniques they've evolved to get through these times, and I've described some of the most reliable ones below.

Being stuck

The simple fact is that everyone gets stuck sometimes, however fluent and creative they are normally. Dwelling on the fact that you're stuck is something to avoid, because you may worry yourself into a worse state and prolong the situation. A far more constructive approach to take at frustrating times like these is to spend your time exploring ways to get past it, which is where this book comes in.

I just can't keep pace with brain research

I mention research and studies about creativity throughout this book. This is a warning that much of the information about the brain will become outdated as a result of the huge amount of research that institutes around the world are undertaking. This research, coupled with frequent breakthroughs in technology, will allow much more precise investigation. Here are two examples:

✔ Thanks to a new generation of MRI scanners at Harvard, neuroscientists have been able to access much more detailed information on the interior organisation of the brain. One of the team has said that, whereas the previous generation of scanners allowed observation of 25 per cent of the brain's activities, new scanners have turned the ratio on its head: the view now is that some 75 per cent of the brain's workings are accessible. The extraordinary images show that the brain's structure is actually a lattice-work, not unlike the matrix in the film of the same name. The implications of this revelation are substantial, and have a direct bearing on understanding the thinking process.

✔ Advances in research on *neuroplasticity*, which is the brain's ability to change its structure, look very exciting. Neuroscientists used to think that upon reaching adulthood, the brain was fixed and could only deteriorate with age. However, it now appears that the situation is much more positive. Recent research shows that the brain continues to change throughout adult life, and in the aftermath of traumatic events such as strokes it rebuilds where possible and generates alternative pathways. Again, the implications of this newly evolving information will provide many clues about brain function.

Whenever you read about the state of the art in neurological matters, remember that this is a science in its infancy. Some of the sharpest minds on the planet are dedicating all their resources to perfecting knowledge of what goes on inside our heads. Ever-evolving technology and breakthrough insights characterise this field. This is creative thinking at its finest. Victorian scientists thought physics was nearly finished and a little mopping up would allow everything measurable to be measured. Then Einstein inconveniently came along and comprehensively upset the Newtonian apple cart. The situation with brain science is similarly fluid.

Getting unstuck

To stimulate your creative juices if you discover you're stuck, you can try a number of simple techniques:

- **Recognise that you're stuck.** This is the first and in many ways the most important step. Don't be in denial, acknowledge the situation, and prepare to take action to change it.

- **Do nothing.** Surprising as it may seem, this often works very effectively. You can do nothing by switching to a different, less demanding activity (such as Sudoku or a crossword), taking a break, or even having a power nap. Don't feel guilty – you're just recharging your creative batteries.

- **Do something.** Make the positive decision to do something equally engaging. You probably have some important stuff to do, so if you're stuck, now's the time to do it. Your mind loves activity, and engaging in a task, any task, can be a great way to rediscover your creative centre. Often, ideas will come just as you commit to the alternative task, so be alert to that possibility.

- **Get help.** Being stuck can be a lonely path. But help is at hand. Have a chat with a friend or colleague. Input from someone not engaged in your task can generate serendipitous ideas, because while you're consciously engaged, your unconscious mind is still on the job, looking for connections. And if you're working alone, dipping into a book – this one, perhaps – can provide stimulation from a different source.

Minding your brain

The terms brain and mind are often used interchangeably, but they are different. The distinction between brain and mind is that the brain is the equipment housing the functions of the mind.

If you think of a car, it has everything you need to get from A to B. There's a powerful engine to provide the motor power, you have control of the steering, velocity and gearing. And you sit in the comfort of an ergonomically designed seat. This is your brain. It's top of the range, and equipped with all the latest extras. It even modifies itself as you use it.

But your brain, impressive as it is, would be precious little use without you in the driving seat. This is your mind, in charge of operations.

So to remember the distinction, your brain is your car and your mind is the driver.

Chapter 2

Living in a World of Creativity

In This Chapter

▶ Connecting spirituality and creativity

▶ Being inspired by the muses

▶ Tuning in to creativity through music

▶ Changing the world through creativity

▶ Using creativity politically

▶ Looking at stereotypes and the downside of creativity

Creativity comes in many forms. You can see it in objects, experience it as thoughts and ideas, and feel it in its emotional impact. From the humblest Neolithic axe head to the vast CERN particle physics installation in Switzerland, every man-made object ever constructed is an example of creativity in action. In short, creativity pervades every aspect of life, and has done so since the dawn of time.

Because creative thinking touches every area of life, it often goes unnoticed. Every man-made object has been through the hands of at least one designer. Every improvement, large or small, in daily life is the result of considered thought.

In this modern world, teams of designers, artists, architects and other creative specialists work endlessly to invent, improve and refine everything that comes into our lives. Many of these evolutionary creative steps sit in the background, but some are conspicuous because of their impact. Attendance at art galleries has never been higher, and cultural events – whether described as popular or high culture – attract huge and increasing audiences.

Think of three man-made products or services created in the last ten years that you can't live without. Then consider what life was like before they existed. Now identify the three that have made the greatest *impact* on your life.

Searching for Spiritual Expression

The need for spiritual expression appears to have been a basic drive throughout history. Many of the oldest archaeological finds, like the Venus of Willendorf (see the nearby sidebar), have spiritual connotations. And many of the oldest surviving structures reflect the spiritual values of their time. The Egyptian Pyramids, the ancient stone circles of Stonehenge and the cave art found at many sites (including at Chauvet in France, dated at around 30,000 BC) all have a thread of spiritual belief.

So it appears that spiritual expression reflects a fundamental need, and in every generation some of the highest forms of artistic achievement have been devoted to spiritual ends.

You can see this sense of profound aspiration in the fact that many religious structures, such as the medieval cathedrals, took several generations to complete: the people who designed them knew they would never live to see them completed.

Embodying spirituality and knowledge in architecture

It appears that, as well as manifesting belief in higher powers, many spiritual structures also served to encode all available knowledge of the time.

The Gothic cathedrals built across Europe from the twelfth to sixteenth centuries, for example, are saturated with symbols of esoteric knowledge, often concealed among the overt images of Christianity. This, of course, was the inspiration for the best-selling book *The Da Vinci Code* by Dan Brown. And much of the current fascination with Maya sites stems from the highly detailed predictive calendars found inside them.

In addition to housing bits of knowledge, these spiritual structures also embodied the latest architectural advances. In the cathedrals, architects invented flying buttresses to permit higher and wider construction. (A *flying buttress* is the external arch on top of a tall column that you can see on the outside of many cathedrals, leaning in to support the area near the roof.) When church, mosque and temple domes grew bigger, the spaces between the spines of the dome (known as *spandrels*) came to be painted or carved and a focus of attention in their own right, often featuring the finest artistic expressions. In this way, such buildings housed each new level of creative thought in an era.

The Venus of Willendorf

One of the oldest artefacts in existence is a small statuette known as the Venus of Willendorf. Carved around 22,000–24,000 BC (according to the latest carbon-dating methods), it was evidently an object of veneration. Similar examples have since been discovered in other locations, suggesting they may have been created within a religion worshipping fecundity (the statue has large breasts and a big stomach, and plaited hair) or an icon representing an earth mother.

As an object, it was skilfully carved (for example, its plaited hair is detailed), but the limestone isn't from the area where it was found, which suggests it may have been carried from place to place. It was also painted.

Creatively, it is a strong image of femininity and would not look out of place in a modern art gallery. This and other artefacts demonstrate that the drive to create artistic objects is as old as mankind.

Connecting body, mind and spirit

One of the strongest growth trends in literature is the field of body, mind and spirit. Whereas it once occupied a marginal niche, it now represents a significant section in bookshops and is a major part of the Amazon.com repertoire.

The growth of the market is a reflection of the current preoccupation with personal growth and the search for physical, psychological and spiritual insight. And creative thinking is central to this process, because part of its function is to break down barriers and overcome limiting beliefs.

Meeting the Muses

Ancient Greece provides another feature of creativity: the concept of the muse. Muses were believed to be goddesses, daughters of Zeus, who were the source of inspiration in the arts. (The word itself is thought to derive from the root *men*, which means 'to think'.) Traditional ideas of the muses and their role have mutated over time, but the term is still a familiar description for a source of artistic inspiration.

Recognising angels and daemons throughout history

The ancient Greeks thought in terms of daemons when they considered the creative process. At that time, the word didn't have its modern negative connotations. Exceptionally creative individuals were considered to have had this gift bestowed on them by the gods. This was a neat idea, because the individual didn't actually own the gift, and the gods could expect recipients to propitiate them for bestowing this blessing – a kind of Greek all-win situation. These daemons inhabited the artists' space and guided their hands, enabling them to create work of special quality.

This notion of the gods blessing artistic talent is closer to our ideas of angels than of daemons.

Following this, the Romans evolved the concept of genius. This was essentially the same principle, but it gave us the word for exceptional creativity. The artist continued to be seen as the fortunate conduit for great work, but the gods still owned the ability.

Then, in the Renaissance, artists emerged as the originators and owners of their own genius, in the way the term is understood now. This was because the rise of wealthy ecclesiastic and merchant patronage encouraged the evolution of *individual* artists. Whereas the numerous guilds had treated artists as anonymous craftsmen on the same level as carpenters and plumbers, this new generation of patrons wanted to be able to flaunt their ability to attract the finest talent. A privileged group of artists found themselves being placed on a pedestal.

Modern concepts of the creative genius developed from this era, and now of course the cult of celebrity has become an added ingredient in the mix.

Musing with Greeks and Romans

The Greeks started with three muses but increased the number to nine eventually. The Romans refined the belief further, giving each of these nine muses a name and sphere of influence:

- Calliope – epic poetry
- Clio – history
- Erato – love poetry
- Euterpe – flutes and lyric poetry
- Melpomene – tragedy
- Polyhymnia – sacred poetry
- Terpsichore – dance

> ✔ Thalia – comedy and pastoral poetry
>
> ✔ Urania – astronomy

The concept of the muses remains a fascinating one because it embodies the idea that inspiration is an enigmatic force somehow bestowed on fortunate individuals.

Meeting modern muses

Although we no longer name our muses, the concept is a charming picture of artistic inspiration. Certainly many creative thinkers personify their sources of inspiration, so perhaps the notion is not so far-fetched after all. Picasso called his many lovers his muses, and his epic Vollard suite of prints tracks the ups and downs of his relationships over his long and turbulent personal life.

Several psychologists working on creative thinking have noted the way inspiration often seems to arrive seemingly of its own volition from somewhere apart from the person who has the creative thought. And sometimes, creativity can appear to hide itself, teasingly just out of reach.

Finding your own muse

Whatever your creative or cultural interests, the current generation of social and informational networking sites gives access to unlimited material. You can explore any topic that interests you in as much depth as you like, and you can also share your experiences in real time. You can both find digital muses to inspire you and provide a muse-like spark to others searching for creativity.

When new technologies arrive, it's almost impossible to recall how the world worked before. Certainly you tend not to retain that sense of wonder you may have had when you first encountered them. But it can be worth trying a little time travel – in both directions – to stimulate your imagination.

Consider the world before online resources existed. Then take yourself on a journey back through time, removing inventions one at a time until you arrive in a world without telephones, radio, television, film and photography, computers or the Internet. How would you have lived and learned? What would you miss most? Now travel forwards and imagine future inventions that may become as indispensable as the ones you have now. You may come up with the next Google, Facebook or Twitter.

Discover your personal muse. Consider the creative activity you're best at and then imagine the muse who could assist you with inspiration:

- ✔ What's she like?
- ✔ What special attributes does she have?
- ✔ What specific extra talents can she bestow on you?

It's difficult to estimate the consequences of modern social networks, although some evidence of the scale of their impact can be gauged from events like the Arab Spring political uprising which began in 2010 and the opening of debate in countries that previously prohibited uncensored communication with the outside world.

It's apparent that social networks are constantly evolving, dividing and merging. And while they may look dated in the not-too-distant future, it's certain there will always be new generations of improved – and sometimes revolutionary – products to build on them.

Tuning In with Music and Creativity

It seems humans are hard-wired for music. Some of the oldest artefacts discovered are musical instruments. A prime example is a Slovenian bone flute, made from the femur of a now-extinct European bear, dated at some 50,000 years ago. Many of the oldest musical artefacts also depict dancing, suggesting that the link between the two is very deep rooted.

Music can be indispensable both to work and play. Where creative thinking is concerned, music can bridge both activities, and everyone has had the experience of tuning in and tuning out when music is playing.

Although some creative individuals prefer the sound of silence, many can't conceive of working without music. Operating theatres are often home to anything from Mozart to heavy metal. And few artists or designers wouldn't dream of working without a sound system.

Discover – or rediscover – the music that hits your creative sweet spot. Notice how you work when different kinds of music are playing. What seems to help, or hinder, your creative processes? And don't forget to ditch the music that doesn't work when you're working.

Music is one of the purest expressions of creative thinking, and in neurological terms it's one of the most complex. If you listen to a song, or compose one, you're employing more parts of your brain at once than for any other single activity.

If you play an instrument, you know that you engage various functions all at once: you use your ears, you track melody, you count time, you engage emotionally, and you probably tap in to your memory too. In addition, you may physically or mentally tap your feet in time and possibly dance, too.

Music is the only creative activity that engages all major regions of the brain. Music engages both right and left hemispheres, and it uses both the new part (the cortex) and the ancient brain that tops the spine (the limbic system). The regions of the brain shown in Figure 2-1 are the main areas that 'light up' when you listen to music or play an instrument, but even this isn't a comprehensive picture, because there is also a huge amount of activity along the neural pathways linking these areas.

Music that makes you feel happy or sad, romantic or reflective, does so by stimulating the appropriate parts of the brain in real time. When you're emotionally carried away, it's because the moment is captured by the parts of the brain those real experiences would evoke.

Different styles of music affect different regions of your brain. For example, dissonant or atonal music (the kind played in films like *Psycho*) can trigger 'fight or flight' responses in the *amygdala*, which is a pea-sized structure in the area where your spine joins your main brain that governs quick-reaction emotions like attacking and running away. And music that violates expectations (like unexpected changes in tempo or key, as in jazz) can stimulate high states of alertness in the parts of the brain concerned with consciousness.

You may not have access to an MRI scanner to measure brain waves, but next time you listen to or play a favourite piece of music, try to step outside yourself:

- ✔ Actually listen to what you're listening to. Monitor the individual sounds that make up the music.
- ✔ Notice where changes occur and the effect they have on you – observe tempo and key changes.
- ✔ Repeat the experience several times, tracking a different aspect of the music each time.

You'll soon find yourself hearing and feeling music in a different way.

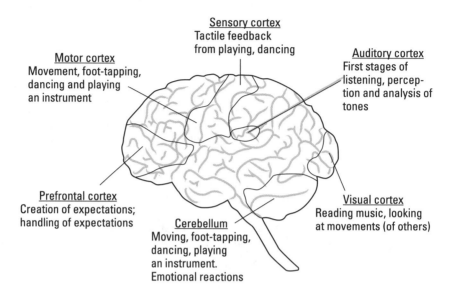

Sensory cortex
Tactile feedback
from playing, dancing

Motor cortex
Movement, foot-tapping,
dancing and playing
an instrument

Auditory cortex
First stages of
listening, percep-
tion and analysis of
tones

Prefrontal cortex
Creation of expectations;
handling of expectations

Cerebellum
Moving, foot-tapping,
dancing, playing
an instrument.
Emotional reactions

Visual cortex
Reading music, looking
at movements (of others)

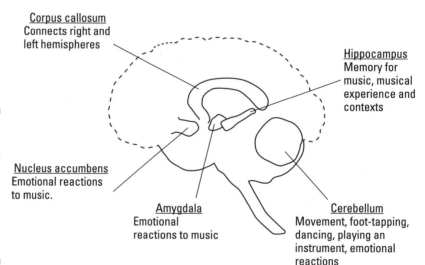

Corpus callosum
Connects right and
left hemispheres

Hippocampus
Memory for
music, musical
experience and
contexts

Nucleus accumbens
Emotional reactions
to music.

Amygdala
Emotional
reactions to music

Cerebellum
Movement, foot-tapping,
dancing, playing an
instrument, emotional
reactions

Figure 2-1:
It takes two
views of
the brain
to show all
the parts
that play-
ing music
affects.

If you don't play an instrument, now is a good time to start. Just as everyone can develop their creative powers, everyone is capable of playing music. Begin by selecting an instrument you really love. It may be the sound it makes, it may be its unique shape, or it could just be because someone you rate plays one. It's never been easier to learn to play, because the Internet has endless free tutorials to take you note by note through your favourite pieces. The *For Dummies* series also has excellent guides on a wide variety of instruments. And remember, every master musician began with the same few notes.

Challenging the Status Quo with Creative Thinking

Every world-changing idea began with one individual's thought. Sometimes, expressing your brave new ideas can provoke opposition. For example, take a look at Mahatma Gandhi and Martin Luther King. They both had dreams that transformed the world. But someone else thought differently, and killers assassinated both men for their thoughts and vision. Now, I'm not saying you will meet the same fate for your ideas, but great ideas are worth a little risk.

And then there's the creative thinking at the visionary level that's channelled in a negative direction – both Lenin and Hitler were visionary thinkers, but of a poisonous disposition. What all visionaries, good or evil, have shown is the power of ideas to change people's thinking on a grand scale.

Playing a revolutionary role

A feature of revolutionary activity has always been the manifesto. This is the statement that defines a radical new thought, followed by a call to action.

Spark your creativity by writing your own manifesto. Take a topic you feel passionate about and write a speech that will have everyone on their feet and eager to join your cause. Pepper it with powerful verbs and strong adjectives. Force your audience to make decisions between the bondage of the present and the liberation you're proposing. (And for added brownie points, choose a really absurd topic to get wound up about.)

Making the difference

Oratory is a powerful form of creative expression, and charismatic speakers have always exploited their ability to arouse crowds, whether from the pulpit or the soapbox.

In ancient Greece, two orators once gave speeches inciting the crowd to attack a local enemy. When Socrates spoke, everyone applauded politely and said, 'Good speech.' Then Demosthenes made his speech, and they cried, 'Let's *march*!'

Turn your manifesto into a speech. Listen to some powerful speakers and note the rhetorical tricks they use. For example, a common device is to repeat the opening words of a sentence, such as: 'I warn you . . .' This works best when you use the same phrase three times in a row. Another tactic is to flip a sentence: 'Ask not what your country can do for you, but what you can do for your country.' Pick some examples you like and weave them into your impassioned speech.

Dressing for the revolution

Fashion can be a significant revolutionary aid. The French Revolution of 1789 had the *sans-culottes* (an early version of Californian baggy shorts, usually in bright revolutionary red), and the term became an identifier for the revolutionaries as well. Mao Zedong, who founded the People's Republic of China in 1949, had high-button cotton coats and jaunty caps. Twentieth-century fascists were obviously fashion victims, though the less said about them the better. The message has always been clear in revolutionary circles: you're in the club or out of it; no half-way measures.

For people who really pushed their message, take a look at the examples of Chairman Mao and Libya's Colonel Gaddafi with a *Little Red Book* or a *Little Green Book* to inspire your followers.

Although these methods may appear somewhat corny to Western eyes, creative politicians have employed them all successfully as tools to win hearts and minds.

Working within the system

It takes a special kind of creative thinking to survive and thrive as a subversive, working inside the system. Many creative thinkers are drawn to the role of the maverick, so for some it's a relatively short step to covert rebellion.

The rebellion can be in the form of small acts of sabotage in protest at perceived unfair regimes. In recent years, covert sabotage has emerged as a major problem in certain organisations, especially when a disconnect exists between unreceptive management and disaffected staff.

On a more significant scale, spies in the camp have always fascinated and shocked in equal measure. When spies like Kim Philby, Guy Burgess and Donald Maclean were unmasked, the most frequently asked question was 'How *could* they do it?' rapidly followed by 'How did they *get away with it* for so long?'

And, of course, the murky world of espionage gave rise to a whole genre of creative fiction, with authors like Ian Fleming, Frederick Forsyth and John le Carré writing best-sellers on the subject.

Nowadays, mavericks looking for adventure often find an outlet in industrial espionage, which is a speciality that's grown on a global scale.

Agent Zigzag

As so often happens, real life has turned out to be stranger than fiction, as the case of Agent Zigzag illustrates. During the Second World War, many kinds of mavericks found their calling in covert operations.

Eddie Chapman wasn't content to be an ordinary spy. He made himself a double agent, and a very successful one. An English criminal (an explosives expert and part of the notorious safe-breaking Jelly Gang), he was recruited by the Germans early in the war while on occupied Jersey. He promptly fed them a stream of misinformation (which continued throughout the duration of hostilities) and was recruited by MI5.

The Nazis never discovered Chapman's subterfuge, and even made him a teacher at one of their spy schools (where he covertly photographed his fellow spies). In an extraordinary twist that the most imaginative spy fiction writer wouldn't have dared to pen, Germany awarded him the Iron Cross for meritorious service.

Chapman was a notorious ladies' man, and while dining with one of his lovers he evaded capture by leaping through a (closed!) window, and then committed a burglary the same night. An MI5 handler wrote of him: 'Chapman loved himself, loved adventure, and loved his country – probably in that order.'

Clearly Chapman relished the creative rush of adrenaline from his exploits, but his isn't a recommended route.

Creating political art

The power of creative expression can be seen clearly when it's functioning in extremely adverse circumstances. Many revolutions have begun with a few individuals finding a voice for expressing opposition to a political institution.

Samizdat is a Russian word meaning dissident activity. It originally described the clandestine copying and distribution of subversive texts, badly printed on cheap paper and circulated underground at great risk. The distinctive appearance of the texts was retained, even when better technology became available. (In the early years, the State owned all printing machines, and had a record of their output, so could trace any printing.)

The power of resourceful and rebellious spirits, coupled with the possibility of danger, creates a heady mix, and this has given energy to several revolutions. This kind of activity toppled the Berlin Wall, and the modern versions of *samizdat*, using Twitter and Facebook, helped bring about the so-called Arab Spring.

Because self-publishing is now so inexpensive, quick and simple, many seeking to find a dissident voice have used it to get their message to a wider world. However, some regimes have used their authority to clamp down on all forms of free expression, including poetry.

Connecting Religion, Politics and Creativity

Creative thinking finds much of its fulfilment in relation to belief systems. Wherever ideas exist about how abstract concepts work, elaborate creative expression is evident. Across the world, two of the most important belief systems are religion and politics. Neither of these is real in the sense that the material world is real, but both excite strong passions and high emotions among their adherents and their opponents.

Pomp and propaganda

Both religion and political movements focus creative attention on dress codes, ceremony and dedicated art and architecture. This isn't confined to certain cultures but is a universal phenomenon.

In their infancy, both religious and political movements often eschew anything but the simplest and most humble forms of expression. In religion, the English Puritans, for example, fought for a return to the unadorned, simple life they thought would emulate the lives of the Apostles. And Buddhist monks go barefoot with begging bowls to learn humility. In politics, many movements have established themselves through a call for basic egalitarian lifestyles. Both the French and Russian Revolutions focused (for a while) on 'the noble peasant', the antithesis of self-indulgent monarchy.

However, the simple life tends not to remain attractive for long, especially among religious and political leaders, and a process of transition begins. Whatever the core of a given belief, the externals – those things that you can see, hear and touch – tend to grow in scale and grandeur. If you trace the rise of any political or religious movement over time, almost without exception a pattern of increasing dressing up and ceremonial activity emerges.

Even in today's climate, where dressing down is a trend, the accoutrements of power continue to increase. The plane named Air Force One is a well-established symbol of the American presidency, and in the UK, Tony Blair established a trend for transforming the short walk from Downing Street to Parliament into a heavily escorted limousine journey. Now, most political leaders have personal jets and fleets of cars wherever they go in public.

Religious leaders typically have a highly evolved wardrobe, and those faiths that prefer their clerics in simple dress nevertheless invest heavily in their places and objects of worship.

As a creative exercise, design your own political party or religion. Disregarding the core proposition, focus instead on the clothes, ceremonial activities and places for delivering your message. Avoid styles contaminated by past fashions, especially those favoured by despots and discredited movements. Reject modesty, and aim for the highest levels of extravagance and flamboyance you can imagine. Then compare your own work with some real examples like the recently deceased Colonel Gaddafi, Saddam Hussein and the current North Korean regime.

Leaders in both the political and religious spheres have always been enthusiastic about using the latest communication techniques to promulgate their messages. Modern politicians have proved themselves early adopters of every new format available. In the public arena, posters were widely credited with winning Margaret Thatcher an election ('Labour isn't working'), and US President Obama's victory was attributed in large part to ingenious use of social networks to track trends and promote his candidacy.

In your fictitious campaign, consider the tools and techniques you would use to get your message across. Compare your initiatives with real-world examples such as posters and social networks.

Nudge – when politicians get ideas

Creative thinking can appear everywhere, even in the world of politics. Politicians have always shown interest in creative thinking, especially when it's rooted in academic research.

The Cabinet Office at Westminster, the hub of the UK Government, has a group called the Behavioural Insights Team. Nicknamed the nudge unit because of its enthusiasm for a book called *Nudge*, based on a system known as behavioural economics, this team is responsible for discovering and applying smarter thinking techniques for government.

Faxing faith

The Wailing Wall in Jerusalem has been a focus for devout Jews since time immemorial. As a holy place, it has always attracted those wishing to pray, and there's a long tradition of the devout leaving supplications in the cracks in the wall.

Shortly after fax machines were invented, tourists were bemused to see a fax machine at one side of the ancient wall so the faithful could transmit their prayers and have them placed in the cracks by rabbis.

When push comes to shove

Professor Richard Thaler, an American social scientist, and his colleague Cass Sunstein developed the thinking behind the Nudge principle of behavioural economics. Both President Obama's administration and the UK's coalition government have enthusiastically adopted the approach.

The Nudge principle is based on the notion that people typically behave emotionally rather than rationally. Even when presented with compelling facts, people often choose something that feels right, however illogical. This isn't a new idea – it's one that's been repackaged and wheeled out many times over the years. Thaler's argument is that, by judicious use of small nudges in the right direction, you can turn to advantage people's tendency to act on their emotions.

You can adopt this technique when exploring ideas in the context of creative thinking. Sometimes you want a blockbuster of an idea, but at other times a gentle nudge may be all that you need.

One frequently cited example is that of using *soft language* (that is, language that avoids harsh and direct turns of phrase in favour of inviting, persuasive and unthreatening alternatives) on official forms such as tax returns, to persuade people to pay the money owing by appealing to their better nature instead of threatening them with dire consequences for failing to do so.

Influencing influential people

Several of the ideas put forward by Thaler appear similar to the work of Professor Robert Cialdini, another academic that politicians on both sides of the Atlantic have embraced. His book is called, appropriately enough, *Influence: The Science of Persuasion*.

Cialdini based his work on six principles which he claims describe the ways in which human decision-making is governed socially. His six principles and their corresponding traps, which are in *italics*, are described in the following list:

✔ **Liking:** We like to buy from people we like, it seems. Cialdini found a consistent pattern of people choosing to purchase from nice sales persons, even on limited exposure. Avon and Tupperware both use friendly local agents in domestic party settings, so customers can form a bond with them. While this may sound obvious when put so baldly, it can be seen as a common, subtle, and effective sales ploy, *my friend. In fact, because I like you, I'm going to share the secrets of Cialdini's other five principles, just with you.*

✔ **Authority:** People tend to obey those they see as authority figures. So people with impressive titles (professor, doctor, superintendent) gain instant deference, as do those in uniform, including men in white coats. The notorious Milgram experiments demonstrated this in in the 1950s, showing that people would follow instructions when ordered to do so by authority figures, even if they thought they were hurting others. *As an expert in this field, I'm reassuring you that this is true.*

✔ **Commitment and consistency:** People trust reliable delivery and respond positively to dedication and promises that are kept. You can see this clearly in fast food outlets, where a basic contract of quality and speed of service exists. Interestingly, once established, a bond often remains even when an initial deal is withdrawn. This is a ploy used frequently in car sales, where an implied offer changes at the last moment. *And if you read the rest of this book, you will be happier, more successful and more creative with every page.*

✔ **Reciprocity:** Scratch my back, and I'll scratch yours. A common tactic, especially in transactions involving several stages, is giving something in order to get something more back. This can be offering a free pen simply for making an inquiry (that's to say, revealing extensive personal details which the recipient can then sell to third parties). *If you recommend my book, I'll recommend yours.*

✔ **Social proof:** Testimonials work because people trust what people they trust do. You're more likely to purchase a product recommended by a friend or familiar trustworthy figure who has used it. (Richard and Judy's book recommendations were a stunningly successful example of this principle at work.) *If you're enjoying this book, let me suggest another one you might like.*

✔ **Scarcity:** 'Sale ends Wednesday!' 'Only five apartments left!' The threat of unavailability is a powerful motivator, and is often used to instigate action. Some exponents rely heavily on this technique, following one 'once in a lifetime' offer with another, like an eternal Groundhog Day. *You'll never have another chance to read this for the first time!*

Of course, you can use more than one of these principles to create a more sophisticated campaign. Cialdini's work was initially the subject of extended academic study into the social factors governing decision-making. The business community then eagerly explored his theories for their insights into marketing techniques. Cialdini subsequently presented his theories to both the UK and US governments, and it's easy to see why they would've been intrigued.

Next time you're watching television, reading a magazine or shopping, notice how many of the six factors are directed at you and have helped you make a purchase decision:

✔ Do you find yourself feeling a bit more loyal towards a shop which provided very friendly service? Has it made you go back to that shop?

✔ Do you trust the advice from the man in the white coat selling you toothpaste on TV? (Did you notice whether he said he was a dentist?)

✔ Are you reassured that your favourite eating place always makes your lunch in exactly the same way and serves it quickly? Would you be concerned if they changed the recipe without telling you or took twice as long as usual to serve you?

✔ Did you decide to buy something recently because the salesperson threw in something extra for free? Did you take advantage of another offer because of it?

✔ Did you buy something recently because a friend or celebrity you trust recommended it?

✔ Did you recently take advantage of a limited offer, perhaps in a sale?

You can make this exercise even more fun if you swap experiences with a friend.

Practising what you preach?

Cialdini's book *Influence* is a model of thorough research, but it's also very amusing. Having spent some three years working undercover in a variety of jobs for background research, he designated himself the worst person he knew at influencing others, and his book is full of self-deprecating anecdotes that lighten the academic tone.

However, there's a serious intent behind his witty observations, and Cialdini makes a convincing argument that much modern marketing is based on ingenious thinking about the subtle factors that drive people to make certain decisions without being aware that they're being manipulated. He's highly regarded by his peers as a leading authority on the subject.

Part of the skill involved in influence campaigns is the apparent innocence of the process:

✔ Did you notice that I got your attention by saying the book was amusing, and that Cialdini put himself down as a bit of an amateur? I made him sound like a nice guy to help you warm to him. That's using *Liking*. (He *is* genuinely a nice guy, by the way.)

✔ Then I pointed out his status among other experts. That's using *Authority*.

These are just two examples of the ways in which the science of influence pervades so many areas, and why it's so attractive to politicians.

Easy come, easy go

In the political arena, some fashionable creative thinking techniques are always at work. Nudge and Influence currently have centre stage. However, in an era in which professional advisors are always on the look-out for creative solutions that they can adapt for political purposes, a tendency to follow fashion exists. New ideas can be dropped as easily as they're picked up.

Shedding Light on the Dark Side of Creativity

Creativity is a subject that attracts a lot of chatter and many assumptions – not necessarily based on fact. There's some residual belief that creativity can't be trusted because it's based on things that can't be seen or measured. And unfortunately, some of these assumptions are fundamentally negative in nature, and provide a darker side to the creative equation.

Limiting beliefs

Many individuals who think they're not creative have that view because of limiting beliefs they have acquired in school and adult life.

What's a *limiting belief*? The term is widely used in psychology and neuro-linguistic programming (NLP) as a description of a permanent frame of mind that inhibits or prevents action. (I explain NLP in Chapter 1.)

Beliefs aren't reality; they're simply a set of rules people impose on themselves. They're embedded within a wider structure of the way we view the world. In NLP, this structure is known as the logical levels. It's best described in a hierarchy, shown in Figure 2-2; read it from the bottom up.

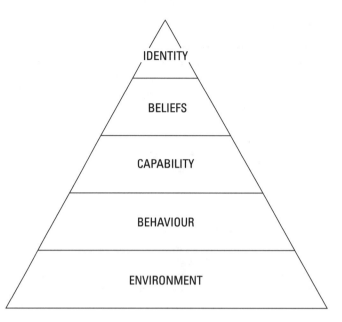

Figure 2-2:
The logical
levels
of NLP.

The following is a short description of each of the levels. If you take the simple sentence 'I can't do that here', different emphasis changes the meaning depending on where you are in terms of your logical levels:

✓ **Identity:** '*I* can't do that here.' This is a statement about the core of your personality – the real you. People often find it difficult to articulate their personal identity, but they know immediately when it's violated in any way. Identity sits at the top of the pyramid as the belief that governs all the others. If you're imprisoned in a non-creative identity, it takes a lot of shifting to change your self-perception.

✓ **Belief:** 'I *can't* do that here.' This is a statement about what you believe deep inside – this is where life-and-death decisions take place. This is also the home of limiting beliefs, the ones that inhibit your ability to use the whole of your creative potential. This is where people say, 'It's just not in me' or 'I'm not talented/smart/young enough to do this.' Limiting beliefs are often accompanied by a great deal of self-talk – the eternal inner commentary that runs in your head. Self-talk tends to get louder and more persistent in the face of a challenge.

✓ **Capability:** 'I can't *do* that here.' This is a statement about how you do things – what you believe you can and can't do. Frequently, this is not reflected in realistic cognitive or physical limitations, and coaching can be an effective method for raising your game. Creative potential is not ruled out here.

✔ **Behaviour:** 'I can't do *that* here.' This is a statement about the rules and conventions you place on situations – whether it's okay for you to do something. As far as limiting beliefs are concerned, this is where the opinions of others come into the equation, often based on assumptions about what you *think* others might think. 'They'd think I was getting above myself' or 'They'd *never* approve of me doing that.' Most of these ideas are merely habit-based, and can respond well to challenge.

✔ **Environment:** 'I can't do that *here*.' This is a statement about context – what's around you and influencing you. Many exceptionally creative individuals have come from poor educational backgrounds or provincial locations: 'You'll never amount to anything' or 'No one famous ever came from there.' Overcoming such limitations is often a first step to a creative life.

At the lower levels, you're mainly dealing with patterns of your daily life that guide the ways in which you choose to act. These are mostly habitual and performed below the conscious level (do you think about how you make your breakfast or how you get to work or your studies?). The belief and identity levels reflect your core values. These are the levels that give rise to 'causes to die for' – sometimes literally. Though they're the most difficult to change, these beliefs are the ones truly creative minds work hardest to challenge.

Beliefs, however strongly held, are always capable of being changed, and many creative thinkers have found the inner courage and resources to free themselves from such limitations.

Draw the logical levels pyramid in Figure 2-2, and at each level write down your corresponding personal belief. If you feel comfortable, do this with a trusted companion. Then consider what you would have to do to release yourself from those beliefs you don't think are helping you creatively.

Generating energy and ignoring burn-out

A perception exists that creativity can lead to burn-out, and like many assumptions it probably has roots in images borrowed from fiction. There's also the notion that you can overdo it, and that somehow creative energy is a finite resource that you can use up. Although some individuals have always fallen by the wayside, as it were, this doesn't chime with most creative experience.

Creativity tends to be an energy-*generating* process, with individuals benefitting from the fulfilment of their imagination. When some form of exhaustion occurs, it's most likely to be associated with conflict or other external factors.

In the modern Western world, stress is frequently cited as a factor in burn-out. Stress and its close cousin anxiety (especially the free-floating variety) both have a deleterious impact over time, and you should heed the early-warning signs. (I discuss stress and anxiety in more detail in Chapter 10.)

Some people experience burn-out as a result of frustration or disappointment. For example, if a major project is cancelled, it's not uncommon for participants to experience prolonged lethargy and feelings of depression, which in extreme cases can result in loss of hope and self-belief.

Stress and anxiety can creep up unnoticed, so it's good to monitor the progress of any project for these factors. Unexpected reverses and disappointments can trigger longer-term problems, sometimes surfacing a long time after the critical moment. Ensure that you notice the impact of adverse events on those you (and your team if you have one) work with. Be open to discussion of stress-inducing factors and the coping levels of yourself and your colleagues.

Melding creativity and personality

When you think of distinctively creative individuals, conjuring up stereotypes, which may or may not be accurate, is easy to do. Certainly, in the illustrations that follow you may recognise someone who fits the profile, but, like most stereotypes, these personalities are exaggerations, often derived from characters in fiction.

This list includes some of the most common perceptions of creative types:

- ✔ **The outsider:** The creative person is seen as an outsider – a loner who's set apart from society. It can be a very seductive image, and many art students and would-be rock stars have cultivated this style, realising that it sets them apart from the ordinariness of everyday life, and is attractive to both peers and potential romantic conquests.

- ✔ **The eccentric:** The *Back to the Future* films featured everyone's idea of the classic eccentric inventor – wide-eyed, wild-haired and in a permanent frenzy of idea-mania. Christopher Lloyd's hilarious portrayal of Dr Emmett Brown was instantly impressive. And Eddie Murphy captured the hysterically nerdy intensity of the love-crazed academic Professor Klump in *The Nutty Professor*.

  Both these images conform to stereotypes (or archetypes) based on the notion that creative individuals have to be cranky or disturbed. The eccentric shares a lot of attributes with the outsider position, placing the creator outside mainstream society. Other oddities are often added to this group, such as the absent-minded professor who can split the atom but not find his own house keys. Or the unworldly judge who announces that a book is so obscene that 'One wouldn't let one's servants read it' or whose colleague has to ask 'And who exactly *are* the Beatles?'

Eccentrics have always been valued as adding colour to life, but being eccentric certainly isn't an integral part of the creative process. Many creative individuals are decidedly level-headed and would not appreciate being lumped in the 'eccentric' category. One of the UK's leading designers, Thomas Heatherwick (designer of the new London double-decker bus and the Olympic cauldron, among many other internationally recognised achievements), rejects the term inventor because, as he puts it: 'In the British psyche the word inventor is immediately linked with mad.'

That said, some individuals of a creative disposition deliberately opt for a different dress code or lifestyle as a way of preserving their distance from those who would not assist their cause, or simply to be provocative. Whether they're eccentric or mad is something best judged by their output, not the way they look.

✔ **The mad man:** The questions about the connections between creativity and insanity have long been with us. Does creativity cause insanity? Or does insanity make you creative? Is there any truth in these notions?

One definition of insanity is the inability to function, and while mental illness has destroyed some creative individuals – and also members of the wider population – many creative individuals have led productive lives despite exhibiting odd tendencies. (See the nearby sidebar 'Creative geniuses or mad men?')

Many creative individuals choose to live outside the normal social conventions – and other people regard them as eccentric or a bit odd for doing so – but otherwise no hard evidence suggests that they're more prone to madness than anyone else.

Creative geniuses or mad men?

It's indisputable that some artists have exhibited disturbed behaviour:

✔ Vincent van Gogh's incident with his ear is often cited as an illustration of madness among creative types (although it may actually have been his housemate Gauguin who sliced it off in a drunken row – the jury's still out on that one).

✔ Tchaikovsky was alleged to have conducted with one hand on his head because he was afraid his head would fall off.

✔ The brilliant mathematician John Nash (portrayed by Russell Crowe in the film *A Beautiful Mind*) suffered debilitating episodes of paranoid schizophrenia.

But these are exceptions.

Outside life

Colin Wilson was a maverick writer who lived the part of the outsider. He wrote his first book, *The Outsider*, while homeless, sleeping rough on Hampstead Heath. The book, published in 1956 at the height of paranoia about the atom bomb, stands as a brilliantly incisive analysis of the role of the outsider as an archetype throughout history.

Wilson drew on an extraordinary range of sources to advance his thesis, and the book remains an original masterpiece, without precedent at the time Wilson wrote it.

The Outsider provided the stimulus for a generation of alienated writers, artists and filmmakers, for whom it became something of a handbook. The various anti-establishment movements and existentialist beatniks of the 1950s and 1960s all emerged from adherents to his themes.

Walking daily to the Reading Room of the British Museum for research, Wilson developed the manuscript wherever he happened to be. By a remarkable stroke of fortune, Victor Gollancz, a noted independent publisher, accepted Wilson's manuscript, realising that it fitted the zeitgeist of a time when alienation was at its most fashionable.

Unfortunately, Wilson never again matched the success of this unique masterpiece of creative insight, and he died in relative obscurity.

Chapter 3

Exploring the Creative Mindset

· ·

In This Chapter

▶ Accepting your creative nature

▶ Becoming conscious of your consciousness

▶ Looking at states of creativity

▶ Understanding creative differences

· ·

Are you creative? This isn't a trick question. If you think you're not, this is unfortunate, because creativity is a universal resource, like language. You learned to speak at an early age because you had a natural facility, and you began to absorb words, then join them up, and pretty soon you could string sentences together.

And while you were learning to speak, you were exploring the world in other ways: drawing, finding out how things worked, and how you could get what you wanted. All these are creative activities.

If you don't think you're creative, it's because somewhere along the way you became disengaged from the creative experience and acquired a belief system that defined creativity as something for other people. You can develop a creative mindset. An excellent starting point is to recognise the creativity in your own environment then to expand your vision to wider horizons.

Creativity comes in all shapes and sizes, and its manifestations take many different forms. Regardless of what you may be inclined to think, plenty of evidence suggests that all people are, in fact, creative in their chosen occupations and their daily lives.

Being Creative – All the Time

If you already understand that creativity is part and parcel of everyone's daily life, you're better equipped to spot creative thinking in action. In general, it helps to nurture a positive and receptive attitude to evidence of creative thinking.

Creativity is an inbuilt response to many kinds of challenges. When a situation demands it, most people are more than capable of pulling a creative rabbit out of the hat. But even if you can't be continually creative at first, you can ensure that you make yourself aware of it and observe the creativity around you.

Develop a habit of noticing the little things that stimulate your imagination. Every time you think 'That's clever!' or 'How did they do that?' follow up by exploring your observations a bit more thoroughly. Many artists cultivate this technique as a way of keeping their vision sharp. It's part of a wider pattern of vigilance and being curious about everything.

Realising that you can't not be creative

If cold hard logic ruled the world, creative expression would have very limited opportunity for appearance. Buildings would be functional, work would be endlessly dull, and leisure time would be very, very quiet. Fortunately, creativity has a tendency to burst through even the strongest barriers, and it crops up in the most unexpected places.

You have creativity in your blood, even if you haven't consciously explored it yet. Creative thinking manifests itself every time you encounter an unfamiliar problem. You automatically enter an interrogative mode: *'What's this all about?'* You search your mental filing system for similar situations, and you begin to formulate hypotheses and test them: *'It looks like one of those I dealt with before. Let's try this. Did that work? What next?'*

Next time you encounter a problem, try to step back and watch your mind at work. Note the kind of questions you ask. Consider the processes you engage as you move to the solution. Notice how you feel when you realise you've cracked it.

As you explore creative thinking in an everyday context, whether it's solving a cryptic crossword or assembling some flat-pack furniture, notice the emotions that accompany the stages of the activity, from problem to solution.

Evolutionary eating

Creative thinking even affects the food you eat. Many commonplace products have taken time to evolve to their current status:

✔ When people first imported potatoes from the Americas, they ate only the leaves – they thought the tubers from the soil were poisonous, and so discarded them.

✔ Pineapples were once so rare and exotic that only the wealthiest could afford them, and people used them as decoration instead of food. Their unique shape was used to adorn public buildings. Noted architect Sir Christopher Wren nearly placed them on St Paul's Cathedral when he rebuilt it after the Great Fire of London in 1666.

✔ Soya has acquired many different applications from its original function as a simple source of protein to its current use in dozens of forms, from sauce to milk to meat substitute. Each new direction was the result of thinking creatively.

Exhibiting everyday creativity

Every day, you and those around you perform dozens of actions, large and small, which demonstrate creative thinking. You may find a better way to juggle your shopping bags and open the front door at the same time. You may discover a shortcut in a task you thought would take a long time. Or you may find a previously undiscovered route to a familiar destination. All these little improvements in daily life reflect your creative mind at work. And if this is happening at the most basic level, imagine what you may discover when your mind is actively engaged in seeking creative solutions.

It's salutary to consider everyday processes like these that must have taken a long time to achieve their current state. Likewise, many now-familiar products haven't always existed in their present form, such as the humble ballpoint pen which gradually evolved from the quill pen over several generations.

In daily life, notice the next time you find a new function for an old product, or a colleague does. Consider anything from using a bottle as a vase to creating funky handbags from old clothing. Then think up another new function.

Knowing creativity when you see it

Sometimes creativity is out in the open for all to see, and everyone recognises it. You may see a great film, read a stunning book or hear an exciting new song. These examples are all conspicuous creativity. But you can find less obvious evidence of creativity if you make the effort to look for it.

Sometimes creativity is hidden from view and has to be unearthed. For example, most graffiti is an eyesore, poorly executed tags scribbled in public places for nuisance value. However, on occasion some diamonds in the rough stand out by virtue of superior thought and execution. Indeed, the American artist Jean-Michel Basquiat was discovered through his graffiti, and in the UK most people now know the work of Banksy, who uses graffiti to make incisive political statements.

Next time you encounter something unusual, whether it's a wall painting, a customised car, or the individual style worn by a teenager, don't just dismiss it, but look beyond the surface at what's being communicated. You may just surprise yourself.

Having the creative touch

In the world of art and antiques, all kinds of experts earn their livelihood through their deep knowledge of their subject. Most of the time they're very good at what they do, identifying and dating even the most obscure artefacts in their specialist fields.

However, the issue that separates the best from the rest is the ability to spot fraud. Galleries and collectors alike fear that on careful examination, a priceless piece may turn out to be a fake. In fact, this has happened many times. Specialists have even exposed as fraudulent copies works that have hung in national galleries for years.

A small group of experts can tell, at just a glance, whether something is real or a fraud. In his book *Blink*, Malcolm Gladwell calls this form of rapid cognition *thin-slicing*. It seems that deep knowledge of a subject allows some individuals to tune in to the essence of a challenge with only the briefest exposure. Gladwell reports this phenomenon in a number of fields including medicine, when doctors are able to make accurate diagnoses with minimal information.

Another manifestation of the creative touch is the talent some artists have for making *good marks*, where every line they draw or paint seems uniquely beautiful. The disciplines of drawing and painting are difficult to master and maintain at a high level, and most artists produce their fair share of second-rate output. Artists offer a wry compliment in the presence of genius, and grudgingly admit about the handful of truly special individuals in every generation that they 'couldn't make a bad mark'.

Picasso was one of this rare breed whose every artistic endeavour was superb. If you visit the Picasso Museum in Barcelona you can see the rapid sketches of doves Picasso made at the age of five, which caused his father – himself a skilled professional artist – to put down his brushes in deference to genius.

Knowing the Moment versus Knowing the Outcome

Creative thinking often has an unpredictable outcome. Indeed, sometimes the aim of thinking creatively is to end up in a new, unknown place.

One well-known example of the unpredictability of the creative urge is the song 'Yesterday', one of the most-recorded and best-selling songs of all time. Apparently the melody came to Paul McCartney in a dream, and when he awoke, he thought it was quite good. However, the only lyric that came courtesy of the dream was the line 'scrambled eggs', which didn't seem very promising. But the melody wouldn't go away, and eventually he found the words that brought the song to life.

Many creative individuals have described this kind of gestation period, which apparently can take hours or years.

A change is as good as a rest

Creativity, unlike rational thinking, tends not to flow evenly. This is both one of the frustrations and one of the joys of the experience. Creative expression often seems to operate on a different clock, with its own timetable. It doesn't necessarily recognise deadlines. In fact, a burst of creativity – sometimes described as an epiphany – often follows a period of frustration or being stuck.

Nowadays, creativity experts recommend that if you're faced with a creative block, change your pace and location. Essentially, do whatever allows your mind to disengage from the task in hand and create some space. The solution may be as simple as getting some fresh air and going for a walk.

If the rough form of a creative thought is present but the complete article hasn't revealed itself, adopting a similar strategy to the one for when you are stuck can be effective.

Changing what you're doing, whether it's mentally shifting your mindset or physically moving to a fresh location, can trigger the next step in the creativity process.

If you experience that distinctive moment when creativity strikes, it's important to respond immediately. Even if you're unable to complete the creative act in full, ensure that you can capture the thought before it dissipates or disappears altogether. Carry a notepad or journal, and in your place of work or study have a pad handy. You never know. . . .

And a rest is as good as a change

A recurrent theme in creative thinking is the beneficial effect of relaxation or even sleep. Sometimes, when you're stuck with half an idea, a few minutes of contemplation, meditation or power napping can provide the cognitive space for the rest of the idea to manifest itself.

If you're wrestling with a creative issue – perhaps a problem you just can't solve – take some time out to relax, close your eyes and meditate, or doze for a few minutes.

Exploring Different States of Consciousness

When you're awake, you're awake. But what *kind* of awake? Many states of consciousness exist, and in the course of a single day you may move through a lot of them.

Where creative thinking is concerned, one of the most useful states is what neuro-linguistic programming (NLP) practitioners describe as a *resourceful state*, which is a state in which you're able to access and use positive, helpful emotions and strategies.

The following sections describe some of the states conducive to creative thinking, both when you are fully conscious and in other frames of mind.

Memories, dreams and reflections

The mechanism of memory has fascinated scientists for years. It was one of the first subjects studied in the 1880s when psychology was a new discipline. Now memory is one of the preoccupations of the current generation of neuro-scientists, who have MRI scanners to provide live access to brain activity.

Remembrance of things past

Memories can be very real, and they can also be misleading. Your brain is capable of playing tricks with your experience, convincing you that you did something you didn't, or you didn't do something you did.

If you've ever had a reunion with friends or family, it's possible that you talked about remembering something from your childhood, only for others to correct you with, for example: 'We never went to Madame Tussauds on that trip!' or 'Uncle Harry was dead then!' or 'It was *you* who pushed your sister in the pond!' You may have been shocked, because you had a vivid – almost photographic – recollection of events.

This false memory is a surprisingly common phenomenon and can occur in relation to both trivial and serious events.

Fitting memory to reality

Police find the identification of suspects by members of the public an extremely unreliable process, and even professionals are prone to misidentification on a huge scale. Having formed a mental image, it can be difficult to displace it when confronted with reality.

Malcolm Gladwell, the author of *Blink*, experienced this phenomenon at first hand: a group of New York cops who suspected him of being a rapist they were seeking suddenly surrounded him. The cops showed Gladwell a photograph of the wanted man. It then took Gladwell an agonisingly long time to point out that he was a different height, build and skin colour from the felon, and their only common feature (the reason the police had targeted Gladwell) was their Afro hair-styles.

Dreaming of something or nothing

Do you remember your dreams? It seems everyone dreams (the evidence is in the rapid eye movements that are tracked in sleep studies). However, not everyone recalls their dreams, and some people can retrieve only fragments.

Some dreams appear to be nonsense (due, it's thought, to the random firing of neurons); others make sense and can provide useful insights or inspiration.

Your dream pattern isn't fixed. It's easy to improve recall of your dreams by keeping a *dream diary* in which you record your dreams upon awakening. As you develop your dream diary, you'll notice that some of your material relates to current preoccupations (because the unconscious mind processes what the conscious mind feeds it). This can be very useful in contributing to creative thinking. Even seemingly intractable problems can sometimes be resolved through the imagery provided by your dreams.

Reflecting on reflections

Reflections are part of the mental reconstruction process. Memories are never just what actually happened. The mind works on narratives and metaphors – the building blocks of memory. So the past becomes a series of stories, and those stories are full of adjustments, embellishments and interpretations. All of these colour the original experience.

With someone you've known for many years, compare notes on an event you shared a long time ago. Try to recall specifics: what the weather was like, what you were both wearing, what you ate or drank, who else was present, and so on. Monitor how much you diverge on the little details. Who do you think is correct?

Daydreams, sleep and meditation

On a typical day, you travel through several different levels of consciousness, usually without noticing. Some of these are what everyone would agree as being awake, but you drift to different levels more frequently than you might imagine. Many of these levels of consciousness are trance or light trance states.

Daydreaming creatively

When you're meant to be working, being caught daydreaming is usually frowned upon. However, for some personality profiles, and in certain circumstances, daydreaming can be a sign of a creative mind at work. Daydreaming is a kind of limbo state, and its cognitive effects aren't unlike the alpha rhythms generated by dozing. The difference is that the reverie of daydreaming is conscious, and it's usually easy to snap out of it. Many individuals of a creative disposition find that daydreaming is their default response when faced with a problem.

If you're daydreaming, it could mean you're on the verge of a great discovery.

Sleeping on it

Just as there are many levels of consciousness, many levels of sleep also exist (which I explore in Chapter 10). The restorative power of sleep appears to be especially important in the creative process.

It's always good practice to ensure that you sleep well when engaged in a period of creative thinking, because the kinds of stress induced by poor sleep or lack of sleep are incompatible with creativity.

Meditating

In recent years, meditation has become much accepted in the West, and its value – from health and wellbeing to improved concentration – has been recognised in many situations. In the context of creative thinking particularly, meditation has proved a valuable aid, because creative thinking flourishes in an environment of relaxation, wellbeing, good humour and access to other states of consciousness, all of which are characteristics of the meditative process. Many varieties of meditation exist, but they all share the attainment of an experience of deep inner relaxation, which is very conducive to thinking creatively. As a prelude to a creative session, a bout of meditation, however brief, can be a powerful stimulus.

If you've tried meditation, you know how enjoyable the feeling of inner calm can be. And if you haven't, you're in for a pleasant surprise. Just follow these steps:

1. **Seat yourself in a comfortable position, and touch your thumb and middle finger together on each hand.**

   If you're able to sit cross-legged, by all means do so – but it's not essential. If you're in a chair, have both feet on the floor and your arms resting on your thighs.

2. **Close your eyes and focus on relaxing your body from head to toe.**

   Notice your head, how it sits comfortably on your neck. If you like, move your head around gently so you can feel your neck muscles relax. Continue down your body, noticing the relaxation of your chest, your arms and hands, then your trunk, legs and feet.

   Don't rush this process; take your time. As you become more experienced, you'll discover that relaxing your body is all part of the whole experience and is valuable in its own right.

3. **Keep your focus on your breathing, your stillness and your relaxation, and let all your thoughts go.**

   As thoughts come (they will!), disregard them and just concentrate on your breathing. Don't adjust it; simply notice the rate of your breaths, and how deep each breath is.

   Continue sitting in this state for as long as you feel comfortable. Allow about a quarter of an hour. After a while, your breathing will gradually become more shallow.

4. **When you feel you've reached the end of your relaxation cycle (you'll know when), don't rush back to consciousness.**

   Gently resurface and, when you're ready, open your eyes and gradually adjust your posture.

The first few times you meditate, keep in mind that it's a completely new experience for you, so don't try too hard. Just notice the feelings that occur. As you become more familiar with the process, you can begin to refine your technique in a number of ways, but this simple experience will introduce you to some of the immediate benefits of contemplative relaxation, and prepare you for some good creative thinking.

Dreaming of results

You can find many stories of individuals having great creative thoughts while dozing or asleep. Everyone knows the story of Newton being woken by an apple falling on his head, and how that experience led to his theory of gravity. (Even though there's no evidence it actually happened like that, the falling apple is a nice little story.)

The kind of sleep most often associated with creative thinking is called *hypnogogic imagery*, and it happens in the lightest stage of sleep, such as when dozing in the sun.

One famous example of hypnogogic imagery is that of chemist August Kekulé (allegedly while on the upper deck of a bus to Clapham during his time in London). Kekulé was working on the structure of the benzene ring (an important

chemical structure, an understanding of which was essential for industry). He was stuck because, lacking modern-day instrumentation, he had to infer the structure from chemical reactions, and nothing seemed to fit. While dozing, he had a vivid image of the mythical ouroborus, a legendary snake that eats its own tail. He realised that this was a metaphor for the structure of benzene, which is a hexagonal ring in which the links consist of alternating single and double bonds, resembling the movements of the snake in Kekulé's dream.

Einstein was not only a famous dreamer, he was also an advocate of accessing the subconscious mind in the search for enlightenment. Many of today's quantum physicists owe their inspiration to this pattern of work.

Being wide awake and curious

Being on full alert, with all your senses turned up to full volume, is a very distinctive feeling. Although you may not be able to sustain that state for long periods, that kind of intensity is a feeling worth having, and it's one of the access points for high-level creative thinking.

Waking up to the wide-awake state

When a venerable Oxford don was asked how he always managed to choose the most exceptional students, he replied that he simply looked for the ones who were bright-eyed and bushy-tailed. He evidently understood the connection between smart thinking and alertness.

When you have a creative-thinking challenge, try turning everything up to 11. Taking each sense in turn:

- **Eyes:** Try to *really* see, rather than passively look

- **Ears:** Listen *attentively* to all the sounds around you

- **Nose:** Sniff the air and *notice* all the smells around you

- **Mouth:** Roll your tongue around and *wake up* your taste buds

- **Touch:** *Feel* everything your body is touching

Notice how you feel afterwards.

Feeling curious about being curious

Being curious helps you think creatively. Questioning how things are is an excellent starting point for the kind of analysis that precedes creative thought. This means not taking things at face value. The corporate giant Procter & Gamble teaches its interns: *'If you assume, it makes an ass out of you and me.'*

Suspend your usual critical faculties, and spend some time in a child-like state of innocence, asking basic questions even about things you think you understand. Ask 'Why?' a lot. The adult version of this approach is known as the Socratic method, but it's much more fun just being a kid again for a while.

Noticing what you notice

You can only take in a fraction of the information that bombards you constantly. So whatever you see, hear or feel, there's always much more than you can absorb. You always have room to up your game and boost your informational intake by actively noticing what's going on around you. Doing so impacts directly on your ability to think creatively.

An excellent technique for increasing your power to notice is being present. This approach involves focusing on remembering yourself (that is, being self-aware), what's happening in the here and now, and excluding self-talk (by which I mean the little voice that provides the continuous commentary going on inside your head) and other distractions. See Chapter 13 for an exercise on self-remembering.

Altered states – sex, drugs and rock 'n' roll

Creative individuals have always experimented with altered states of consciousness, and have explored every conceivable method for changing their minds, sometimes literally.

Ian Dury's song 'Sex & drugs & rock & roll' encapsulates the three principal methods used in the search for creative inspiration throughout history.

More sex, please, we're creative

'Love is the Drug' sang Roxy Music, and so it has proved for many creative souls. Historically, many artists have thrown themselves into passionate affairs in the belief that love enhanced their creativity. Picasso was a renowned lover, and intense new relationships marked each phase of his long career. (Regardless of the artistic style he embarked on, at the start of each new romance he painted an intimate portrait in conventional style as a marker.)

From Sanskrit wall paintings through ancient Greek vases to many of today's pop stars, erotic imagery has always had a central role in the creative process.

Whether as the act itself or depictions of it, sex appears essential to many forms of creative expression.

It's the drugs, man

Creativity has a long association with drugs of all descriptions. In the endless quest to stimulate the parts ordinary consciousness can't reach, creative individuals have employed mind-numbing, mind-expanding and mind-warping substances.

The problem is that while drugs may be fascinating for those taking them, with very few exceptions the outpourings of users are anything but creative. Fortunately, many individuals have realised in time that the human mind is perfectly capable of producing exceptional output without external assistance.

It's only rock and roll but I like it

Rock and roll emerged in the 1950s as a powerful aphrodisiac for performers and fans alike. This aspect of creative expression definitely speaks for itself.

Exploring the subconscious

The subconscious grabbed the popular imagination at around the turn of the twentieth century. Some artists became very interested in the new theories of the subconscious advanced by psychoanalysts like Freud, Adler and Jung. Those who were creatively inclined must have felt it was like opening a door to another world.

Surrealism – any form of art dealing with dreams and the workings of the subconscious mind – quickly became a substantial international movement with dreamscape artists from Magritte to de Chirico teasing the public imagination. The most famous surrealist was Salvador Dali, a shameless self-publicist, and many of his and his companions' images are part of the universal visual vocabulary – who can forget bowler-hatted men with apples for faces, deserted eerie spaces or soft pocket-watches? Advertisers and designers picked up on ideas about dream life and the subconscious with enthusiasm.

Now you see it. . .

The fascination with the unconscious mind resulted in a phase of interest in subliminal advertising in the 1950s and 1960s, which generated some unusual ads until the practice was eventually banned.

One example was a magazine ad for a brand of gin in which the ice in the glass spelled out the word 'sex' if you looked carefully. This kind of encoding was thought to register in the subconscious, although the theory remained unproven.

In another attempt to use subliminal messages, some cinemas participated in an experiment whereby they increased the temperature of their auditoriums while advertising a cooling ice cream. Again, the results were inconclusive.

Doing it for Dada

If you wonder why a pickled shark can be described as art, the blame probably lies with Dada. Dadaism was a radical artistic movement that began in the early part of the twentieth century in response to the horrors of the First World War. As an art form, it grew out of some of the experiments with Surrealism.

Where classic Surrealist art was primarily concerned with dreams and the unconscious mind, however, Dadaism introduced a distinct political edge.

The Dadaists were discontented with what they saw as the complacency and conservatism of the artistic mainstream, and they were sensitised to the massive upheavals all around them. Capitalism and bourgeois values were under attack across Europe, and revolution was in the air. The shock of the First World War caused Dadaists to explore the destructive urge, and some Dadaists even declared themselves to be anti-art.

In this charged atmosphere, artists experimented with new forms of expression designed to challenge the status quo: Stravinsky wrote *The Rite of Spring*, based on discordant musical structures; Marcel Duchamp hung a urinal in an art gallery and declared it art; and George Grosz produced viciously satirical cartoons attacking politicians.

Creatively, this brief but intense explosion sowed the seeds for changing perceptions about art and culture, and the repercussions continue to this day.

Going punk

In the footsteps of Dada, punk kick-started a similar revolution in the 1970s, with a similar anarchic energy that quickly spread across music, fashion and art. Punk has lasted longer than Dadaism, and you can see its influence in design, film and many other creative manifestations.

Understanding Different People and Different Kinds of Creativity

We're all the same and we're all different, the cliché goes. The precise ways in which people share certain aspects of personality while differing in others has always fascinated scientists. The current study of personality gained a great deal of momentum from the work of the Swiss psychologist Carl Jung.

Jung's theories and the foundations of modern personality assessment

Jung was 20 years younger than Freud and suffered to some degree from being in his shadow. However, while Freud's legacy appeals primarily to a diminishing group of psychoanalytic loyalists today, Jung's influence has grown steadily.

As science has become progressively more engaged with what may be described as the human side of human beings, the study of Jung's humanistic psychology has moved centre stage.

Jung had a far-reaching vision of humanity. Unlike most of his professional contemporaries, he was interested in wellness rather than illness (which was one of the causes of his eventual dispute and separation from Freud and his colleagues). Long before most thinkers, Jung proposed that a universal unconscious connected humankind – a vast cognitive network that allowed individuals to tap into a collective mind. Jung was one of the first to explore *synchronicity* (when apparently unrelated events occur at the same time), which is a recurrent topic in creative thinking.

Jung believed that *archetypes* (specific psychological personalities) were the key to understanding the human psyche, and that humankind was somehow wired to comprehend and incorporate aspects of these archetypes into individual personalities. (I describe several archetypes in Chapter 6's section on classic stories and the book *The Hero's Journey*).

Here are some archetypes. Looking around at people you know, observe which archetypes best describe their personalities: jester, artist, wise old man, earth mother, goddess, trickster, child, hero.

One of the foundational building blocks of Jung's vision was the concept of introverted and extraverted personality types:

✔ **Introvert:** An introvert is primarily driven by interior motivations. If introversion is your style, it means you're likely to be happy with your own company, work best without interruption, separate work from play, and avoid unnecessary distractions.

✔ **Extravert:** An extravert is driven by external forces and events and tends to search for a stimulus. If you're an extravert, you probably like working with the radio on, enjoy interruptions from colleagues and friends, and like to have several things on the go while you're working or relaxing.

There's no right or wrong here. Your personality type is simply how you're wired up.

Jung saw these types as each end of a continuum. At one end, introverts live inside their heads, with a rich interior life. Extraverts, on the other extreme, seek stimulus from the outside world and have a need to express themselves in relation to others.

This basic polarity gave rise to many of the personality assessments in use to this day. Several of them also incorporate other Jungian concepts, such as the spectrum from feeling to thinking and from judging to perceiving.

Using the MBTI – Myers–Briggs Type Indicator

The MBTI is still the most widely used personality assessment tool (practitioners don't like the word *test*) in the business. MBTI is an acronym for Myers–Briggs Type Indicator. The tool is named after the two women who devised the system. Isabel Briggs Myers and her mother Katharine Cook Briggs gathered masses of personality data on index cards long before the advent of computers. And despite this rather basic method of information gathering, their model has proved robust.

The system uses four pairs of preferences based on Jung's work. These are:

✔ Introversion – Extraversion

✔ Sensory – iNtuitive (intuitive is always represented by the letter N, so as not to duplicate the I from Introversion)

✔ Thinking – Feeling

✔ Perceiving – Judging

These pairs produce a matrix of 64 combinations of personality profiles, identified by their dominant initial letters. So an individual can be described as, say, ENTJ (your humble author's profile); this personality type is summarised as representing life's natural leaders.

Extraverts outnumber introverts by around three to one in Western society. To give a flavour of the temperaments behind the acronyms, Table 3-1 shows the one-line descriptions of the most and least common personality types.

Table 3-1	Most and Least Common Myers–Briggs Types
Most Common Types	**Least Common Types**
ESTP: The ultimate realist	INFJ: An inspiration to others
ESFP: You only go around once in life	INTJ: Everything has room for improvement
ESTJ: Life's administrators	INFP: Performing noble service for society
ESFJ: Hosts and hostesses of the world	INTP: A love of problem-solving

The MBTI is used at all levels of business and is also applied as a method of assessing teams. It's also used in family dynamics, and a children's version exists.

The creativity index for the MBTI, called the MBTI-CI, identifies an SFP cluster (nicknamed the artist profile) as being the most likely to reflect more creative types.

DISC jockeying

DISC profiling has emerged as a popular challenger to the MBTI in recent years. Designed and developed by psychologists, the DISC model is both statistically *valid* (it measures what it purports to measure) and *reliable* (it's a repeatable measure). DISC is used both by individuals seeking insights into their own behaviour and motivations, and by groups wanting to understand the dynamics of, for example, families and work teams.

DISC is based on four main behavioural types (see also Figure 3-1):

- ✔ **Dominance,** which relates to assertiveness and the desire for power and control. Ds typically like to be in charge and make decisions quickly. Others can sometimes find Ds a little remote and obstinate, especially when thwarted.

- ✔ **Influence,** which relates to communication and social situations. Originally called the 'Inducement' group, Is tend to be at ease in social situations and are good facilitators, persuaders and motivators. They're often popular, but can seem somewhat 'slippery'.

✔ **Steadiness,** which relates to persistence, patience and thoughtfulness. Originally called the 'Submission' group, they are at their best in situations requiring quiet efficiency. Not likely to be the life and soul of the party, they are nevertheless fiercely loyal.

✔ **Compliance,** which relates to organisation and structure. These individuals tend to be found in highly structured situations with clear rules and boundaries. They're likely to have a conservative outlook, and resist ambiguity. Some versions of DISC also describe people with this behaviour type as 'cautious' and 'conscientious'.

Figure 3-1:
The DISC
profile.

Most individuals embody a combination of more than one type.

The DISC assessment yields a highly detailed series of profiles and takes into account differences between 'natural' and 'work' frames of mind, acknowledging that people adapt their behaviour to different circumstances. As with the MBTI, several versions are available.

Spoilt for choice

Personality assessment has become a large industry in its own right, and many methodologies are available to suit every, er, personality. Some are very simple, if not simplistic, and provide a quick snapshot – usually in one of four, six or eight personality dimensions. Other methodologies, like Spiral Dynamics, are based on much more elaborate conceptual frameworks and require deep study and commitment for users to gain the full benefits. Unsurprisingly, these are used much more rarely.

For fans of profiling, it's possible to use any of these personality-assessment systems in conjunction with the others.

Liam Hudson, creative maverick

Hudson was a scientist who definitely walked the talk in his chosen subject of creativity. Much of his work was truly original, setting the foundations for the study and practice of creativity.

In many ways, Hudson was ahead of his time. He had a great sense of mischief and enjoyed upsetting the academic establishment with his controversial views. For example, he proposed

the then wildly unfashionable view that art and science should be considered as interdependent (echoes of Leonardo da Vinci there) rather than as separate disciplines to be kept in separate academic boxes.

His pioneering work on creative thinking has assured him a place as a leading thinker in his own right.

Convergent and divergent thinking

Like lateral thinking, the concept of convergent and divergent thinking has entered the public consciousness, and most people know that convergent thinkers are rational, left-brain types not given to idea-generation, whereas divergent thinkers are open-minded, right-brain types who can, well, think of lots of uses for a brick. As with many cognitive models, there's more to it than that.

One thing experts seem to agree on is that more than one 'creative mood' exists. Just as there are individual differences in other aspects of temperament, it's the same when you seek to be creative.

Where the creative process is concerned, people tend to revert to type. So some get into the creative swing gently, and gradually build up speed. This approach resembles a long-distance runner, taking it steady and reserving energy for a final finish. Others start with a burst of speed, much like a sprinter, and generate masses of ideas at a rapid pace.

Gender

Are men or women the most creative? This question is trickier than it may appear at first sight.

Most of the research (and there's a lot of it) draws a safe tentative conclusion that both women and men are creative (hardly a surprise, because the evidence is all around), but that they tend to excel in different areas. For example, while there are many female writers, there are (historically) more male artists.

However, given the cultural changes today, the situation is fluid and the best advice is to watch this space.

Age

A great deal of evidence suggests that people become less creative as they grow up. Young children are naturally creative and perform well on all kinds of tasks designed to measure their creative output. But tracking young people's creativity through school, college, and into adulthood reveals a steady decline.

Sir Ken Robinson, the respected educationalist, and other experts attribute this to the moulding of a conservative education system designed, as they put it, to produce academics.

But it's not all bad news. There's growing evidence that during adult life and into middle and later age, the brain rewires itself and gets smarter at insight and intuition, both of which are conducive to creative thinking.

Creativity across cultures

Creativity is a universal human characteristic, and it can be seen everywhere, at any time in history. However, creativity isn't evenly spread. Historically, it seems that creativity ebbs and flows over time. The ancient Etruscan, Byzantine, Greek and Roman cultures all showed patterns of creativity in the arts, sciences and architecture – growing, flourishing, then declining and ultimately failing.

Some historians have pointed to an architectural sequence of:

- ✔ Classical, in which the style, like the prevailing culture, is in its purest form
- ✔ Baroque, in which the style reflects increasing success and abundance
- ✔ Rococo, in which the style becomes overblown and decorative, showing signs of decay
- ✔ Dissolution, whether from outside interference or internal collapse

The implication here is that the style of architecture accurately reflects the creative state of the civilisation. If that's true, start to worry if you see evidence of Rococo architecture being built around you!

The 2,000-year-old computer

In a remarkable feat of archaeological detective work, an international team of archaeologists, historians, computer engineers, astronomers and mathematicians recently reconstructed an artefact discovered on a dive in the Mediterranean.

As the team pieced the rusty object together, they gradually realised that they were looking at a sophisticated computer designed to track and predict comprehensive details of planetary cycles, including eclipses and phases of the moon. The artefact also included much about earthly activity that would be of use to sailors. About the size of a laptop computer, this object used a complex series of cogs and trip mechanisms to display its information, and the maths behind the system involved a profound knowledge of prime numbers.

The team deduced that the inventor of this extraordinary device was probably Archimedes, the leading mathematician of his time. In any event, the item was almost certainly constructed during Archimedes' lifetime (circa. 287–212 BC).

Basically, this was a particularly sophisticated *astrolabe*, a device used to calculate astronomical, astrological, navigational and other time–space movements. It was unlikely to be the only one of its kind. After the cultures of the Mediterranean fell, it appears the knowledge moved eastwards, and today Islamic museums, like the one in Qatar, house fine examples of this superb craftsmanship, though none (as yet) are as sophisticated as the 2,000-year old computer.

Discovering pockets of creativity

One classic example of a pocket of creativity is Renaissance Florence, where circumstances conspired to generate a hotbed of creativity. Thousands of artists were at work in that era. Michelangelo and Leonardo da Vinci rubbed shoulders (probably reluctantly, because they despised each other).

This period of exceptional creativity came about for many reasons. Artists were beginning to emerge from an artisan role, in which they were mainly anonymous members of a guild, to have individual status. The emergence of wealthy patrons, in the form of merchants and the Church, fostered this situation. And international exploration enriched the culture and the thirst for knowledge.

Does this seem a bit like the recent history of the music industry, with anonymous performers mutating into stars, and international influences growing the market exponentially? It should, because this kind of pattern occurs in all sorts of cultures, especially in cities.

Breeding creativity

When considering where creativity is most fertile, it's better to think in terms of cities rather than individual countries. Recent research has shown that people are up to three times more creative in cities than in other environments.

Using a series of measures, psychologists have concluded that the diversity of cities – the melting pot effect – and the constant informal interaction are major factors stimulating individuals to fresh thinking and absorption of new ideas and concepts.

Locations like Silicon Valley in California, Grenoble in France and Cambridge in England – and other clusters of similarly inclined people – are also considered as natural breeding grounds for creative thinking. It seems that the extended suburban sprawls of Silicon Valley feature many coffee bars and eating places where like-minded nerds, geeks and technophiles hang out. But research has shown that homogeneous groups such as these – clusters of people who are on the same wavelength – are still not as creatively enriching as the city environment.

Beyond the five senses

How many senses do you think you have? The usual five? Or perhaps more? Perhaps you feel that you experience some of those senses in combination? Conventionally, you expect to have sight, hearing, touch, smell and taste. But do those basic five explain all the sensory information you experience?

- ✔ Have you had that moment when you're aware someone is watching you or standing behind you? (It's called *proprioception*.)
- ✔ Have you entered a room and noticed an 'atmosphere'?
- ✔ Have you 'just known' a loved one is in trouble?
- ✔ Have you correctly predicted that the phone is about to ring?
- ✔ Have you tasted a particular colour, or smelled a particular sound?

Each of these remote experiences is beyond the normal sensory apparatus, but if you recognise any of them you'll know they feel very real. It seems that many people experience events like these frequently. Biologists are becoming interested in these experiences and how they work.

Happenstance and coincidence

Consider the experience conjured up by the two magic words *serendipity* (which is the experience of a 'happy accident') and *synchronicity* (where seemingly unrelated events happen together). You may find that when you're working on something, a magazine article or voice on the radio will produce a word or image that corresponds precisely to your topic. Or the phone rings just when you're thinking of a loved one, and you hear a familiar voice. . . .

There's increasing interest in additional senses, and biologists like Rupert Sheldrake have made extensive study of extrasensory experiences (much to the annoyance of orthodox scientists, some of whom have branded him a heretic and even called for his books to be burned). A brilliant and original thinker, Sheldrake specialises in working at the margins of knowledge, and is fascinated by subjects like proprioception. His work is a brilliant example of creative thinking, because he dares to challenge assumptions in his field of biology and ask questions that few others dare to. The hysterical reaction of some dogmatic scientists to this spirit of inquiry is reminiscent of the treatment received by Galileo (see Chapter 15).

Smelling the colour of the coffee

Another sensory dimension is *synaesthesia*, a condition in which the experience of the senses is somehow mixed. Some people are born with the facility to experience mixed senses. They see sounds (a musician acquaintance uses this to remember compositions – A is green, B flat is blue, and so on). Others feel colours – so sandpaper is yellow for them. Apparently, synaesthesia can be a mixed blessing: some find it a useful way of enriching their sensory experience, while others resent the interference with their normal sensory repertoire.

Close your eyes and invent your own synaesthetic vocabulary. Start with textures and discover what colours you choose for them. If you're musical, give notes colours or textures. Continue through all your senses.

Part II
Preparing Yourself: Creating Your Creative Mindset

The 5th Wave   By Rich Tennant

In this part...

You get into creative thinking and commit to creativity. You discover how to prepare yourself for creative thinking by developing your creative mindset, then you set your creative stage, build your creative environment and use the principles devised by Leonardo da Vinci to establish a creative lifestyle.

Chapter 4

Preparing to Be Creative

*W*hen you're in a creative frame of mind, you can be unstoppable. You have the bit between your teeth and you're raring to go. If you've experienced this feeling and the energy it generates, you'll know without doubt how exciting and involving the experience can be. Unfortunately for most people, creativity isn't a tap that can be turned on at will.

If you decide to do some DIY at the weekend, tidy your desk and filing system, or begin that pressing project, you probably know that characteristic moment of hesitation between intention and action. Suddenly it's time to make a cup of tea, check your lottery numbers or phone a friend. That feeling, of course, is procrastination. It crops up in the most unexpected places, and it can be very inconvenient.

When you're embarking on a new project, whatever the scale, one of the biggest problems in getting started can be – getting started! And preparing to be creative is no exception. However exciting or engaging your challenges, it's a fair bet you've hit the buffers on more than one occasion.

So is there a way through this barrier? No magic bullet exists, but this chapter outlines some tactics that can help smooth the path.

Understanding the Creative Process

One of the great things about creative thinking is that it attracts creative thinkers, some of whom have devised ingenious methods for enhancing creative thinking skills. I talk about many of the abundance of tools available in the chapters in Part III. But, as you prepare to get into creative mode, the main thing to know about these tools is that most of them are designed around a process divided into three basic parts: opening up, closing down, and changing your mind. I discuss each stage in the following sections.

Opening up to ideas and originality

The first perspective on creative thinking is opening up or idea generation. For many, this is what comes to mind when creativity is mentioned. In this phase, you can make use of various techniques designed to shape, structure and stimulate the creative thinking process.

Sometimes, this process is genuinely open-ended, in the search for something entirely original. Here, the tools used may be ones designed to help the imagination soar, and to get as far from the here and now as possible. You may, for example, want to create an entirely new product or product category. This kind of thinking generated products such as Polaroid cameras, the Mini, Swatch watches, and the Apple range.

In other situations, you may be searching for ways to stretch something that already exists. Food and drink manufacturers are constantly seeking innovative ways to extend their product ranges. Examples include cereal makers moving into snack bars, drink makers extending their products into different niches like diet, youth and energy, and confectioners packaging products in a variety of size and shape configurations.

Closing down to solve a problem

In the second phase, the goal is to solve a specific problem. You tend to deploy more structured tools here to lead the creative thinking process through a funnel towards a specific outcome. An example here is the development of an advertising campaign required to meet a number of specific communications objectives.

This closing down process also occurs frequently in product development, where existing products may need updating, upgrading or modernising. Increasing concern for the environment has led many manufacturers to rethink their products in terms of energy-saving, often with exciting and unexpected results.

Changing your mind for a different perspective

The third arena is where the intention is to evolve a different mindset – a conceptual shift – in order to facilitate fresh thinking. This can involve developing the ability to dream or visualise, sometimes aided by tools such as meditation.

Many artists and scientists try to work in this creative space where they can suspend the normal conventions and allow themselves to dream beyond any limits. Thinking of this kind allowed physicists to evolve concepts such as about the existence of 'black holes', which have never been seen but are believed by some to be the very stuff of the universe.

Capturing Your First Ideas

Coming up with creative ideas is intrinsically interesting for most people, whether it's thinking up a better way to organise your filing system or inventing a new kind of mousetrap. Neuroscientists believe that curiosity is a key factor in survival and development. Satisfying your curiosity and expressing yourself are fundamental drives.

Unfortunately, ideas can come and go with alarming ease. A common problem in creative sessions – especially traditional brainstorming sessions – is that exceptionally good ideas can occur out of thin air almost before the session has begun.

Often the very first moments of idea generation produce a rush of energy. Harness this initial burst of energy by capturing your first thoughts as they emerge. Don't censor them by saying to yourself 'This isn't good enough' or 'It's not quite right yet.' Sketch those first ideas using pictures and/or words, depending on your personal preferences. You'll probably be the only one to see these early thoughts, so don't hold back.

Sometimes the creative magic can happen even before a creative-thinking session. I vividly remember setting up a workshop at a well-known advertising agency; one of the arriving participants turned to another as he strolled through the door, and said, 'So this is where we make . . .', and in that moment came up with one of the best-remembered slogans in advertising history. Luckily, his off-the-cuff comment was recorded for posterity. On this occasion.

I've seen groups ignoring these fleeting moments and moving on to progressively weaker thoughts, simply because the best ideas didn't happen when the group expected them to. However, research suggests that idea generation is often front-loaded, with the best quantity and quality of ideas happening at the beginning of a session.

So it pays to be prepared. And that brilliant idea? You may already have had it!

If you give your creativity free rein the moment your imagination kicks in, you can sail right past the procrastination phase almost without noticing. You may not know exactly when your initial rush of creativity will happen, but you certainly know it when it does. And because your brain is wired to recognise and repeat behaviour patterns, you can prime your brain to repeat the experience.

In those early moments of creative thinking, a common source of frustration can be the simple issue of not having anything available to capture the ideas. Much has been said about great ideas written on the back of an envelope, and it's true that anything is better than nothing on which to note a thought before it flies away forever. But being prepared and having a notepad and pen or the notes facility on your mobile phone on hand at all times is better. Who knows, a simple scribble may be the difference between the world having your brilliant anti-gravity machine or never knowing what it missed!

Getting into the Right Space – Mentally and Physically

I'm always surprised when I encounter companies where creative thinking is sandwiched between other activities such as sales forecasts and brand reviews. But it's not just in companies that creative thinking is denied its proper place. I've coached many entrepreneurial individuals who expected creativity to somehow happen as part of the business process.

What's wrong with this picture is that just as a painter sets up for work by mounting a canvas on an easel, preparing the brushes and choosing paints for the palette, you want to set up your creative stage for best results.

Getting in the mood

Doing anything is difficult if you're just not in the mood. So is there such a thing as a creative mood? For some people, the answer is a resounding 'yes!' They know when they're ready to be creative and when the muse is upon them. Some people describe it as an almost tangible presence. They're fortunate enough to be naturally creative and have no problem establishing the right mood. However, this is by no means true for everyone, and at the other end of the scale, some people struggle to get creative. If this scenario sounds familiar, it helps to be prepared.

The mindset you're aiming for is what's called *being in the moment*. If you've ever been totally immersed in a task to the exclusion of everything around you, and forgotten the time, your surroundings, or even how long you've been working, then you've experienced a variation of being in the moment.

The film *The Karate Kid* provides an excellent illustration of this state, when Mr Miyagi, the karate master, makes the reluctant kid perform a series of apparently mundane tasks at his house, such as waxing his car and hammering in nails. Eventually, after much resistance, the kid gets the point, and starts experiencing what it's like to really be in the moment.

Like many features of creative thinking, being in the moment often happens spontaneously, and you only realise what's happened as you emerge from that state. So can you control this state and make it happen at will?

One way to achieve control is to cultivate *self-remembering*, in which you consciously remind yourself of where you are, what you're doing and how you feel. (I look at self-remembering in more detail in Chapter 13.) The aim is to become mindful, a state many people who meditate achieve. Briefly, *mindfulness* describes a condition of attentive awareness, being actively alert to what's happening around you. (You can read about Mindfulness in depth in *Mindfulness For Dummies* by Shamash Alidina (Wiley).) You don't have to be a practising Buddhist or on any kind of spiritual journey to appreciate this state, which is very conducive to creative thinking.

Self-remembering and mindfulness can be hard to do at first, because you're asking yourself to change established habits of thought. When you first attempt it, you're likely to find that you get distracted almost as soon as you start. However, if you begin with small chunks of time, allow for those early distractions and gradually increase the intervals as you gain confidence, it's possible to experience the state quite quickly. And like all new habits, the more you practise, the better you get.

The benefits of being in the moment quickly become apparent as you get used to the process. You'll find that your ability to concentrate increases, as does the way you can filter out extraneous sounds and other distractions.

Setting the scene

Before you begin a creative session, preparing the stage with appropriate primers can be helpful. For example, if you like to work with music, have a selection of your favourite tracks on hand. And if you prefer silence, make sure you get it.

Listening to the sound of silence

When composing, musicians tend to have clear ideas about what works for them and what doesn't. At one end of the scale are those who withdraw from the world and banish all external stimuli, especially other music. At the other end are those more comfortable when immersed in what's going on. These musicians are gregarious and want to be abreast of all the latest sounds. So is one approach superior to the other?

Both Pink Floyd and the Beatles used the Abbey Road studios, but whereas Floyd valued the isolation of an acoustically perfect environment, the Beatles worked with friends constantly dropping in and the radio on (you can hear it on parts of the *White Album*). Both groups achieved their creative aims and produced highly creative ground-breaking albums, but their paths couldn't have been more different.

The same is true in other creative fields. If you visit artists' studios, you find many contrasts. Some studios are austere temples where silence reigns; others resemble a medieval market, with a cacophony of sound and vision bombarding the senses.

What works best? The answer has to be measured by what works for the individual artist and by the quality of the output.

Whatever environment you prefer is fine so long as it's conducive to your way of working, and the outcome is what you were aiming to achieve. If you've found your own creative centre of gravity, you'll probably want to defend it and will work hard to make sure you get what you want in terms of preparation for creative thinking.

To get yourself into a creative mood, try literally setting the scene. You don't have to come up with an elaborate scenario, although it can be fun to go the whole hog and devise your own creative oasis with all the trimmings. At its simplest, you can select a small area of your workroom, or even just part of your desk space, and make this your personal creative area. In the same way that you may create a small shrine for religious or meditation purposes, you can set aside space for when you want to stimulate your creative side. This approach works on the same principle as all behaviour patterns: the more you do it, the better it works. Eventually, turning to your creative space will start your creative juices flowing.

Use as many senses as possible for your mood-setting space. Stimulate your vision with illustrations you associate with creativity. One colleague of mine has pictures of his creative heroes and speculates about what they would say to him about his ideas. This is a variation on the theme of the 'dinner party' recommended by some creative thinking specialists who suggest creating a 'guest list' of creative A-listers whose contributions to the conversation would be invaluable. (Consider what Leonardo da Vinci or Albert Einstein would have to say about your latest idea.) Another colleague has postcards of her favourite artists' works above her desk, which always seems to work for her.

You can play music you find conducive to thinking, perhaps even creating a soundtrack to stimulate the creative juices.

Many people are also subject to the 'fiddle factor' – the tendency to play with any object within reach. Fiddling is the tactile equivalent of doodling and can be a significant aid to creative thinking. Decorate your creative space with a selection of favourite objects you pick because of their shapes, textures or sentimental value.

There are, of course, no limits to what you choose – do what works for you. Whatever you choose to do, just make sure that the scene you set promotes pleasurable, creative feelings.

Surrounding yourself with creative stimuli

When Francis Ford Coppola made the film *The Godfather,* he filled the sets with memorabilia from the era. While rehearsing, the actors could wear clothes and accessories from the period to help create the right atmosphere in their minds, and several of them spoke in interviews about how this total-immersion method worked for them. Apparently, Al Pacino in particular thought that the period Armani ties and heavy cigarette lighters gave him the key to his character and the way he would move and behave. Of course, Coppola isn't the only director to use this ploy, but it clearly worked for him, and it's hard to watch that film without being transported back in time.

The idea of dressing spaces is very relevant to the creative thinking process. You may select favourite visual stimuli such as paintings and photographs that inspire you. Smell, the under-rated sense, can contribute directly to a creative atmosphere, and many artists, sculptors and photographers confess to being addicted to the unique smells of their studios.

Atmosphere may not be tangible, but it's certainly discernible, as many musicians will testify. Some musicians, for example, travel great distances to work in particular studios, sometimes with much more basic equipment than they could afford to hire, simply because of a special quality in the air.

Other ways to make your creative space your own can include colours, textures and personal mementoes to trigger the imagination. Sigmund Freud's consulting room (recreated in the museum that was his Hampstead house), was full of rugs, throws, furniture collected over the years, primitive art, and all sorts of memorabilia – every item imbued with some personal significance.

Of course, you needn't confine the idea of dressing to your chosen creative space. Some creatives I know wouldn't dream of beginning a project without donning a favourite garment or picking up a personal talisman. Some go further and dress for the part. Dickens wouldn't consider writing without wearing one of his favourite brocade waistcoats, and the novelist Wilbur Smith has written every one of his many books with the same fountain pen, given to him by his wife. These quirks may seem odd or trivial, but if their owners believe they aid the creative process, who's to knock them?

Finding creative office space

Apparently, there's a time and a place for everything, and this often seems to be the case with creative thinking. In this crowded world, space is at a premium, and this is certainly true of the typical office environment. The cartoonist Scott Adams has become world famous for his sardonic depictions of his character Dilbert's stressed daily life in the cubicles of a bog-standard open-plan office. In such offices, businesses often conduct their workshops and brainstorming sessions in small, crowded meeting rooms within tight time schedules. If this is a familiar description for you and your work space, it's hardly surprising that creative inspiration can sometimes be hard to come by.

When I conduct workshops on creative thinking, I often begin by asking participants to produce two drawings: one of their own work area and one of their favourite space for spending time at home. Sometimes they draw their living room or study, sometimes the kitchen or bedroom. Some even lovingly sketch their bathroom! But whatever home space they choose, the important point is the difference between where they work and where they like to live. Often, the contrast is dramatic. The point is that many people spend the biggest and best chunk of the day in a space that's not as pleasant as home.

Napping on the job – and finding space to do it

US President John F Kennedy surprised his aides during the Cuban missile crisis and other turbulent moments of his presidency by taking frequent power naps, a habit he'd picked up in the Navy. He often caused consternation in the Oval Office by stretching out on one of the sofas while everyone scurried around him, under orders not to wake him. Of course, if you're the president, no one's going to object to this habit!

Although napping may not yet be culturally acceptable in many places, an increasing body of research evidence suggests that shifting from our normal wide-awake state (in which beta waves dominate the brain) to a neutral, drowsy or meditative state (mainly alpha waves), can be helpful in achieving cool objectivity and insights in relation to a problem.

Some companies have introduced special spaces – quiet zones – where employees can go to meditate, sit and think, or even doze briefly. They provide a sanctuary from the hustle and bustle of everyday working life.

Many professional creative types value the opportunity to get away completely from the problem they are working on, and a change of location can be beneficial. (James Webb Young, whose technique is described in Chapter 8, regarded 'dropping it' as an essential step in the creative thinking process.)

Unfortunately, even in enlightened businesses, the notion of sleeping on the job is still frowned upon, despite evidence that it can be conducive to improved thought processes.

Working environment evolution

When I began my career, the workspace was clearly defined: desk, chair, phone, filing cabinet. Visiting the offices of some clients and their advertising agencies and designers came as something of a revelation. One office, belonging to a senior executive in the music industry, had no conventional desk, but instead looked more like an art gallery, with original paintings and sculptures, and a soft seating area with a huge coffee table piled with books on art and music. Its owner explained that he spent most of his time thinking and in conversation, so had no need for a desk, but a great need for visual stimulation. This approach made a lot of sense, and he had gained a major reputation for creativity in his field.

Current trends indicate that, as work practices are changing, so are the ways in which many people view the work environment. Technology has made working a more portable experience, with laptops, tablet computers and mobile phones replacing traditional desk-bound equipment. In addition, many more people have the option of choosing where they work. Sometimes this means working from home, and increasingly, temporary offices or membership clubs fulfil the need. Several of my colleagues divide their time between home and a location conveniently close to their main clients, in order both to have a comfortable work environment and avoid the trials and tribulations of commuting.

Crafting your own creative environment

What would your own unique creative environment look like? Maybe you've had the good fortune to create your own special space, or to work in one of the increasing number of businesses that have invested time and energy in creating special working environments. One London advertising agency had its own oasis – a room complete with sand and palm trees! Going to such extremes isn't necessary, of course, but you can certainly personalise your space in many different ways.

Your ideal creative environment needn't be purely physical. Design your personal creative world in terms of *all* your senses. Being aware of all your senses and utilising them can be a great aid to the creative thinking process.

When you're in your ideal creative space, consider:

- ✔ **What you see.** Wherever you look in your creative space, what you see should help you think and have ideas. One way to plan the visual context of your space is to consider it as a manifestation of what's in your own head. How would you define your own visual taste: patterns or plain; traditional or modern; casually comfortable or formally organised?

  What are your visual preferences? Paintings, drawings, pieces of sculpture, photographs – or something else entirely? Works by famous artists or reminders of your family? Perhaps you're fond of mementoes and memorabilia. Whatever you really like or value, having it around you while you work can be a great stimulus. Recent research shows that the colour blue has a significant positive effect on creativity, so you may want to choose this as a background colour.

You may want to strip your space bare, so nothing intrudes on the purity of your inspiration. If that works for you, fine, but it certainly won't feel right for most people. (If you find the notion of being creative in a blank environment challenging, consider how many organisations expect to run creative sessions in bland, neutral-coloured meeting rooms. . .)

✔ **What you hear.** You may like the sound of silence so you can work undisturbed. Or you may want the latest sounds or your old favourites. Some find they can't work without the radio on in the background.

✔ **What you smell.** Most of the time you may not be conscious of smell, partly because the brain habituates to odours very quickly. But at a subliminal level, the sense of smell is always at work (you can close your eyes voluntarily, but not your nose – you have to pinch it).

You can choose to use particular odours to stimulate or relax yourself while you work, and these scents can be a powerful aid to creating specific states of mind. You may find that you rapidly form associations with particular smells, and these can help you achieve a desired state more quickly.

✔ **What you feel.** Like smell, your sense of touch often exists in the background. However, in this special space, you'll be touching things all the time. Explore the positional sense of your body. How are you sitting (or reclining if that's your preference)? Are your feet on the floor or something else? Are your shoes on or off? What are you sitting (or lying) on? Is it exactly right? If it's not, what can you do to perfect it? Do you need to stand up and walk around? Would a short walk in the countryside boost your creativity?

Even dedicated workers need to play sometimes, and indulging your fiddle factor – the tactile equivalent of doodling – by having some toys and games within arm's reach can be helpful.

How about what you touch? Are you using tools and equipment that please you? A respected designer colleague said, 'You can't have a big idea on a small sheet of paper.' He also insisted on using high-quality paper of a certain weight and choosing pencils and coloured pens with great care. He may have been an extreme example, but he felt that his choosiness directly benefitted his work.

✔ **What you taste.** Some creativity workshops use an exercise in which you eat a strawberry 'for the first time in your life'. This is always a revelation for several participants, because they discover that the experience doesn't match their memories. Select a type of fruit to try periodically, savouring it bite by bite and chewing slowly.

Can you eat something familiar in a different way? Even a simple apple is different depending on whether you bite into it, peel it or slice it into sections. What about other fruits? And then consider the vegetables. . .

You may want to keep more exotic products to hand. Confectionary, leaving aside dietary implications, can be fascinating. Sweets and chocolate are often used as a reward, so you may choose to award yourself a nibble when you've attained a goal. But it can be more interesting if you treat confectionary like you do your fruit. Select something interesting – hand-made truffles or Turkish delight, perhaps – instead of common-or-garden varieties. Notice the texture of the first bite, how it changes as you suck or chew the confectionary, and how the flavour comes through.

The same applies to drinks. You need to ingest liquids as you work, but you can go beyond the typical workplace beverages of coffee, tea and water.

Why get so intense about taste? Taste, as Proust proved with his famous Madeleines (the biscuits that triggered a flood of memories about his childhood), is an extraordinary stimulus for memory and association. If you're intending to think creatively, certain tastes can remind you of other times when you've been exceptionally creative.

✔ **What ambience you want.** The atmosphere of your unique space will be peculiar to you. Whatever works for you, you'll absolutely know when you've got it right.

If you don't have total control over your space, these suggestions may have made you a bit envious. But whether you have a magnificent studio at your disposal, just an alcove in your home, or a tiny portion of your cubicle, you can still enjoy the pleasures of customising your creative space for all your individual senses.

Flying Solo versus Working in Teams

The choice of working alone or as part of a team is a complex one, with no right or wrong answer. If you work alone, it can be difficult to co-opt others into your creative time, and if you're part of a team, the culture may determine that you have to work as a group. You may not have a choice in the first place. However, if the choice is under your control, you can consider the benefits of each approach.

Working alone

If you're predisposed to work alone, the presence of other people, even those whose company you normally enjoy, can be very counterproductive. Soloists feel most comfortable without the distractions of others who are only too prone to interrupt your creative flight at precisely the wrong moment. If you like to drift around mentally, gently floating in the idea space until solutions begin to coalesce, it can be enormously disruptive if a goal-orientated colleague demands to know 'Are we there yet?' Alternatively, if your natural approach is driven by an 'idea rush', where the thoughts come tumbling one after the other, you won't take kindly to someone slowing you down by picking ideas apart or introducing distractions at critical moments.

Sometimes an aversion to working in a group comes down to personality differences, where the interpersonal chemistry doesn't gel for some reason. Or it can be connected to patterns of work, such as preferred pace. But flying solo has certainly been the preferred mode for many creative individuals past and present. Leonardo da Vinci wasn't a team player, and the painters David Hockney and Francis Bacon, both highly gregarious individuals, couldn't bear to have other people around when they were working.

Some who prefer the solitary path have been highly critical of teamwork. Undoubtedly, it was one of these individuals who made the observation that a camel is a horse created by a committee.

Working together

A key element of the creative thinking process is that it should be fun. And unless you're strongly predisposed to working alone, the company of others can prove very stimulating and conducive to creative thinking.

The advantages of working creatively in a group can be substantial. Sometimes working with others comes in the form of a permanent or semipermanent team, and many professional creatives develop permanent teams that work together on every project.

Some artists found great inspiration over the years in working with fellow artists. Picasso did some of his most innovative work with others. In his early Paris years, he lived in Le Bateau-Lavoir in Montmartre, a chaotic commune of artists who worked and lived cheek by jowl; he and Braque created Cubism together, and his later ceramic work was produced in close collaboration with other potters. Other artists throughout history have merged into both formal and informal groups to explore fresh creative territory together. John Lennon and Paul McCartney famously wrote most of their best songs together.

Passing it on

For several hundred years, artists commonly worked in the *atelier system* in which a master artist works in the same space as the apprentices. This system began early in the Renaissance period as artists grew in status from being lowly guild tradesmen to having individual reputations.

In that period, no ready-made products existed and artists had to work laboriously through every stage of production. They stretched and primed their own canvases, ground their own paints and even made their own brushes. Part of the apprentice's role was to learn these mundane skills in preparation for the more sophisticated activity of mastering the painting of less important parts of the master's canvas.

This rigorous grounding meant that generations of artists grew up knowing the craft behind every masterpiece, and each generation was able to build on the achievements of its predecessors. This practice declined at the turn of the twentieth century for a number of reasons, although some artists continued the tradition.

In the 1920s the architect and artist Walter Gropius revived the concept in a radical way with the Bauhaus, a revolutionary kind of art school, which survived until the Nazis put a stop to these intellectual practices as part of their purge on creative expression in the 1930s. However, especially in Britain, the Bauhaus concept survived in modern art schools, which imbued the principles of an apprentice-style education based on hands-on experience of every aspect of creative thought and production in generations of twentieth-century students. The impact on creative industries from art to music, fashion to film and beyond, was enormous.

Ateliers, and their cultural successors, provide convincing proof of the viability of teamwork in the creative process. If you're planning to work in a creative capacity, these principles make a sound foundation for embedding creative thinking and practice.

However, creative teams don't have to be permanent, and creativity can flourish by using a more informal approach. Some creative agencies deliberately throw very different individuals together to stir the creative pot. So a professional creative team may be supplemented with, say, a student, a housewife, a sea captain and an engineer. The thinking behind this approach is that in order to create the unexpected, you must work with the unexpected.

Sometimes an even more unstructured approach can produce results. The philosopher Gurdjieff was an inveterate people-watcher and spent much of his most productive thinking and writing time in European cafés, where he could overhear daily chatter and observe passers-by as he worked.

In another field, Edison, one of the most prolific inventors of all time, built a workshop deliberately populated with other inventors, and many of his best products came from joint ventures with them (he was just a lot smarter at claiming the credit when it came to patents!).

Teamwork in the creative field obviously works for some individuals, and they tend to actively seek the company of others as an integral part of their work. When this is a matter of choice, the working partnership or team can be very productive.

Partners and groups have created much exceptional music, of course, and it's common for them to explain their achievements in terms of a chemistry whereby the whole is more than the sum of the individual parts. Interestingly, even after working intimately together for many years, such musicians often find the experience difficult to put into words, other than the fact that 'something happens' whenever they get together.

You can see an example of the continuing magnetism of the group dynamic with the Eagles, who largely defined the Southern California sound in the 1970s. Their acrimonious split in 1980 dictated the name of the album they released when they reunited in 1994: *Hell Freezes Over*. The point is that your role in a team may not be a smooth ride, but if you work best in the company of like-minded people, the ups and downs can often be just a temporary glitch in a much longer relationship.

Working in a team also offers the possibility of benefitting from mixed disciplines. Benefits may come to light as people working together discover their own and each others' strengths and weaknesses. Friends and families who start businesses together often find that, as their businesses grow, they naturally fall into particular roles they may not have explored previously.

You can also create your own custom-built team by spotting talented individuals who are able to fulfil specific roles. In many situations, this approach may sound easy; but it may be much trickier in practice because, of course, teams don't consist only of skills – the interaction of personalities is also involved. Those on the creative side of a business may sometimes find the more methodical attitudes of the engineers and accountants frustrating.

Having it both ways

A third option, of course, is to have the best of both worlds and to explore your creativity both alone and with others. You may find, as a number of creative thinkers have, that there's a right time for each option as you progress from gestation through to a full-grown solution.

You may, for example, want to be alone during the initial embryonic process, when you're just playing around with half-formed thoughts and not yet ready to share. Or your way of working may be to chuck a few ideas around with your team-mates before knuckling down to some more disciplined individual thinking. There really is no 'one size fits all' solution, but when you find the pattern that suits you, you'll know it and want to develop that rhythm of work.

Brainstorming the Harvard way

Conventional brainstorming involves a group of people – 8–12 is typical – brought together to generate ideas based on a specific problem, usually under the guidance of a facilitator. They work within a set of ground rules, such as not criticising each others' output. (Go to Chapter 7 for more on brainstorming.)

Harvard experiments on brainstorming techniques provide some interesting insights on group versus individual approaches. In a search for better methods of idea generation, researchers varied the normal brainstorming structure in a number of ways.

The Harvard researchers found that the most successful option was to divide a brainstorming session into 20-minute segments, alternating individual and group activities. This approach was markedly superior to conventional approaches in terms of both quality and quantity of ideas produced.

Of course, idea generation is only one aspect of the creative thinking spectrum, so it would be interesting to play with the individual–group concept, applying it to other stages of creative thinking such as problem-solving.

Many writers on the subject of thinking stress the importance of regular breaks as a way to avoid getting tired or stale. In a similar vein, switching between solo and group activity can be an effective way of sustaining the quality of your creative thinking. You can organise your work in this way formally, allocating periods in your timetable to each alternative, or leave it more to chance (even if this outcome is actually less random than it might appear at first glance). For example, some companies, including Apple and Pixar, have designed their work areas so employees cross paths several times a day. It's possible to engineer random meetings in many ways, from planning the location of toilets to the seating arrangements.

One option, adopted by some design and advertising agencies, is the 'big table' – a place where employees are encouraged to spend time interacting with anyone else who happens to be there at the time. This random element gives people the opportunity just to chat with, discuss ideas, and get feedback from people they might not normally come across during the working day, and in a much less formal environment than a meeting.

Assessing Outcomes

Sometimes the answer to the question of whether you solved the issue at hand is obvious. You know you're where you wanted to be and that what you've done works. However, the situation isn't always that clear-cut, and you may find that evaluating your efforts is more complicated or subtle.

Glowing Orange

In the early days of the mobile phone industry, much of the running was made in the Far East. Mobile telephony rapidly became widely used during a tumultuous 'gold rush' period, when many mistakes and reputations were made as rivals fought for supremacy.

Following his audacious success for Hutchison Whampoa in Hong Kong, Hans Snook was asked to do a similar job for the company on its ailing UK brand, Rabbit.

Snook's team, tasked with developing what eventually became Orange, faced a classic complex creative problem with issues at every possible level, all of which the team had to overcome if the project was to succeed. The problems were:

✔ The brand was fourth in a crowded market.

✔ That market was confused and chaotic.

✔ The focus was on the business market. Few of the major players thought there was much opportunity among the general public.

✔ Hutchison's product, Rabbit, was a curious system based on phones that could only make outgoing calls within 100 metres of a transmitter. (Surprising as it may seem now,

several other major players at the time also explored this system.)

Snook and his team decided, against prevailing wisdom, to create a unique brand at the heart of the business. This brand would embody lifestyle values (everyone else focused on the technology). It would create a new language free of the prevailing jargon and gobbledygook. It would be simple (people were baffled by these new-fangled products and how to use them). It would be trusted in a market notorious for unreliability.

This was a very complex creative challenge. Were the sniping critics right who insisted it couldn't be done? Or did the team succeed in cracking this complex creative problem?

Well, Orange met its initial target of 1 million sales within two years of launch, and it's still glowing. The team achieved success by segmenting the problem into its individual components and addressing these within the context of the single big idea of the brand. This allowed them to see both the strategic big picture and deal with more tactical issues in an appropriate context.

If your problem is both big and complex, dividing it into segments can be an excellent way to tackle it.

For example, a solution may be the best of a bad lot – not ideal, but the least worst outcome. You may be aware that you didn't totally achieve your objective, but what you have produced could have been a lot worse.

So what are your options in a situation like this? If time and resources permit, the best solution may be to revisit the situation and work for a better outcome. However, sometimes doing so isn't possible, and you either have to accept the situation or resort to a quick fix that delivers a partial improvement.

Did it work?

Evaluating creativity is, by its nature, tricky. Even to raise the subject can be a provocative act in some quarters. However, in the real world, creative output is subject to assessment, whether it's welcome or not.

Sometimes, especially if your problem is complex or multi-faceted, it can be hard to tell whether you've succeeded. Many reasons for this lack of clarity exist. For example, if a problem has several facets, you may have had to devise several partial solutions and, like the proverbial curate's egg, some of these part answers may be better than others.

Here, the emphasis is on how to assess creative outcomes. Say you work in a team that's handling a complicated problem requiring creative thinking. There may not be one single measure of success but a series of interlocking variables, each of which has to work for the project to succeed.

If you need to measure the results of your creative thinking (perhaps to get a course of action signed off at a higher level), you can use standard measures – creativity scales – which you'll find in systems like TRIZ (see Chapter 8). These measures are designed to make creative assessment more tangible, and in the right context they generate very useful information. But like many aspects of creativity, measuring its results is fairly fluid and very situational. Whether you can measure creativity depends, for example, on what exactly you want to measure. If you're looking for a straightforward index of success, then you must define total failure and total success, and calibrate the distance between these two points.

In what you want to measure, is the outcome *binary* – either on/off, go/no go, with nothing in between – or are there gradations in which you could be moderately, mostly or totally successful? Then, if you have gradations of success, how many do you want? Would it make sense to have a scale with a few points (say, five grades between failure and success) or a percentage scale ('We were 78 per cent successful')? The simplest approach is generally the best.

Whatever scale of assessment you adopt, consider two points:

- ✔ Come up with a clear definition of both success and failure and each point in between before you start.

- ✔ Determine what you'll do with partial success. Say you got 3 out of a possible 5 score, or perhaps 69 per cent success. What are the implications for your project? It's crucial here not to get bogged down in statistics but to stick to simple principles.

Creativity and intelligence

You might expect there to be an obvious link between creativity and intelligence – that naturally intelligent people are the most naturally creative. However, the connection between the two isn't quite as black and white, and is more complicated than you might suspect.

Once upon a time, as all good fairy tales begin, intelligence was a simple topic. Some well-meaning men (this was the Victorian era, and they were all men then) wanted to measure intelligence, so they devised scales to assess reasoning and related abilities, and hey presto! – intelligence could be measured as precisely as everything else in the Victorian physical world. However, their methods of measuring intelligence came to be viewed as outmoded.

To begin with, intelligence is no longer understood as a single cognitive dimension, but as a complex interaction of a wide variety of features. Psychologists have defined a range of contributory factors, including the following:

- Spatial
- Linguistic
- Logical/mathematical
- Bodily kinaesthetic
- Musical
- Interpersonal
- Intrapersonal
- Naturalistic

Where intelligence was once thought to be a single measure, it's now recognised as being subject to a host of social, educational and cultural influences. And to top it all, it may be that intelligence is not as useful as an assessment tool as once thought. Research – and a lot of it exists – has shown that the relationship between intelligence and achievement can be tenuous, to say the least. Some individuals who seem highly intelligent on the basis of their success turn out to be of average intelligence, while many measurably intelligent people are relatively unsuccessful in the real world.

As examples, a good mechanic may be able to fix your car perfectly, without being able to articulate how he spotted and fixed the problem. And a medical consultant may be able to diagnose your illness without having the fine motor skills necessary for performing the essential surgery. Both people may have high IQs, but one has performance skills and the other has predominantly verbal skills. Both are valid, and both can be successful in their chosen careers.

Added to this, a phenomenon called the Flynn Effect (after James Flynn, an American academic) demonstrates that IQ scores have risen substantially in the last century, something that is also true of many measures of creativity. So are people getting smarter, or just better at doing these kinds of tests, and does measuring intelligence serve any purpose?

For these reasons, and more, posing the question about the relationship between intelligence and creativity can be like stepping into a metaphorical minefield. One of the most creative thinkers of the twentieth century, the Nobel-prize-winning physicist Richard Feynman (see Chapter 15), had a high, but not exceptional IQ, and he dismissed intelligence tests as 'not real science'. Given the continuing confusion over the topic, perhaps that's not a bad point of view.

Establishing parameters at the outset of a creative thinking session is a good idea. A parameter may be as straightforward as a yes/no verdict, but life is rarely that simple. If the scenario has more than a single dimension, you may need to consider what the individual factors are, and how you can calibrate them.

The most productive approach to complex problems is to segment them into their component parts in order to evaluate them individually. Clustering these components around a single, central concept can help you retain coherence.

As interest in creativity has increased exponentially in recent years, so has the body of research analysing it. Much of that research is concerned with individual performance, which I discuss in Chapter 3.

A useful concept of measurement is the *Law of Big Numbers*, which is based on the notion of simple chunks of information rather than specific details. For example, how much is 66 per cent? Well it's roughly two-thirds. And 19 per cent? That's about a fifth. And 51 per cent? More or less half. In most real-life situations, these approximations are close enough, and they're clearly easier to grasp than abstract numbers. Where decisions about creative output are concerned, it's probably best to describe success or failure in solid numbers rather than approximate fractions.

Working on the principle that simplicity is the best option, try to avoid getting bogged down in complex statistical analysis, and trust your judgement. If your output is basically sound, then it's probably viable, but if it seems flaky, it won't help to know that it's 43.67 per cent okay.

What to do next

It's all very well having a creative experience, and sometimes the euphoria generated by a successful session can be exhilarating. Unfortunately, the downside to all this excitement is that you have to find a way to implement your good outcomes. Workshops often suffer from 'the honeymoon effect', where the creativity experience is delightful, but the good feelings cease when the session is over.

The best course of action is to maintain the pace while the glow of creativity is still strong, and to embark on the practical phase as soon as possible after the event.

From talent to genius

The scale of creativity from talent to genius is easier to see than to describe. One definition of talent is ability in the raw state – a person having the potential to achieve, but awaiting development and refinement.

In the early stages of childhood, a talent for creative thinking can be cultivated, and many educationalists have become interested in developing methods for growing creative ability. Some of this interest is driven by clear evidence that, for most children, creative thinking ability actually deteriorates markedly during school years.

Schools that educate using the Montessori method focus on the natural creativity and curiosity of children, and use a wide range of educational tools to enhance skills. From its raw beginnings, talent can thus be nurtured.

At the other extreme, genius is an accolade awarded to very few individuals who have achieved exceptional outcomes. Where true genius is concerned, a history of precociousness in childhood exists, giving early indications of the promise to come.

Even though few people can aspire to genius, building on your innate creative talent is certainly possible. Start with the belief that you have that ability, foster it by regular practice, and use creative thinking tools like those described in this book.

Chapter 5

Committing to Creativity

· ·

In This Chapter

▶ Achieving creative continuity

▶ Imitating Leonardo's life

▶ Being hit with inspiration

▶ Creating your own style

· ·

*T*he subject of creativity raises all sorts of questions and remains a much-misunderstood aspect of our lives. Those who perceive themselves as less (or not at all) creative wonder about creative inspiration: is it something that happens to you? Or can you initiate it? If so, how? Does it continue to flow or is an allocation granted that you somehow use up?

This chapter addresses the question of when creativity strikes and what form that takes. It examines the difference between creative manifestation as a one-off event compared with a constant flow of creativity. It appears that some individuals experience occasional creative flashes, some work with a continuous flow, while others appear to enjoy the best of both.

Some people seem to have creativity in their veins. From their earliest years these prolific creators deliver a torrent of original work of the highest quality. Mozart wrote his first proper symphony at the age of eight; Picasso was already producing exquisite drawings at five. Such prodigies are rare but not unique. You may not be the next Mozart or Picasso, but you can adopt some of the patterns commonly found in highly creative individuals.

If you work in a creative environment, you'll recognise the need to place some structure on the creative process. You may not be able to plan for flashes of inspiration, but you can work to create conducive conditions.

As you take a closer look at how creative experiences work for different people, consider what naturally fits your behavioural patterns. And remember to examine the ones that don't currently fit for you – they may be worth exploring!

Creating Continuously – Keeping the Tap Running

In many walks of life, you need to be creative on demand and your ability to generate ideas, solutions or dreams is an integral part of the job. Disney calls the members of its creative teams *imagineers*, a term which neatly captures the relationship between dreaming something and making it real.

For many people who work in a creative profession, it's important to keep creative juices flowing. Those with a talent for creativity, in professions like architecture, music, advertising and design, depend on a constant flow of fresh thinking for their livelihood.

As an example, the creative director of a large advertising agency may see hundreds of ideas from creative teams in the course of a year, and each of these teams has to generate a number of solutions for a number of accounts on a regular basis. At team level, the creatives at the sharp end are under constant pressure to deliver enough ideas to enable the directors to make good choices. At director level, the top decision-maker uses years of experience to make quick evaluations in order to sift the nuggets from the dross.

The two main criteria for judging the quality of creative work in the advertising world have become part of ad agency folklore:

✔ An idea has legs, which means – literally – that it can stand on its own two feet. Given the fiercely competitive environment in which marketing schemes have not only to survive but also cut through the clutter to make their point, successful ideas (*concepts* in ad agencies) must not only work in their own right, but also be differentiated from the competition.

✔ Ideas must have *campaignability*, meaning that they can work over a period of time and in a variety of media. In addition, a variety of other criteria are often brought into play, meaning that the chance of a winning idea getting broadcast is roughly equivalent to a single sperm fertilising an egg – fewer than one in a million survive and thrive.

Being creative for a living

In a world where creativity is at a premium, professional creatives have evolved a variety of tactics to ensure that they can maintain an adequate flow of ideas. At the heart of this is a paradox which lies in the balance between stress and creativity. In recent years, stress has been recognised as a major problem in the commercial world, and a body of research is being developed to help better understand it. One aspect of this research has addressed the impact of stress on performance, including creative performance.

A Belgian who used his little grey cells

René Magritte produced some of the most powerful and original images in modern art. Although he is classified as a Surrealist, his oeuvre is unique and resembles nothing else. His style is the stuff of our deepest dreams and darkest nightmares. Once seen, Magritte's images embed themselves in our psyches, unforgettably disturbing our imagination.

So how did Magritte achieve this unique perspective on the world? Did he dream away his days in opium dens, cavort in wild drug-fuelled orgies of the imagination, or drink himself into stupors while chasing his demons? Nothing could be further from the truth. A middle-class Belgian, he lived in an affluent suburb. Every

morning at the same time he walked the short distance to his studio, where he worked all day until it was time to return home. Not for him the smock and beret; his attire was a meticulous three-piece suit with all the accoutrements, not unlike his fictional fellow countryman Hercule Poirot.

Here, Magritte's methodical, humdrum routine serves as an example – perhaps deliberately exaggerated as a Surrealistic gesture – of how exceptionally creative individuals often order their lives in a very disciplined manner, which belies the notion that creative types are eccentrics living anarchic lives on the social edge.

Many individuals who work creatively for a living evolve personal systems and routines, perhaps as ways of avoiding the build-up of toxic stress. They structure the day, and they follow certain superstitious rituals or idiosyncratic patterns. These patterns can be based on, for example:

- ✔ **Time:** Working only certain hours
- ✔ **Output:** Working until they meet a specific goal; writers setting themselves word targets, for example
- ✔ **Location:** Setting aside a space conducive to creative thought; for example, Roald Dahl and the founder of IKEA both worked in their garden sheds
- ✔ **Organisation:** Gathering and preparing all the tools they need ahead of time; for example, sharpening all their pencils and making sure they have paper before starting work

Stressing about creativity

One longitudinal study, conducted by Harvard Business School, reveals that too little stress can be as counterproductive as too much. Apparently the optimum creative context requires enough light stress to keep momentum, but not so much that high stress levels kick in.

Beyond a certain level of stress, the brain activates the limbic system – the part of the brain that tells you to fight or run away – the so-called fight or flight response. And of course it's hard to feel creative if you're battling an enemy or running for your life!

Achieving the magic 10,000 hours

The writer Malcolm Gladwell, himself an original and highly creative observer with a unique perspective, has drawn attention to what he describes as the magic 10,000 hours, which is the time it seems to take for creative individuals to master their craft. This principle seems to apply across all kinds of creative fields.

Ten thousand hours is equivalent to a thousand ten-hour days. So even working several hours a day, most days of the year, you'd have to commit around three years to achieving this target.

As an example, people who knew the Beatles from their early days say that before they went to Hamburg on a punishing two-year contract that required them to play many hours a day, six or seven days a week, they were just another average Liverpool group. After playing several hours a day, several days a week for more than two years, the lads from Liverpool had become, well, the Beatles.

That kind of intensive routine is typical of that completed by many artists in all fields of expression: truly successful people seem to share an early period of extraordinary devotion to practising.

Drawing on this concept of creativity through routine, some people maintain their creative edge simply by repetition. They set themselves a pattern of behaviours – a series of routines if you like – that they perform regardless of whether they're feeling creative or not. This is often allied to a demonstrable passion for the subject.

Preparing for good results

Creativity experts do everything in their power to create an environment that helps participants get into the creative spirit.

Workshop rooms are typically dressed with positive colour schemes and filled with light and air. A team of people, experienced in guiding the process to a positive conclusion, introduce participants to the location in a carefully orchestrated sequence of events. In other words, everything is done to set the scene for the desired outcome.

It may not be possible to dress your environment as the professionals do, but these few tips can help get you in the creative frame of mind:

- ✔ Make the workspace blue. Research has demonstrated that blue is the colour that generates the most creative results, by a wide margin.
- ✔ Surround yourself with colour and light. Put up bright posters, place flowers and other colourful objects around, and open the curtains and turn all the lights on.
- ✔ Play your favourite positive music (avoid anything moody or depressing).
- ✔ Treat yourself to pleasant tastes and smells while you work, and take frequent breaks to nibble some fruit or smell the flowers.

These are ways of stimulating all your senses together and it helps your mind tune in to imaginative thinking.

Living Like Leonardo – Working with Creative Continuity

If you want to commit to a creative life, it helps to have a game plan. One of the best was that which Leonardo da Vinci wrote in his extensive journals, containing detailed descriptions of his precepts. He not only wrote one of the first how-to manuals, but personally lived the life he recommended.

It appears that da Vinci set himself a routine to which he adhered throughout his life, which gave him a framework for his work. He taught his routine to his apprentices and recommended it to his patrons.

Living like Leonardo

Michael Gelb, a highly regarded expert on creativity, with several books to his name, spent several years researching Leonardo's life. Gelb wanted to understand the unique mind of Leonardo, and felt the best way to achieve his aim was to emulate the patterns of Leonardo's life. Thanks to the copious notes on his methods provided by contemporaries and by Leonardo himself, Gelb was able to follow Leonardo's daily routines to the letter and immerse himself in the experience of living like him. Gelb spent time living in the locations where Leonardo worked, and retraced Leonardo's footsteps from Florence to Milan and other important locations in the master's life, emulating his daily routines.

Gelb's research gave rise to his book *How to Think Like Leonardo da Vinci* (and other books), and a series of workshops delivered to corporate clients around the world. The seven steps summarised here are the elements Gelb described as essential to the Leonardo da Vinci ethos.

Leonardo described seven facets of his daily activities which he applied as the foundation of his prodigious output. What is remarkable is how modern they appear, reflecting many current preoccupations with personal development and the need to follow a disciplined approach on the path towards individual evolution . . . without the psychobabble.

The following sections explain da Vinci's seven principles along with their original Italian terms, most of which are easy to translate into English because they sound similar to their English equivalents. This tour of Leonardo's precepts offers an insight not only into his unique view of the world, but also into how you might adopt some useful approaches to more creative ways of thinking in your own life.

Leonardo advocated living in the moment, which is a practice endorsed by many wise individuals across the field of personal development. Living in the moment is also defined as *mindfulness* – essentially being aware of yourself and the world around you. The subject of mindfulness is covered exhaustively in *Mindfulness For Dummies* by Shamash Alidina (Wiley), which I recommend.

Being insatiably curious – curiosità

This facet of Leonardo's ethos can be summarised as 'an insatiably curious attitude to life and unrelenting quest for continuous learning', which is how he eloquently put it in one of his journals.

This characteristic marks out many great creative minds. They constantly ask questions, wondering how things work or how they can do things differently. Like small children, they're not afraid to ask questions that might embarrass or mystify adults: 'Why is the sky blue?' 'Why can't we fly?' 'How do birds find their way home?'

Google, a business that employs some of the smartest people around, prides itself on choosing individuals who ask good questions. The general principle at work here is simply keeping an open mind and *noticing*.

To emulate da Vinci's approach, it helps to take some simple steps, the first of which is keeping a journal. Da Vinci used his journals as a means of monitoring his curiosity, recording anything and everything that caught his attention, from major projects to everyday chores (some of the journals even have shopping lists cheek by jowl with designs for weapons and flying machines). This process of continual recording acts both as a method for tracking the evolution of ideas and as an ongoing stimulus for creative imagination.

TECHNICAL STUFF

Leonardo or da Vinci – what's in a name?

The question of correct nomenclature for Leonardo di ser Piero da Vinci has caused much debate. Well, like the man himself, it seems nothing is straightforward (even da and Da are used interchangeably). And the name of the village where he was born isn't a proper surname, although birthplace was often used as a reference at that time.

Dan Brown's novel *The Da Vinci Code* sparked a lively debate in the art history community. Leaving aside the controversy surrounding the theme of the novel, Brown raised many historians' hackles by referring to his subject as 'da Vinci'. As an illustration of the continuing ambiguity over what we should call the artist, I read a review of *Da Vinci's Ghost*, an interesting

analysis of da Vinci's Vitruvian Man drawing, in which the reviewer, like so many writers, consistently calls the subject *Leonardo*, regardless of the inference of the title.

The man himself loved ambiguity and deliberately cultivated it as a thinking skill, so it's tempting to think he may have been amused by all the debate over something as mundane as his own name.

For the purposes of this book, following the convention adopted by various respected writers when speaking of his work, it seems right to refer to da Vinci, and when discussing the man, to call him Leonardo.

My personal recommendation for developing the journal habit is to do so by taking these steps:

- ✔ Choose a high quality A5 or A6 journal with a sturdy cover and either plain or grid paper rather than lines. Writing on lined paper encourages left to right linear thinking. Grid or plain paper gets you away from subconscious reminders of linear thinking – and you may want to draw as well as write.

- ✔ Get a decent pen and preferably a small set of coloured pencils or pens, because colour adds another dimension to even the most rudimentary sketch.

- ✔ Rather than using your journal from left to right (another linear habit), turn it sideways – a tip I borrowed from mind maps and use myself. This simple action generates a different mindset, as you'll discover if you try it.

- ✔ Following Leonardo, it's good practice to use your journal every day, and to write your thoughts as they arise, along with some statements such as 'I wonder how/why . . .'

These actions also help personalise your journal, making it truly unique to you. Interestingly, after adopting this practice for a while, you will find it feels slightly odd if you revert to the conventional view. This is a small example of the way you can retrain your thinking processes.

If you want to develop the journal habit (which can be rewarding and addictive in equal measure – so be warned!), seeking out the journals of artists such as Leonardo is a good idea. Part of the fascination is that they capture odd fragments: mistakes, abandoned projects, personal reminders, work-arounds, and so on. An intriguing jumble of thoughts in progress.

One inveterate journal-keeper was landscape artist JMW Turner, and some of his greatest works started life as rough (but exquisite) sketches in the tiny journals he always kept with him. Other artists with the journal habit are easy to find on the Internet. You can find many examples on YouTube, and it's worth checking out an artist called Suzi Blu, who actually runs artist journal workshops.

In these days of sophisticated technology, would it not be simpler to rely on an iPad or similar tablet rather than a journal? For me, the answer is both/ and, rather than either/or. An electronic tablet is incredibly useful for all sorts of creative activity, but it's hard to beat the experience of expressing your personal thoughts directly onto paper.

Try to observe your world according to a daily theme you set yourself. For instance, you may choose 'ideas' as a theme and spend the day noticing examples of good and original ideas around you. It's worth bearing in mind that this is a personal exercise, and your notion of a good idea might not correspond to someone else's. As an illustration, looking around my study I notice some objects:

- ✔ I see a remote control, and remember when changing channels involved physical activity. What might a remote control of the future look like? (Apparently, a UK firm has produced a Harry Potter wand – a universal remote control that's selling like hot cakes. What a great idea!)

- ✔ I look at my shredder and speculate on how the course of political history might have changed without this instant disposal device.

- ✔ I consider the Post-it notes all over my work and think of how the scientists at 3M couldn't come up with a use for weak glue until one of them wanted bookmarks that didn't fall out of his Bible.

And so on. Each good idea I notice, however mundane, tells a story and ignites my imagination. Plenty of fodder for my journal, right at my fingertips – who knows what might become of some of these streams of thought? And I'll choose a different theme tomorrow.

Another route is to generate a *stream of consciousness*, just letting your thoughts tumble out randomly without trying to put any structure on them. Begin by selecting a topic or issue that interests you then record your thoughts and associations as you go, without censoring or editing them (you may need to try this several times to break old habits).

Word games

In a twist borrowed from the author William Burroughs, David Bowie made collages of words and phrases clipped from newspapers and magazines to aid his composing. He found the odd juxtapositions generated this way gave rise to some of his most intriguing lyrics.

This kind of thinking isn't limited to writers. Artists in many media have free-associated to arrive at great works. Stravinsky produced a delightful piece based on the song 'Tea for Two' celebrating his love of American culture. And the quirkily absorbing film *Being John Malkovich* is clearly based on a free-association 'what-if' scenario.

Einstein famously used stream of consciousness to stimulate his unique imagination, and one frequently quoted example is his imagined ride on a wave of light, which apparently helped him conceive the theory of relativity. It's important not to edit or censor yourself, but to keep writing. Many writers and composers have used this stream of consciousness technique successfully to stimulate their imaginations, from writer James Joyce to musician and artist Brian Eno.

 Some writers claim to avoid writer's block using the *three-page technique*. This is a simple routine of starting the writing day by producing three pages about – well, anything really. The idea is that the act of writing is in itself creative, and this three-page jotting (sometimes called *free writing*) acts as a kind of warm-up technique, much as a runner warms up the leg muscles before attempting anything strenuous.

Testing knowledge through experience – demostrazione

Demostrazione exemplifies Leonardo's 'commitment to test knowledge through experience, persistence and a willingness to learn from mistakes', as Michael Gelb neatly puts it.

This reflects the more scientific aspect of Leonardo's complex personality – that he sought tangible proof for his observations. You can clearly see evidence of demostrazione in the extraordinarily detailed anatomical drawings da Vinci produced at a time when knowledge of the human body was very limited and doctors relied more on superstition and hearsay than the evidence of their own eyes.

To understand the true power of da Vinci's work (and that of his contemporaries who sought to understand the human body), it's necessary to go beyond the sanitised, refrigerated world of the *CSI* TV series, where bodies are neatly laid out on slabs surrounded by an exotic array of clever technical equipment designed to expose every anatomical secret. In Leonardo's world, human dissection was a crime against Church and State, carried out under cover, with decaying bodies of criminals and the diseased – plus the accompanying stench! Only the most determined pioneers had the stomach for this kind of work. Yet what Leonardo produced in these stinking, candle-lit confines were masterpieces. As drawings, they're sensitive works demonstrating incomparable control of line and form, and in a very real sense, life. As anatomical illustrations, they stand the test of time for their accuracy and clarity.

Implicit in demostrazione is the accumulation of wisdom through *experience*. Begin by checking your belief systems. What beliefs do you hold that you can verify by experience?

Play the three-points-of-view game with yourself to test your beliefs through experience:

1. **Make a strong case *against* a belief you hold.**

2. **Take a *distant* view about this belief, as if you came from a different culture or world.**

   Ask yourself, 'What would a visitor from Mars make of this belief?' and argue from a Martian's perspective.

3. **Get friends to give you *different contributions* from their own viewpoints.**

   Be prepared for some surprises as you adopt these different views on beliefs you may never have questioned before.

As a further exercise, you can try this forensic approach on advertisements. Look at some of the adverts you like in magazines and on TV, and think about what appeals to you and why. Draw up a list and see whether common patterns exist in those you like. Now consider them objectively. Instead of being the passive consumer, think about the strategy and tactics used by the agencies that created them. Notice the language used and the visual tricks of the trade.

Another way of demonstrating experience to yourself is to consider the opposite of what you'd normally do. As an exercise, find yourself some *anti role models* – individuals you don't want to resemble, whose mistakes you want to avoid, and who are the opposite of what you'd normally think of as role models (role models being people you'd like to emulate). Observe the traps they fell into so that you can avoid them.

Contradicting yourself can be dangerous!

The French film *Ridicule*, a beautifully observed tragi-comedy based on the Court of Versailles, contains a scene in which a verbose philosopher entertains Louis XVI by proving, through an elaborate argument, the existence of God. Emboldened by the delighted applause of his king (and, of course, the court), he foolishly declares, 'And, of course, I can prove the opposite!' Unfortunately, he doesn't retain his head for long enough to make the counter-argument.

Refining the senses – sensazione

In English, the word *sensation* is rich with layers of meaning, and Leonardo used it in a similar way to summarise 'the continual refinement of the senses, especially sight, as the means to enliven experience'.

Leonardo believed that we can best practise his notion of demostrazione through our senses, and he emphasised sight. This is why one of Leonardo's mottos is *saper vedere* (meaning 'knowing how to see') – one of his foundations in both the arts and science.

Following Leonardo, try this exercise in sensazione:

1. **Write a detailed description of an experience.**

    For example, select an experience full of meaning for you, such as watching a sunrise, and immediately write about the event in your journal.

2. **Note where you were, what mood you were in and how that changed as the event unfolded.**

3. **Record what colours stood out.**

4. **What did you hear?**

5. **How did you feel at the end?**

Make your account as vivid and real as possible. At a later date, re-read your account and see what effect it has on you.

Smells like teen spirit – when you notice it!

Smell is one of our most evocative senses, and it permeates our lives as much as sight. However, it's easy to relegate smell to a background role, only using it consciously when an odour is particularly good or bad. So as an exercise, try to describe a smell in as much detail as possible:

1. Capture the smallest element of the smell and the biggest impression.

2. Did it remind you of an event or experience?

3. Did it generate a special emotion?

4. Did you recall the first time you experienced it?

5. What else comes up as you immerse yourself in this review process?

6. Can you find words to capture the essence of this smell?

Once again, write everything in your journal, and illustrate it.

Try this exercise with taste and touch. And if you're feeling adventurous, play with less-well-known senses such as *proprioception* (knowing where the parts of your body are), and consider your posture, what your hands are doing, and whether you're feeling tense or relaxed during the exercise.

Active listening

Hearing is another primary sense that deserves special treatment. Normally, you hear in a passive way – sounds come to you and form much of the daily backdrop to your life. Because sound is there all the time, it goes largely unnoticed unless something disrupts the pattern, like a loud bang or a scream. However, you can learn to sharpen your hearing skills through a process called *active listening*, which involves you consciously paying attention to the different kinds of auditory experience all around you.

As you practise active listening, you'll discover elements you hadn't noticed before, and this can be a major stimulus for your creative imagination.

Here are some ways to get started with active listening:

1. Try noticing the quietest sounds, such as your own breathing.

2. Pay attention to the loudest sounds – heavy traffic, a baby screaming.

3. Think of the effect each type of sound normally has on you.

4. Deliberately change your response and emotion in relation to each sound.

This exercise is further material for your journal, and, as with the other experiences, it's always worth re-visiting your journal at a later date to review your responses and make further notes on them.

Drawing on your drawing skills

In any discussion involving Leonardo da Vinci, drawing is an essential component.

Smoke and mirrors and sfumato

In the original Italian, sfumato means 'smoke', which nicely evokes the ambiguity Leonardo loved. It also describes a painting technique in which he excelled.

In painting, sfumato involves applying a series of transparent glazes in layers. This process adds luminosity and depth to surfaces (it works especially well depicting skin). It also permits the artist to play with ambiguity.

Da Vinci's most famous portrait, the *Mona Lisa*, has prompted endless discussion of the expression playing on La Gioconda's lips. This ambiguity was deliberate on Leonardo's part, because he painted the mouth using the sfumato technique so you can't tell whether it's a hint of a smile or the effect of shadow.

Learn to draw, even if you believe you can't. You can find many resources available to help here, and Betty Edwards' books, notably *Drawing on the Right Side of the Brain*, remain outstanding and should convince even the most self-deprecating non-drawers of their innate ability.

Embracing ambiguity – sfumato

The word *sfumato* doesn't translate into English as easily as some of Leonardo's other terms, but his intended translation is 'a willingness to embrace ambiguity, paradox and uncertainty'.

Experts agree that one of the features that distinguished da Vinci was his love of a sense of mystery. Some of his paintings may seem straightforward on the surface (a portrait; a madonna and child) but da Vinci layered each one with symbols, codes and multiple meanings. Even today, art historians are finding fresh evidence of da Vinci's ingenious ability to embed mystery into each work.

Most of us instinctively avoid ambiguity and gravitate towards certainty. However, a willingness to befriend ambiguity can lead to a whole new way of seeing. Ambiguity is essentially to know something, although its meaning may be indeterminate.

As an exercise, try holding two different emotions at the same time. Picture a time when you were really sad, and a time when you were equally happy. Now put them together and see whether you can experience both at the same time. (Don't be discouraged, it can be done: Country and Western artists are experts at bittersweet!)

A second technique is to use what's generally known as the Socratic method, a process of continually asking questions while not giving answers. (Parents of three-year-olds will recognise this only too well!)

A simple demonstration of how effective – and frustrating – ambiguity can be is provided in what lawyers call the 'one too many' tactic. The lawyer asks, 'Why did you kill your wife?' The defendant protests that he did not. So the lawyer repeats the question, 'Why did you kill your wife?' Again, the defendant denies the charge. Once again, the lawyer demands 'Why did you kill your wife?' and by this time the defendant is so exasperated he blurts out, 'Alright! I hated her!'

In day-to-day life, the key to following this process effectively is humility: don't assume you or anyone else knows the answers for certain, and question every premise.

Unsurprisingly, Socrates was criticised during his lifetime for his relentless use of this method, and I recommend that you refrain from using this powerful technique in social situations if you want your host to invite you back!

Balancing art and science – arte/scienza

Here, the emphasis is on 'the development of the balance between science and art, logic and imagination'. In essence, this refers to what we now call *whole-brain thinking*.

The Western world has a history of separating art and science, treating them as though they're independent of each other. Modern educational thinking is now moving to a more integrated approach, recognising that both art and science have a role to play, and that each can benefit from the other.

Mapping your world

One very powerful technique you can use to blend art and science is mind mapping, which I describe in detail in Chapter 6. This technique is now well established and is widely used in many fields from business to education.

Its strength is that it combines logic and imagination in a unique evolving process – the signature spider-web pattern – using words, shapes and colour in a way thought to be analogous to how the brain itself works.

Mind mapping is based on a simple set of guidelines designed to help everyone attain rapid mastery of the process. You can make up your own rules, of course, but following the creator's path will help you get to where you want to be more quickly and effectively. This topic is covered in depth in *Mind Mapping For Dummies* written by Florian Rustler with a foreword by mind mapping inventor Tony Buzan (Wiley).

The best of both worlds

It's often thought that Leonardo da Vinci was left-handed, and his name tends to come up in that context. However, it's not true. Leonardo was ambidextrous, and you can see this in his work, where the shading and brush strokes show that he used both hands with equal dexterity. In addition, Leonardo advocated ambidextrousness as an essential skill for the rounded individual.

Recent research shows that people with this ability are more likely to recover fully from brain injuries such as strokes. The brain appears capable of re-wiring itself to adapt to adverse situations (in a process called neuroplasticity), and ambidextrous individuals have a head start here.

The science of art and the art of science

Some of the most interesting art now being created is based on the latest scientific developments. Several artists are exploring the visual beauty of, for example, the patterns created in genetics and quantum physics, and the mathematics of fractals. And scientists are using drawing and sculpture to help them grasp some complex and abstract issues.

The Science Museum in London is a great starting point if you want to see art and science intersecting in ways that would have fascinated Leonardo.

Cultivating the finer aspects of life – corporalita

We don't have an exact English equivalent of this word, for while corporeal means 'of the body', this doesn't quite convey Leonardo's 'cultivation of grace, ambidexterity, fitness and poise'.

Contemporary accounts suggest that Leonardo was something of a dandy, with long flowing locks and the most fashionable and expensive clothes (in contrast to his rival Michelangelo, who dressed in peasant garb and rarely washed, and whom Leonardo enjoyed teasing). The mirror-writing in Leonardo's journals has fascinated generations and is just one example of his extraordinary physical dexterity.

How do we achieve corporalita? Creativity is of course cerebral, but it helps to house it in a fit body.

Develop a personal programme to cultivate your physical fitness, focusing on three key elements:

✔ **Flexibility exercises:** Techniques such as yoga, Pilates and tai chi are excellent methods for developing physical flexibility. They also benefit balance and poise. A flexibility programme should also include attention to the hands and hand–eye co-ordination. Learning to juggle and ambidexterity are both useful here.

✔ **Strength training:** It's said that Leonardo could break a lock with his bare hands. You can achieve physical strength in many ways. *Isometric* exercise – flexing and contracting muscles – provides an excellent workout without the need for bulky and expensive equipment.

✔ **Aerobic conditioning:** Better breathing has many beneficial results: increased lung capacity, oxygenation of the blood and release of feel-good endorphins among them. Any sustained physical activity such as swimming, cycling, jogging or power walking will achieve this.

The benefits of these types of exercise become apparent relatively quickly. You can easily incorporate these activities into your daily routine. It's also worth checking out these refinements:

✔ **Develop your body awareness.** As you develop your overall physical fitness, consciously become more aware of your body. Whichever techniques you use as part of your fitness regime, try a variety of other techniques that co-ordinate mind and body skills, such as yoga, tai chi or qi gong, juggling or dance – whatever takes your fancy. They're all great fun once you get the hang of them, and you stay fit almost without noticing.

✔ **Become ambidextrous.** Often cited as an example of the supposed link between left-handedness and genius, it would be nearer the mark to describe Leonardo as truly ambidextrous, for although many of his drawings show left-handed shading, his paintings reveal brushwork using each hand. He seems to have been the embodiment of the corporalita he so eloquently describes.

To become ambidextrous, you can use this simple sequence of actions:

• Start by performing simple routine tasks with your non-dominant hand, such as cleaning your teeth or eating with a spoon.

• As you gain confidence (and your brain creates new neural pathways to help you) you can graduate to writing. Begin with capitals, then single letters and finally joined-up writing.

As a bonus, you may want to teach yourself to write upside down, which can be very impressive across a desk in meetings!

Taking a tiger by the tail

The novelist Elizabeth Gilchrist (*Eat, Pray, Love*) tells a fascinating story about when she interviewed the American poet Ruth Stone, then in her nineties. Ruth lived on the prairies – vast empty landscapes where nothing much happened.

Periodically, from this great space, she'd experience an extraordinary sensation as inspiration literally rushed towards her out of nowhere. She would have to drop everything and rush to find pen and paper before the moment passed and the inspiration sped on to find another receptive soul. Sometimes she had to grab the inspiration by the tail as it swept overhead. When this happened, she reported, she usually managed to capture all the words – but in reverse order.

The legendary American designer Raymond Loewy, creator of the Coca-Cola bottle and many other American icons, used to draw his designs across a table from his clients, enjoying their amazement at his virtuosity as the images appeared the right way up for them. He credited many wins to this technique.

Connecting everything – connessione

Meaning *connection*, for Leonardo connessione was 'a recognition of and appreciation for the interconnectedness of all things and phenomena'. Today we recognise this concept as *systems thinking* or what some businesses call *interdependence*.

Much of Leonardo's output is based on his ability to form new patterns through connections and combinations of different elements.

Ways to follow his example include:

- ✔ Find ways to link things that seem to be unrelated. The more unlikely they are, the better. Find similarities between a bear and a diamond, a ship and a brain, a shoe and a palace. If you think this exercise is silly, consider that the logo for BP the oil corporation is, at a subliminal level, a flower (a chrysanthemum to be precise). Also much humour is predicated on the juxtaposition of two or more highly unlikely ingredients ('A horse goes into a bar and says to the barmaid . . . ').

- ✔ Play the dinner party game. Imagine you've invited some of your real life and fictional heroes (and villains if you want to enrich the mix!) to your dinner party, and imagine the conversation. Feed them a topic and enjoy the spectacle. What does Gandhi say to Hitler about quantum physics? What do Margaret Thatcher and Steve Jobs discuss about modern art?

> ✔ Think about how things originate. What has to happen for certain things to exist? Take examples from nature (how do plants re-populate after a forest fire?) and from the man-made world (what do you need to make a motorbike?).

Experiencing a Creative Burst

When we hear the word creativity, the first association for many of us is a sudden moment of revelation exemplified by the cry 'Eureka!' (meaning 'I have it!'). This notion of creativity as a sudden discovery persists in many forms, as the next sections explore.

Lighting up – the light bulb effect

We speak of the light-bulb moment when someone has a bright idea. It's a powerful metaphor, and many of us have experienced a distinctive feeling of lighting up when that tricky crossword clue is solved, or a better way of doing something suddenly occurs out of the blue.

Eureka! Striking gold

Although the story of Archimedes discovering the properties of displacement as he stepped into his bath and noticed how the water rose in proportion to his body entering it is something every schoolchild is supposed to know, its significance is often under-rated.

At the time of Archimedes' famous bath-time discovery, the King of Sicily had offered a prize to anyone who could determine how much gold was in his crown. The king suspected his goldsmith of duping him; rightly, as it happens. The discovery Archimedes made enabled him to measure the proportion of gold to silver in the crown, and to prove that the goldsmith was indeed a thief. This breakthrough immediately had much wider ramifications, for Syracuse was a major port, and the ability to make an accurate assessment of ships' cargos was invaluable.

As the greatest mathematician of the era, Archimedes had already measured the area under a hemisphere, defined the relative volumes of a sphere within a cylinder and approximated pi – all huge achievements which earned him an enduring reputation as a giant in mathematics. The sphere within a cylinder adorned his grave, as Archimedes had apparently considered it his highest achievement, above even the measurement of displacement.

These apparently sudden events often seem to occur not entirely spontaneously, but as a result of a set of circumstances that predispose you to be ready for the occasion. Archimedes was no doubt preoccupied with the conundrum of how to measure an irregular object. After all, there was a major prize to be won, and the port of Syracuse would find such a solution immensely valuable; in addition, he'd worked on related problems for many years.

Also, when we suddenly get that crossword solution or resolve that intractable problem in an instant, we've actually been thinking about it over a period of time, both consciously and subconsciously, so the solution has had time to gestate. This is not to diminish either Archimedes or our own achievements in any way – what we perceive as a miraculous one-off is often actually the product of considerable background mental activity.

It appears that the Eureka moment can happen spontaneously or it can be induced. However, although the light-bulb moment is undoubtedly exciting when it happens, especially for the individual experiencing it, it represents only one part of the creative experience. For many individuals, this occasional burst is their only direct taste of creativity, and the notion of a creative life is outside their daily experience.

But if creativity is part of your job, then it's time to be more systematic in your approach by applying principles like those of Leonardo, as discussed in the 'Living Like Leonardo – Working with Creative Continuity' section earlier in this chapter.

Exploding with creativity

For many of us, creativity has a special quality, and at least some of this experience is the result of the rush of energy that characterises the creative moment. Some have described this as an explosion, and research on the activity of the brain at the instant an idea strikes reveals that a burst of activity does indeed occur in the areas of the brain associated with this kind of thinking. So in a way, an explosion literally does happen. Some neuroscientists have related such events to concurrent activity in the pleasure centres of the brain, which suggests, if true, that creativity is literally – chemically – a pleasurable experience.

Some companies that work with creativity – teaching the techniques, and helping businesses become more innovative – use models that include an explosion phase, and many of the processes they employ are designed to instigate that magic moment. Typically, these techniques use a combination of sequences that compress – packing a lot of activity into a short space of time – or amplify – increasing pace and volume (sometimes literally!) – to create a crescendo of experience. Either way, the intention is to attain a state in which the idea can be born. Scenarios like this can be quite intensive.

The real light-bulb moment

Despite the light-bulb legend, the real-life experience of Thomas Edison's light bulb was anything but such a moment. Embodying his own dictum that genius is 1 per cent inspiration and 99 per cent perspiration, Edison laboriously tried thousands of filaments before hitting on the right solution, only to find that someone had beaten him to it with a patent – the English inventor Joseph Swan, who'd been pursuing a parallel path. Then, showing the creative inspiration for which he was renowned, Edison promptly brought Swan into his company as a joint venture partner.

Finding Your Own Creative Style

Take a look at your own natural style in relation to creativity. Do you try to be creative every day, adopting a routine that helps you into a productive pattern? Many home-based workers report that the most difficult aspect of the day is getting started. Endless procrastination, making coffee, putting the pens in the right order, just touching base with the news or sports results. Such displacement activities can help pass a lot of time. Have you found a way through that impasse? Do you simply just do it regardless of how you feel?

Perhaps you manifest your creativity in sudden bursts that come from out of the blue. Do you find that you have to drop everything and grab something to capture your idea by the tail before it escapes forever? You never know when the magic could happen. In the past, many creators kept a notepad by their bed in case the big idea came to them as they slept.

William James, the psychologist behind many modern insights about human motivation and behaviour, once awoke during the night convinced he knew the Secret of the Universe. He scribbled it down before falling back to sleep, and awoke the next morning anxious to discover what the secret was. He read his scrawled note, which said 'Higamus hogamus women are monogamous. Hogamus higamus men are polygamous.' Some thought it proved that all this subconscious stuff was arrant nonsense, whereas others considered it a perfect insight into the human condition. You decide.

Part III
Getting Creative –
The Practical Stuff

The 5th Wave   By Rich Tennant

CREATIVE
VISUALIZATION
SEMINAR

In this part...

You get creative with the practical stuff and explore the tools and techniques of creative thinking. You open your mind with idea-generating processes from brainstorming to lateral thinking, and close in on the answers to your creative problems with problem-solving processes designed to engage your whole brain. In these chapters you discover how to change your mind through mapping, language and visualisation. And you also get to play creatively!

Chapter 6

Changing Your Mind with Creative Thinking

*T*here's an old story about someone asking a local person for directions. 'Well,' said the local, after a bit of thought, 'if oi was you, oi wouldn't start from 'ere.' Sometimes, on the journey from problem to solution, creative thinking needs to start from a different place, and conventional approaches just won't do the job.

Changing your mind is about putting yourself into a state that could be more conducive to creative thought. What this means in practice is disrupting the conventional patterns of thinking you'd normally bring to a problem and replacing them with other approaches that could be better suited to the task.

According to Einstein, doing the same thing over and over again and expecting different outcomes was one definition of insanity. So how can you do things in other ways and achieve the different results you want?

What you need at times like these are fresh ways of facilitating a creative mindset. What specific tools and techniques can you employ to approach this problem? Are there different mental states or frames of mind that may help you achieve your aims? Changing your mind involves discovering and engaging those different kinds of mental activity. You can use the processes and techniques that I describe in this chapter as ways of unlocking your creative mind, or as processes and techniques in their own right.

Discovering Ways of Changing Your Mind

When you start a project, whether it's inventing a new product or planning your shopping list, the conventional mindset is to be organised about it. You want to focus on the task, planning your needs and considering the outcomes. You may make a list of what you need and another of things you need to do. More often than not, you will have a timeline in mind within which to handle your problem.

Take the example of a shopping trip. A straightforward timeline may look something like this:

> Leave home by 10.
>
> Go to shops first for eggs, butter and milk.
>
> Meet friends for coffee at 11.
>
> Go into town for treats from my favourite deli.
>
> Home for kids' lunch by 12.30.

Even this simple shopping list has a timetable with deadlines, specific goals, tasks to accomplish, and measurable outcomes. With bigger projects, the complexities increase.

This type of conventional problem-solving generally falls into the category of *left-brain thinking*, which is shorthand for activities that require logic, order and planning. Most people, confronted with a problem to solve, adopt the list strategy – analyse the components, construct a sequence of tasks and goals, address each issue, and perhaps include a timeline for delivering specific results or achieving goals.

In many situations, that's all that's required, and you can achieve your desired outcome by relying on logical analysis. Using the shopping list example, you knew what you wanted and where to buy the various products, you planned a sequence for accomplishing your tasks, and you had a timeline to work to. You knew when you'd achieved your goals because you'd bought the required items, you'd met your friends, and you got home in time to meet the children, enjoying a small reward on the way.

But when your aim is to generate creative thinking, that conventional left-brain mental state may not always be the best frame of mind. Imagine another kind of shopping experience. This time you've decided to have a dinner party with some friends and you want to impress them with your exotic cooking. Here, the left-brain approach won't deliver, because you don't know what you want yet; that success will be defined only by the surprise and delight of your friends.

Sometimes it can be more productive to approach your issue in a different way altogether:

- ✔ What if you were deliberately *not* focused?
- ✔ What if you were intentionally *not* fully awake (perhaps choosing to relax and daydream about the upcoming event)?
- ✔ What if you specifically decided *not to* impose goals or timelines?

Would the outcome be chaos? Or might such a radical approach open up different – and perhaps more interesting – possibilities?

You can think about your problem and gain access to different cognitive resources through the following tools and techniques:

- ✔ **Create a mind map:** In creating a mind map, you mix your senses. Instead of relying solely on verbal analysis, you also engage visual elements (colours and shapes), and remind yourself of smells, tastes, textures and memories, all at the same time.

  So, in planning your dinner party, you spend time depicting various foods you like, tastes you know your friends like, past dinner party successes, favourite shops for giving you foodie ideas, chefs who inspire you, and so on.

- ✔ **Lay your problem out like a game:** Using objects and/or words, you stimulate your imagination through exploratory play. You move away from linear thinking and enter a much less structured state where you can indulge in random actions and allow yourself to go where ideas lead you.

  You may choose to set out a representation of your dinner, and work from there to decide how to meet everyone's expectations, and where and when you'd have to perform the tasks required in order to succeed.

- ✔ **Immerse yourself in creative visualisation:** You engage some of the techniques associated with trance, meditation and hypnosis, using dream-like experiences to create new possibilities.

  You could imagine a perfect dinner where your friends are congratulating you and praising the unique meal you created. Now you know what to buy!

If you find that you get 'stuck' at any point, the process of changing your mind can be a positive contribution to handling the problem. Just putting yourself in a different frame of mind is often sufficient to get you past that awkward stuck moment. You can, of course, continue with the same process and see where it takes you in relation to your problem or, alternatively, you may prefer to switch to another technique if that seems more appropriate. The choice, as ever, is yours.

The next sections describe these and other techniques in more detail.

Getting to Grips with Mind Mapping

Mind mapping is one of the most powerful tools in the creative armoury. A *mind map* is a graphic diagram showing the elements of a project in picture form. Tony Buzan developed the form of mind mapping most widely used today, although varieties of map diagrams have existed since ancient times.

Anyone can create a mind map: instead of writing a conventional list or set of notes – left to right, top to bottom – try starting in the centre with your main topic then draw a series of spider-lines out from that central topic. These lines are called *theme lines* because they lay out the themes of your map. That's the most basic way to create a mind map. But that's not the whole story.

True mind maps can give you much richer results than simple spider diagrams can, especially if you incorporate the straightforward guidelines Tony Buzan has devised over many years of practice and teaching around the world. I explain these guidelines in the upcoming 'Creating excellent mind maps' section. By applying these principles and avoiding some of the common pitfalls, you can quickly become proficient in creating first-class maps that benefit many kinds of work, especially if your interest is in creative thinking.

Mind maps appear to correspond to the way our brains process information. Mind maps resemble the form of neurons – the threadlike pathways in the brain that connect the different areas – and some speculate that mind maps work so well because they mimic the way our brains store information. There is broad agreement that mind maps work and are very effective at assisting organisation, memory and idea production.

Designing a mind map

Mind maps are, by their nature, flexible and personal. If you decide to use mind maps, you'll soon evolve a style that's individual and unique to you. Some simple guidelines do exist, however, which help produce better results, whatever your personal preferences.

As with all creative thinking processes, a good guiding principle is to keep it simple. Begin with your single, central idea and work from there. As you build your map, a clear layout helps you depict the information and remember it, because your brain is very responsive to the patterns and colours you use.

Gathering your tools

Before you start a mind map, you need to select your materials. Several sophisticated software products are available for your computer, tablet, or smartphone, which make mind mapping very simple. These programs perform most of the creation and management tasks automatically, with the facility to customise as you get used to the tools.

When gathering your tools, here are some simple tips:

✔ If you're using traditional pen and paper, select a pad of paper with large plain sheets, so you have plenty of room for your map to grow.

✔ Position your paper landscape (sideways) because this gives more space for your mind map, utilising your peripheral vision.

✔ Use quality paper, so your colours and design look their best.

✔ Choose quality pens – a good set of coloured fibre-tip pens is inexpensive. Some pens have two nib thicknesses, one at each end, which is ideal for rapid mapping.

Creating excellent mind maps

Use these steps, based on Tony Buzan's guidelines, to create a perfect mind map:

1. **Start drawing your mind map in the centre of the page, so branches can radiate in all directions.**

2. **Have your first image represent your central idea, and make it as colourful as you can to help fix it in your mind.**

3. **Use key words on each branch to describe your theme, using capitals for main themes and lower case for subsidiaries.**

4. **Make the branches radiating from the central idea thick close to the main idea, getting thinner as you extend to subsidiary themes.**

5. **Use words, images and symbols to draw individual themes radiating from your central idea, using a different colour for each theme.**

6. **Write the name of each theme along the branch connecting it to the central idea or to its parent theme.**

7. **Make each branch the same length as the word.** This makes the themes clearer and easier to remember.

To show you what your mind map should look like, take a look at the example mind map I've included in Figure 6-1. My mind map summarises the structure of this book.

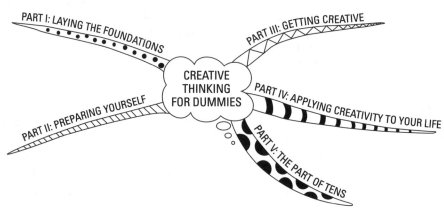

Figure 6-1:
A mind map.

Keep these tips in mind as you construct your map:

✔ Colour is an important feature of mind maps, so feel free to make full use of your colour palette. Using a range of colours also makes things easier to recognise and memorise. Keeping one colour for each branch and sub branches helps differentiate key areas.

✔ Make the map your own; don't just copy other maps. If you see a map with eight themes, for example, it doesn't mean you have to produce eight themes in your own mind map. And if each theme has several subsidiaries, that doesn't mean you need the same. Every mind map is unique to the individual or team that produced it, and you'll quickly develop your own style.

✔ Use different colours and thicknesses of line for emphasis.

✔ Try to avoid thinking in a linear way. A mind map is less likely to be of use to you if you remain in a linear frame of mind; you may as well write a conventional list. (If you're cautious about mind maps, you could try using traditional lists and a mind map side by side for a while, and comparing the outcomes.)

✔ Keep your mind map clear by controlling the layout with your selection of branches and sub-branches, colours and symbols, and numbers, if necessary.

In some situations, you may not be able to make use of colour, for instance when your work will be faxed or published in black and white, as in this book. If you can use only black and white, make sure you make full use of all the other techniques, such as line thickness, emphasis and graphic depiction. Figure 6-1 shows how a black and white version can work.

Rebutting the mind map nay-sayers

No hard and fast rules apply to mind maps; for many people, this is one of the benefits of mind maps. However, some common mistakes and misperceptions are still associated with mind maps, such as the following:

✔ **Don't like the way mind maps look.** Some individuals dislike mind maps for aesthetic reasons – they just don't like the look of these spidery pictures.

This dislike is unfortunate, because substantial evidence shows that mind maps can help users absorb complex information. Users describe other benefits, including the fact that they can generate mind maps rapidly (for example, during a lecture or meeting).

✔ **Mind maps aren't serious.** Some more traditionally minded individuals feel this way because, with the colourful freehand appearance of mind maps, they don't look like real work.

This is not, however, a view shared by some of the world's leading businesses, which have chosen to deploy mind maps to solve some of their biggest and most complex problems. CNN, for example, reported that a giant 25-foot mind map manual (at that time, the largest in the world) created for Boeing saved months of training time and netted an estimated $11 million in savings. Bill Gates is also an advocate of mind mapping, describing it as 'leading the world into the next stage of our information democracy'.

✔ **Mind maps are just lists.** Some sceptics have dismissed mind maps as coloured lists, but this really misses the point. Lists may look organised at a superficial level because of the familiar linear format, but often they lack a central theme, especially if they grow beyond a certain length.

Mind maps, on the other hand, are built from a single central idea, and have a coherent composition because of their radial structure, regardless of the scale or complexity of the subject.

Employing Table Games

An excellent way of working creatively is around a table. Whether you're alone, in a pair or group, or part of a roomful of people at a workshop, a table provides a natural, comfortable setting for all kinds of activities.

When organising table games in workshops, I like to place participants in multiples of two, depending on the individual tasks I'm inviting them to undertake. Odd numbers – three, five or seven – tend to result in one participant becoming an observer. Depending on the number of participants in total, groups of four, six or eight are ideal. Be aware that whenever you have a group larger than eight, the members tend to fragment into smaller groupings. This is a common phenomenon which happens in all sorts of social groupings from focus groups to people dining in a restaurant.

Table activities range from formal undertakings to open-ended games. A wide range of tools and techniques have been developed to assist creative thinking, as well as for a host of other purposes outside the scope of this book.

Building with Matchbox and other games

Designed at the instigation of the UK's Design Council as a way of introducing entrepreneurs and designers to creative thinking to help them achieve better design solutions, Matchbox has wider applications.

The game uses three sets of hexagonal cards: challenge cards, business suggestion cards, and design suggestion cards. Starting with a challenge card that best reflects the aim of the session, players add business solution cards then design suggestion cards – explaining their choices at each stage – to create a step-by-step map of the problem and a basis for exploring a solution.

Matchbox is loosely based on some of the same principles as mind mapping, which I explain in the preceding sections. The game can be played individually, but is designed to work best with a team.

Hexagons are the best shape to use for developing an open-ended table layout, because the six sides enable you to explore ideas in several different directions, as I show in Figure 6-2. The hexagonal format of Matchbox cards is ideal for open-ended thinking; you can prepare a customised pack based on this shape, as a way of exploring any given problem, relatively easily. A customised pack can also use different combinations of words and images to help visualise aspects of the problem.

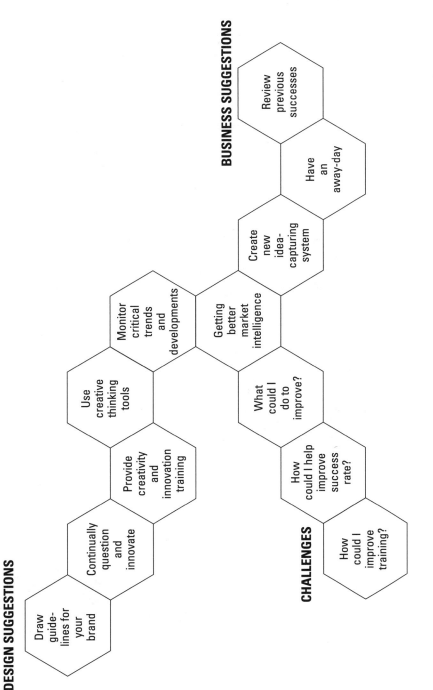

Figure 6-2:
A typical Matchbox layout.

Some creative thinking specialists also use variations of classic board games like Monopoly, Snakes & Ladders, Ludo and roulette. These games are adapted to help players determine their route along a journey or to introduce random and unexpected events into a given scenario.

Using creativity cards

Tables and cards were made for each other, like strawberries and cream. Tables provide a focus for activity and social interaction, and cards operate as the stimulus. Typically, creativity cards are packs of playing cards that feature inspirational or creatively stimulating images and statements.

One of the best-known packs of creativity cards is Roger von Oech's Whack Pack, a set of 64 cards designed to 'whack' you out of habitual patterns of thought. You can use the cards on your own or in a game to trigger creative thinking. The Whack Pack cards each feature a provocative or ambiguous open-ended statement, such as:

- Ask 'What if?'
- Muzzle your barking dog
- Conform
- Don't force it

In addition, each statement is supported by a short story illustrating the point. So, for example, for 'Don't force it' an anecdote describes why delaying a course of action can sometimes be the best option.

Other packs of cards like the Whack Pack employ similar features. Each pack has an individual perspective reflecting the personality of its author.

Packs of cards like these have proved popular in fields like neuro-linguistic programming (NLP). In NLP, the cards are used as shorthand reminders of NLP principles that can be employed to stimulate or change thinking and behavioural patterns.

You can play games using creativity cards individually or in group situations. Participants play the cards according to pre-agreed rules, which are either supplied (most sets come with suggested game formats) or made up by the moderator to fit a given scenario. Some cards are now also available as apps.

Playing with Language

Language is one of the distinguishing human characteristics and is deeply embedded in our psyches. This can be both an advantage and a disadvantage when it comes to creative thinking:

- ✔ On the plus side, a decent command of your native tongue allows you to describe your whole world and convey all kinds of possibilities. Not only can you talk about what's in the real world, but also you can imagine things that haven't happened yet or dream up things that don't exist. In this way, language can make a positive contribution to creative thinking.

- ✔ On the minus side, language can be a limitation precisely because of your familiarity with it. Because the brain works on patterns, those patterns associated with language are some of the deepest rooted. It can take real effort to escape ingrained ways of using words. Thinking creatively sometimes requires major changes in cognitive style, and that can include language.

Fortunately, some effective ways of escaping from your normal linguistic habits exist. Some of the best ideas are at the very edge of language.

Harnessing the power of metaphor

It's no exaggeration to say that almost all language is *metaphor* (where you speak of something as being something else that it resembles), or more accurately, metaphor piled on metaphor. The language in daily use is mostly built by creating associations with other words. Sometimes those associations are obscure, but often they lie just beneath the surface and can be accessed with a little delving. In fact, a whole science of meaning, called semiotics, examines exactly this territory.

Something up my sleeve?

As an illustration of how pervasive metaphors are in everyday language, I used several metaphors in the previous paragraph:

- ✔ **'metaphor piled on metaphor':** I didn't literally construct a wall of metaphors there, but I bet you clearly understood the image of building up one thing on top of another.

- ✔ **'language . . . is built from . . .':** Of course, language isn't actually built, that would be absurd, but again the meaning is clear enough.

✔ **'often they lie just beneath the surface':** It would be surprising if you thought I meant submarines or *Jaws*! Once again, you understood that I was saying that meanings are sometimes only slightly hidden.

✔ **'a little delving':** Anyone got a shovel or a long stick? It's obvious I wasn't searching the undergrowth but giving you an image about making an effort.

✔ **'examines this territory':** Clearly, semiotics doesn't have a geographical location like Arizona or Zanzibar, but you know I'm trying to convey a kind of space – in this case a cognitive one.

So in one short paragraph there are several metaphors. In each case, if my writing was clear, you got my message and weren't confused by thoughts of walls, sharks, shovels and exotic locations. That's how deeply metaphors are embedded in day-to-day language.

Often we only notice metaphors when they're mixed badly – so if the writing's on the wall, wake up and smell the coffee!

Using the metaphorical thinking technique

Although depending on metaphor can sometimes be a limitation, it's possible to turn it to advantage through the *metaphorical thinking technique*, a tool that deliberately plays with similes and metaphors in innovative ways. (Here, the term metaphor covers both metaphors and similes, although strictly speaking similes declare that something is *like* something else, whereas metaphors make a direct substitution.)

One option is to take your concept, idea or problem and try to redefine it in new language by using progressively more obscure and outrageous metaphors, which you can select from a prepared list or generate during the session:

> My love is like . . . a red, red rose/a battleship/an aardvark/tobacco/ Birmingham/yoghurt . . .

> My new coffee shop will be . . . a refuge from the real world/a place to dream/where Harry met Sally/the source of the beans for Jack's beanstalk . . .

> Starting my new novel is like . . . the siege of Leningrad/swimming the English Channel/packing for going around the world in 80 days/making an omelette without breaking eggs . . .

You explore each new metaphor for all its possible associative connotations before moving on to the next one.

Another option is to group a number of metaphors together and make leaps of imagination about how your concept or problem could link them. This technique is useful as an ice-breaker in a group scenario, because it quickly leads to laughter and testing limits. It's also effective in its own right, especially if a team is temporarily stuck.

Talking about narrative and trance

One way into a different frame of mind is through narrative. Narrative is deeply embedded in all cultures. The oral tradition has existed from time immemorial, so it's to be expected that you not only recognise a good story when you hear it, but also you routinely turn many of your own experiences into stories. But how does telling stories assist creativity, you ask? The next sections provide some answers.

Making up stories

When you're chatting with friends, you don't usually confine your narratives to the bare facts, in the way that Mr Spock would talk to his colleagues in *Star Trek*: 'A car hit mine, causing little damage. I did not know the driver. We exchanged details. Then we drove away to our respective destinations.' Not exactly something to have you gripping the sides of your seat! More typically, you embellish a little: 'You know how I hate that corner on Acacia Road, and I've always said it was an accident waiting to happen. Well, you'll never guess – last Tuesday, tell a lie it was Wednesday, no anyway, it was raining so it must have been Wednesday because I remembered my mac was still at the cleaners. And then suddenly out of nowhere this lunatic . . .' This tale is well underway, and there's no sign of the shunt yet!

In a creative thinking context, this tendency to embellish, exaggerate, dramatise and generally enrich any story can be used to great effect. You can explore a concept or problem through story-telling. The point of story-telling as a creative thinking tool is to weave a web of fantasy. The subject itself may be mundane. Perhaps, for example, you want to devise a campaign to attract new customers to a café you've opened in the town but, because other local cafés are already up and running, you need to make yours appear different. This is ideal territory for a story-based approach.

The story you weave can be fact or fiction, or a mixture of both. It can be set in a specific genre: 1001 nights, a murder mystery, a treasure hunt, superheroes, a movie, and so on. The tale can be told by one individual, or it can be played like the game of Consequences, where each player in turn takes the story to a new and unpredictable stage. Or each member of a team can inhabit the role of a character as the story plays out. Your aim is to explore imaginative scenarios and see where they lead.

So thinking again about cafés, it's worth remembering that the hugely successful international Hard Rock Café franchise was built on the myth of a typical American roadhouse and what its creators, inspired by classic American road movies, imagined it might look like. Neither the owners nor any of their customers had ever been to such a place in real life (they don't really exist!), but once you cross the threshold, you are immediately part of that dream.

You need a really good facilitator to guide the narrative. In most groups, at least one member emerges as a natural story-teller (perhaps the one who tells the best jokes or has a naturally fluent conversational style). If you're unlucky enough to get stuck with the pub bore though, consider rotating the story-telling through different individuals!

In a sense, the story itself isn't what matters. The heart of the process is the engagement of the players as the story unfolds and subconscious influences come into play, often revealing exciting insights into the core issue. (In the Hard Rock story, the original concept included the dream of a place with bigger portions, friendlier service and more comfortable seating than normal, and the idea that travelling musicians might have hung their instruments on the walls as they passed through on their road trip to fame.)

Telling the classic stories

Looking more closely at the way stories work, and the power they have to drive your imagination, it's worth taking a brief tour through one of the most influential memos ever written for the Disney Corporation.

As a film-maker, Disney employs specialist story analysts whose job it is to examine the world's stories for plots and narrative structure. This meticulous research process resulted in one analyst distilling what he learned about Joseph Campbell in the book *The Hero's Journey*, and noticing how frequently many of the themes Campbell described in his extensive writings on mythology appeared in popular films and novels, as well as in classic tales. He wondered whether there was a common denominator, deeper than the surface stories. The result was the celebrated Disney memo, which lays out the hero's journey – a journey that demonstrates the underlying themes of so many of the best-loved stories.

See how many of your own favourite books and films sound familiar in the context of this sequence, which mirrors that in the Disney memo:

1. **The ordinary world:** The story starts with the hero in his or her familiar world. Typically this is calm, peaceful, even boring. Here is Harry Potter in suburbia, Luke Skywalker on the farm, Julia Roberts working on her computer at the start of *The Pelican Brief*, Sigourney Weaver preparing for the voyage in *Alien*, or the beach at the beginning of *Jaws*. In some versions, you may sense a hint of something not quite right in the air, but mostly all is peaceful.

2. **The call to adventure:** Something unexpected happens to disrupt normal life. A sudden raid by an invading enemy or a shocking event such as the forest fire in *Bambi* or the tornado in *The Wizard of Oz*. Alternatively, the event may be a messenger bearing dramatic news or a warning, as when Obi-Wan Kenobi asks Luke to join the quest. In themes based on the Holy Grail (and there are many of them, often thinly disguised), the event is the news that the sought-for article exists.

3. **Refusal of the call:** Initially, the hero may resist or refuse the call to adventure. Or another character may cast doubts. But the dramatic event proves a powerful motivation, and the hero decides to embark on the adventure, albeit with misgivings. He may be acting for the greater good, as Harry Potter did when he understood the scale of threat posed by the return of Voldemort.

4. **Meeting the mentor:** The hero meets a seasoned traveller who helps him prepare. In *Lord of the Rings*, this is Gandalf; other magicians include Merlin advising Arthur, and Professor Dumbledore at Hogwarts. Or the hero may reach within himself for a source of courage.

5. **Crossing the threshold:** This is the critical transition to the second act, where the hero makes the commitment to leave the old familiar world and journey into the unknown. In many stories this is literally a path or journey, such as Dorothy's Yellow Brick Road, or the trek to Mordor in *The Lord of the Rings*. Sometimes the journey is an interior one, conquering inner demons or struggling to find new strength, like conquering fear to take on the shark in *Jaws*.

6. **Allies, enemies and tests:** Along the way, the hero recruits support, learns about his enemies and is tested. On the Yellow Brick Road, Dorothy recruits her weird and wonderful characters and is threatened by the Wicked Witch's flying monkeys. This is the moment when an initial skirmish is likely to occur, with the hero winning an early minor victory which intensifies the enmity of the foe.

7. **Preparing for the challenge:** Now is the time to face the challenge, with a life or death outcome in prospect. This is where doubts surface as the hero wonders whether he's worthy. The enemy further tests the hero's resolve, perhaps with a despicable act such as killing a loved character.

8. **The ordeal:** This moment, when the hero faces his greatest fear and achieves his goal, is pivotal. Often, this is a near-death experience, and the hero may seem to die at one point, as in the moment when Luke Skywalker is sucked below the surface in the rubbish crusher.

9. **The reward:** The hero has possession of the reward, but danger still exists. After the dramatic high point, the hero takes possession of the grail, which could be an elixir, a real treasure or the maiden. Indiana Jones flees the temple with his prize, pursued by a boulder.

10. **The road back:** This is the third act, where the hero crosses the threshold back to his familiar world. There may be further struggle and a race to get home in one piece. This is often a thrilling and dangerous chase, with the enemy in hot pursuit and many precarious moments for the hero and his allies. Mad Max escapes the encampment with the precious fuel, chased by the army of frenzied crazies determined to stop him at all costs.

11. **The resurrection:** Almost home, the hero faces a final supreme test, where final victory resolves outstanding issues. This is often the sudden reappearance of the enemy, or an unexpected twist such as the revelation of a traitor in the hero's midst. In *Jaws*, the shark makes a final dramatic lunge after its pursuers thought it was dead.

12. **Return with the reward:** Having been transformed himself, the hero arrives home with the power to transform his world. He can bring peace back to his village, marry the maiden, or restore the fertility of the land. In modern versions, the ending is often false because the enemy is not completely vanquished, allowing for the possibility of a sequel. Voldemort may be down, but he's not out yet. . . .

I've sprinkled a few illustrations from well-known adventures, but of course creative writers don't just follow formulas in their original work. However, they tend to acknowledge and understand the deep roots of powerful narrative and use them to great effect.

Thinking creatively, these eternal themes can provide a rich background for exploring ideas, especially in the context of a workshop, where there's time to develop a complete story. Here's an example from the formative period of one of the world's most successful businesses.

In the organisation's early days, Apple was a puny David to the Goliath of the major US computer corporations, and it had to work exceptionally hard to justify its outrageous vision. A conventional business plan just wouldn't cut it for attracting and retaining ambitious young computer specialists tempted by competing offers from the giants.

Legend has it that Apple conducted a story-based workshop about the brand and the philosophy of the company. It's said that, with typical ingenuity, Steve Jobs took a lateral path with this narrative workshop, designed to appeal to the independent spirit of people like himself. Participants in the story considered how different adventure scenarios might look and the parts the characters would play. Seafaring emerged as a theme. The outcome of this workshop was the conclusion that corporations like IBM were the Navy (hierarchical and conventional), but the maverick Apple team were the Pirates. Much more exciting. And motivating!

Building the house of memory

A useful by-product of creative thinking can be an improved memory. This is often the case if you use visualisation techniques as part of your thinking. Many creative thinkers apply variations on the concept of the house of memory. This builds on a practice that goes back to classical Greece. The story goes that, following a tragic fire at a large banquet, one of the guests claimed he could identify all the burned bodies by recalling where they had sat.

This impressive feat of memory allegedly gave rise to the notion of fixing memory items in a special space like a house. You create a series of rooms in your mind's eye and place anything you want to store and recall at certain locations in these rooms. Professional memory-act performers use this device to track long strings of random numbers, packs of playing cards or apparently unrelated objects.

If you're facing a creative challenge – starting a new business, embarking on a novel or work of art, or perhaps overcoming a major obstacle – the narrative sequence of the hero's journey can generate valuable insights for you. Whether you're working alone or as part of a team, you can dramatise your story – as a personal fantasy or in a workshop – and pursue your own goal, overcoming difficulties along the way, ingeniously winning against adversity, and bringing the prize back home. And in case you think this route may seem a little far-fetched, bear in mind that some of the world's most sophisticated organisations use strategies like this to explore their options.

Finding a way into trance states

One common consequence of story-telling, as every parent knows, is what's called a light trance state. Story-time, for most small children, is the prelude to drifting off to sleep, with that magic in-between moment of being awake but drifting.

When you're awake as an adult, it's normal to think of yourself as being alert. After all, you know when you've been asleep or when you feel drowsy, don't you? So you must *know* when you're awake, surely? But the waking state isn't always as simple as that.

Several levels of awakeness appear to exist. You know, for example, how a sudden shock like a near-miss while driving can propel you into a super-awake state where everything is greatly intensified for a while. Colours are more vivid; sounds are brighter; you seem to notice much more of what's going on around you.

At a different level, you can be awake but not actively alert. This is when you are likely to find yourself gravitating towards what's known as a trance state. It doesn't mean that you've been hypnotised, but, instead, that your brain has moved into running on autopilot for a while. Autopilot can engage when you're bored, or when you're involved in a repetitive activity, or when what you're doing is part of a well-practised routine.

So what does this state feel like and how do you know when you're in it? Surprising as it may seem, we spend a lot of our waking lives in a light trance state. If you follow a familiar route to work, the shops or school every day, you've probably had the experience of arriving at your destination without recalling precisely how you got there. That's a light trance state.

Another classic example of a light trance is the 'supermarket shuffle'. This is where you find yourself at the check-out without a clear memory of what you put in your basket. While you were wandering around the aisles with your mind somewhere else, your subconscious self was efficiently choosing the milk, butter and eggs you routinely buy.

If you find yourself running on autopilot when you weren't intending to, it can be inconvenient or even a little embarrassing. However, you can turn trance to your advantage, especially when it comes to creative thinking.

You may have found that when you start considering a problem, especially a creative one with many possible outcomes, you somehow start to drift. You may find yourself coming back and realise you've been in a kind of limbo for a short while. If that's happened to you, then you've experienced that trance state. Your brain spent a few moments switched from the busy beta state that characterises normal waking to a gentler, dreamier alpha state, where the subconscious starts to get to work on your problem.

In many educational and work environments, drifting off is considered socially unacceptable, of course: 'Pay attention, Jones!' However, a light trance is an ideal state for encouraging new thoughts to surface. So provided no one tells you off, feel free to indulge.

Now you know that light trances happen naturally, and often when you're thinking creatively, aim to take control of this useful resource. If you want to initiate a trance state, the simplest route is to relax: sit comfortably, close your eyes, and let your thoughts drift around the topic that's preoccupying you. Ask yourself 'What if?' and if the answer seems silly or off-beam, don't censor it – just follow wherever it leads, because that's a signal your unconscious mind is kicking into action on your behalf.

Using Random Input

Most of the time, your world is probably quite structured. Our brains are designed to make patterns, and we see order in everything. When it comes to creative thinking, the natural tendency is to make sense of the subject in hand. You may want to start by making a list of the main factors, sketch a diagram of the problem, or perhaps draw a mind map. All of these methods are good for beginning the thinking process, and for many people they work a lot of the time.

However, what do you do if your tried and tested approaches fail? Random input is one method for getting into a problem by a different route. It works by deliberately disrupting the normal patterns of thinking and introducing different perspectives.

The creative expert Edward de Bono described how, when he was a student, he would spend part of his study time reading magazines unrelated to his subject, and how he often came across articles that unexpectedly proved relevant to his studies. He has since written extensively on the value of serendipity and the use of random input in creative issues. (It obviously worked for him, because he first graduated at the age of 15 then gained several further degrees and doctorates, including in medicine.)

Several effective ways exist to use random input as part of your creative working routine. You may choose to use these when you're stuck or perhaps just to kick-start the creative process.

Playing word games

Single words can provide a rich source for idea generation. The point of using words is to break your normal thinking patterns quickly. Random words work precisely because they're illogical. Using single words is an example of what creativity experts call *provocation*. (Strictly speaking, provocation, as defined by de Bono, is the deliberate selection of an outrageous utterance.)

Like many creative exercises, this one is deceptively simple, and may even appear too simple at first sight. As you come to trust this approach, you'll find that it can generate unexpectedly productive outcomes. You can play word games by yourself or as part of a team.

Cutting up creatively

If you like detective stories, you'll no doubt be familiar with the classic ransom-note format. The kidnapper cuts letters and words from a selection of newspapers so the police can't trace the source.

A similar process called the *cut-up technique* has proved useful for several creative artists. The process works by cutting out lines of text from various sources and assembling them into some kind of order. David Bowie says he's used this technique to write several of his songs (which explains the surreal quality of some of his lyrics). Bowie claims he learned the technique from the author William Burroughs, who was a major influence on many art students like Bowie in the 1960s and 1970s. Burroughs used the technique in novels like *Naked Lunch, The Soft Machine* and *Nova Express*.

Using dictionaries and other sources

You can use a dictionary or thesaurus as a starting point for random-idea generation. Simply close your eyes, open the book at any page and then run your finger down to a point where you decide to stop. The selected word should be a noun, so if it isn't just carry on down to the first word that is. If you want to enhance the process, you can add another filter by opting only for nouns that describe something tangible (such as tree, skyscraper, sofa) instead of concepts (like religion, jealousy, friendship).

Alternatively, you can try the same exercise with any book or magazine. Remember, you're not looking for any kind of context, just an individual noun.

A third option is to create a ready-made list of random words which you assemble using the dictionary technique; 50–100 words should be enough for most purposes. Blindly pick one word from your list. You can do this using the eyes-closed method, or, like sticking the tail on the donkey, by turning the page over and sticking a pin into the blank side, and then seeing what you speared. You can also number the words and then choose a number at random.

In each case, you use the word you picked as the starting point for thinking about your problem. Creativity experts agree that no word can be too random, and ideally your chosen word will have nothing whatsoever to do with your problem. The purpose here is to stimulate your thinking by forcing you to make associations. In fact, if the word seems at all close to your subject, it's best to pick another one.

Being persistent

Don't give up at the first hurdle. Some words you choose will be dead-ends, producing nothing useful, but persist with the exercise because you'll find that other words stimulate interesting new associations and contribute to your problem-solving activity.

The essence of this process is serendipity, and what you seek is the unexpected, so continue until you're happy with the result.

Making complexity simple

A recurring theme in creative thinking is the drive towards simplicity. Many problems can appear bafflingly complex or intractable at first sight. This can be because they really are that difficult, but in many cases they can be made more accessible if you examine them from a different perspective. Ruthless *deconstruction* of a problem (that is, breaking it down in different ways) is often a prelude to solving it. The concentration required can provide useful stimulation of your thinking as well as generating new perspectives.

Several techniques described in this book are useful in deconstructing a problem. For example, the SCAMPER process, which I describe in full in Chapter 7, encourages you to discover new and different ways to view your problem. Using SCAMPER, you can make your problem bigger or smaller, break it into smaller pieces, add things to it or take things away, look from a different perspective, and so on. Often, the simple act of changing perspective can help you towards a solution.

Transforming language

Taking thinking to the limits of language can be a very productive process. Creatively, you can think of nonsense and surreal language as going to the edge of language. Sometimes it pays to discard linguistic conventions and look for new ways of expressing yourself. As examples of this:

- ✔ Lewis Carroll, an accomplished mathematician, wrote the *Alice in Wonderland* books. Carroll delighted in playing with words and ideas, and he embedded some of his astute mathematical observations within the surreal language and events he described.

- ✔ Nonsense was the term used by Edward Lear to describe his own verse (although it was very carefully crafted nonsense!). And John Lennon, a fan of both writers, was similarly playful with words, which resulted in some of his best song lyrics.

- ✔ *Neologisms* (made-up words) can be very productive and memorable: Carroll used the word fumious, meaning furious and fuming, in his poem *Jabberwocky*. Nowadays, chillax, used to describe chilling and relaxing, uses a similar construction. In other well-known examples, the word nylon came about because the product was first developed in New York and London, and television is a combination of Greek and Latin words meaning, roughly, 'far away seeing'.

Try combining some of the processes by making up new words for your problem from random elements, nonsensical words and verse, with a light sprinkle of trance as you dream about transforming your thoughts into something entirely new.

Visualising Success

In recent years, increasing interest has been shown in visualisation as a technique for idea generation. Strong evidence suggests that visualisation is very effective. Basically, the technique works by fooling your brain into believing that what you imagine is real.

Some years ago, sports coaches discovered that they could prove the power of visualisation by splitting teams in two during training. One half team went through the normal training procedure, rehearsing and playing physically. The other half team remained on the bench, with the players imagining their playing techniques. The results were surprising. When combined on the playing field again, the visualisers consistently outperformed the players!

Experiments like this transformed sports coaching in every field. Books like *The Inner Game of Tennis* by W Timothy Gallwey (Pan) helped popularise the notion of visualisation as a legitimate training method. Now visualisation is widely taught across many sports as an integral part of the training regime.

Creative visualisation has applications in a number of fields aside from sport. It's widely used in self-development, both as a method of continuous self-improvement and for the attainment of specific goals such as health, happiness, and success in the workplace and personal life.

A rapidly growing body of evidence from the field of neuroscience also supports the notion that your brain has a remarkable capacity to turn thoughts into reality, which has major implications for many aspects of everyone's life.

When it comes to creative thinking, much interest is shown in the process of visualisation as a quick and effective method of enhancing creative power.

When you want to learn a new skill, the natural approach is to practise it, repeating your performance until you've mastered it. That's fine, but this time spend an equal proportion of your practice session simply visualising your desired outcome. Here's how:

    1. **Sit quietly, in a relaxed posture, both feet on the ground, hands in your lap.**

2. Gently press your thumb and middle finger together on each hand.

3. Close your eyes and breathe slowly and evenly – in through the nose, out through the mouth.

4. When you're ready (you'll know when), start to picture in your mind what success will look like.

5. Intensify the image by brightening the colours, sharpening the focus, making the mental picture bigger or adding sounds.

6. See yourself mastering the skill, performing it faultlessly, time and time again.

7. See yourself from the inside. Repeat to yourself: 'This is me. I am doing this now. I am an expert.'

8. Continue this step until you feel you've completed the exercise (you'll know when).

9. Gently let the image fade, release thumbs and middle fingers, and return to normal breathing.

   This last step is important, because it allows you to warm down, just as athletes need to warm down to let their bodies return to normal after intensive exercise.

Note how you feel now. When you're ready, try your new skill and see how much you've improved.

Putting visualisation to work with image streaming

One of the best techniques for creative visualisation, and a personal favourite of mine, was devised by the respected creativity expert Win Wenger. He called his version *image streaming*. Enthusiasts make strong claims for its effectiveness, saying it leads to increasing intelligence and generating extraordinary levels of creativity. So how does it work?

You can practise this technique alone or with a partner. A session will probably last from five to 15 minutes. Just follow these steps:

1. **Gather your tools for the exercise. Use either a hand-held voice recorder (or smartphone app) or sit in front of your computer and use your PC mic to record your session.**

   You can do this exercise with a partner who records your observations, but many people find using a recording device here more satisfying and liberating.

2. **Find a quiet place where you won't be interrupted, turn off your mobile phone and make yourself comfortable. If you prefer, you can darken the room and even lie down if you want (just make sure you don't doze off!).**

3. **Switch on your recorder.**

4. **Close your eyes. Begin to calm your breathing, making it soft and smooth. Breathe in through your nose and out through your mouth. Do this for a little while until you start to feel yourself becoming calmer and more relaxed inside.**

   This process is similar to that when your brain waves progress from beta to alpha waves, like that feeling you get when beginning to doze lightly under a tree on a warm summer afternoon.

5. **Start to focus on your mind's inner screen and become aware of the continuous flow of consciousness you're experiencing.**

6. **Immediately begin to describe out loud what you're seeing. Engage and use all your senses to capture and describe every detail of what you're experiencing.**

   If you're doing a session alone, be really uninhibited in making your imagery as rich, deep and wild as you like. It's important not to hold back or censor yourself but to say everything as it happens in your mind's eye. Just how powerful your imagination can be may surprise you.

7. **When you've completed your image streaming, play back the recording and listen to your description, or discuss it with your practice partner.**

   Don't leave out this essential step. According to Wenger, listening to your audio recording helps you create a feedback loop with your brain that stimulates intelligence and creative functioning.

Discovering other creative visualisation techniques

Many techniques are available nowadays and some of the best are described in Robin Nixon's excellent *Creative Visualization For Dummies* (Wiley).

Enjoying a power nap

It's hard to over-emphasise the importance of your state of mind when you seek to be creative. The so-called 'power nap' can be a useful tool to aid creativity. In the conventional work environment, the idea of dozing off periodically is viewed with disapproval (even if operating heavy machinery isn't involved!). Some enlightened organisations, however, are now incorporating quiet areas into their offices, where employees can retire to a comfortable space in which they can meditate.

The power nap is part of the repertoire deployed by many creative thinkers to achieve a quick change of state. A few minutes switching off is increasingly recognised as an effective component of the creative process. It works for several reasons. First, it enables access to the alpha state (conducive to daydreaming and meditation). Second, it literally takes the individual out of the moment, and this has long been recognised as a way of allowing the unconscious to do its work.

Of course, going to sleep isn't essential – just relaxing and closing your eyes for a few minutes can achieve the desired objective. However, many advocates report that a brief nap has the effect of re-energising their little grey cells.

Among Nixon's fascinating suggestions are:

- ✔ **Going on a hunting expedition:** Imagine yourself on safari tracking down an elusive idea, learning its habits, finding where it lurks and then returning to camp with it in a sack to discover what it is.

- ✔ **Riding the idea train:** Use a journey as a source of random stimulation for the problem or idea that's preoccupying you.

- ✔ **Flying over your mindscape:** Imagine being able to fly over your personal land of ideas where you can pick and mix from a rich source of inspirations.

Nixon also offers many practical methods for perfecting visualisation techniques and overcoming obstacles along the way.

Where creative thinking is concerned, visualisation can be a powerful means of introducing resources from areas not normally accessible to the conscious mind. Two of the main applications for creative visualisation are:

- ✔ Finding a quick solution
- ✔ Exploring the deeper recesses of the mind

You can start by conjuring a favourite creative personality to assist your visualisation sequence. This may be an artist, an inventor or anyone you fancy as a creative hero. This individual is the living embodiment of all you love and value creatively. Your creative personality will work intimately with you as your personal advisor on your visualisation journey. The more you bring this character to life, the stronger your visualisations will be, so find this person's voice and notice his or her mannerisms, style of dress, and so on. The underlying question is always 'What would my hero say about this?' except that you phrase your questions directly and listen to the responses face to face.

Another option is to make yourself the creator. In this scenario, you're a hugely talented artist in your favourite field of endeavour, so you may be a painter, sculptor, musician – anything you choose as your true creative self. Because visualisation works best when it's repeated, you may want to create your own gallery, concert hall or home environment in which to show off your priceless work. This will be the starting point for all your visualisations, so choose to begin with the bare walls and floors and then populate them with your work.

Alternatively, you may prefer a more relaxed environment, reflecting your ideal. A friend who taught creative visualisation in England always envisaged a house by a beach as his ideal base for visualisation. He recently announced that he's set up his practice in a new location: a beachfront luxury apartment overlooking Sydney's Bondi Beach.

Whatever result you want to achieve, relaxation is an essential starting point; you can use processes like those described in this section. At the simplest level, you should be comfortable, without any distractions.

Chapter 7

Opening Your Mind with Creative Thinking Techniques

*M*any of the greatest inventions and concepts have begun from the spark of a single idea. But where does that idea come from in the first place? For some fortunate individuals, the creative switch is always on and ideas seem to flow effortlessly. But such people are the exception, and most can use some help when it comes to generating ideas. The tools and techniques described in this chapter offer a little assistance in getting the show on the road.

No single technique covers all aspects of creative thinking, and it's best to think in terms of a repertoire, or toolbox. This chapter looks at some of the most popular processes for coming up with ideas. The techniques described here reflect the foundation of best-practice methods that have been used extensively and have stood the test of time. Essentially, they consist of *unstructured techniques*, where the aim is to encourage a flow of unrestricted creative energy, and *structured techniques*, which use a framework within which the creative processes can flourish.

Personal preference is also important. What works smoothly for someone else may not be your cup of tea. Also, if you've relied on a single approach in the past, trying on some different techniques for size and seeing whether they suit you may be a good idea.

Regardless of which techniques you decide to use, always bear in mind that the best fertiliser for creative soil is laughter – if you're having fun, you're probably on the right track.

Pausing for creativity

The Creative Pause is an excellent technique for getting into a creative frame of mind. If you want to enjoy a film you've been looking forward to, the preparation is an essential part of the process. The ritual of buying a favourite drink and popcorn or a hot dog adds immeasurably to the anticipation.

Adhering to a ritual works for creativity too. You don't need snacks here (although some people like to reward themselves from time to time), but some kind of ritual, brain food if you like, can help you build the right frame of mind to get the benefit. This simple process provides a moment of stillness before you embark on creative activity.

You need to create a ritual of preparation to help ease yourself into the right frame of mind. Follow these steps:

1. Make yourself comfortable and then, on each hand, touch your thumb to your middle finger.

2. Breathe steadily and slowly – in through your nose, out through your mouth.

3. Now give yourself a few moments to consider what you're about to do, in a calm and positive way.

That's it!

This sequence is a good, reliable starting point for many kinds of creative processes.

The principle behind this technique is that you're training your brain to help you get into creative mode. The relaxation, the steady breathing and the finger–thumb touching are simple anchors (to borrow a term from neuro-linguistic programming) that tell your brain to recognise this pattern and to shift into creative gear. You may be a little self-conscious at first, but you'll find this ritual easier and more natural with practice.

Generating Ideas with Brainstorming

One of the oldest-established techniques for idea generation is *brainstorming*, which is the catch-all description of idea-generation sessions with groups or teams. Many years ago, brainstorming had a precise definition, which I explore in this chapter, before becoming the preferred term for any kind of group idea generation.

Unfortunately, in recent years brainstorming has become a generic term for any kind of creative thinking process and is widely misunderstood and misapplied. Part of the problem is that brainstorming is a technique almost everyone has heard of. Moreover, most people think they've already done it. In a recent survey of US businesses, more than 70 per cent of respondents believed they had participated in brainstorming sessions.

Processing the rules

The concept of brainstorming has probably existed in some form since humans first wanted to generate ideas.

However, the most commonly used rules for brainstorming weren't devised until the twentieth century. That's when Alex Osborn – best known for being the O in BBDO, the innovative advertising agency – came up with the term and process he called brainstorming. Osborn defined five basic rules for brainstorming:

- ✔ **Criticise nothing.** Criticism is one of the deadliest enemies of creative thinking, especially in the fragile early stages. Many people are nervous of sharing a tentative idea and feel crushed by a smart remark or a scornful snort, to the point that they never share an idea again.

- ✔ **Go for large quantities of ideas.** It's no accident that Osborn called this technique brain*storming*. A single idea can sound good, but always see what else comes up. The more ideas you have, the richer the potential harvest. And it often happens that the better ideas cluster, and together trigger bigger ideas.

- ✔ **Encourage freewheeling, wild and even nutty ideas.** Don't limit yourself to 'sensible' ideas or those you think meet with everyone's approval. Be daring. Be outrageous. Don't hold back. The more ideas you have, the richer they get.

- ✔ **Build on ideas.** Nourish the good ones and actively encourage their growth. Ask a lot of 'what if . . .?' and 'what else . . .?' questions and see where they take you.

- ✔ **Stay focused on the task.** Start with a single topic, even though it may evolve into something more. Avoid drifting off topic, which easily happens when several people are talking through ideas. Keep bringing the group back to the subject at hand. Some playful digression can be fun, but always keep in mind why you are there.

As a creative director at BBDO, Osborn lived by the success or failure of the teams working for him, and he learned through years of observation what made creative thinking sessions work and what didn't. If you intend to facilitate a brainstorming session, take some time to consider the rules from both sides; ask yourself, 'What happens if we don't do this?'

Brainstorming the right way

Brainstorming is a great technique for encouraging creative thinking but, perhaps because the term *brainstorming* is so well known, many people don't work through it correctly, and so deny themselves the full rewards of their efforts. Most shortcomings in brainstorming sessions occur when participants breach the simple rules in the preceding 'Processing the rules' section. To brainstorm correctly and avoid the most common problems, be sure to follow those rules and use the guidelines in the following list:

- ✔ **Be prepared.** 'If you fail to prepare, prepare to fail,' says the old adage, and it's as true in brainstorming as it is in any other context. Don't be so eager to jump into being creative that you forget to set the parameters first. Plan your brainstorming session properly:

  - Decide on your main topic and key question(s).

  - Select a good cross-section of participants (don't just choose the obvious ones – often the best sessions result from individuals bringing experience from different parts of the business or even different walks of life).

- ✔ **Use the rules.** You need rules (such as those explained in the preceding section) governing the process. Brainstorming without rules is like playing tennis without the white lines: the result is a mess. Rules can be very useful, especially if you use them intelligently.

- ✔ **Switch on.** You don't go jogging without a preliminary warm-up, and you can't engage in strenuous brainwork without limbering up first. Treat your brainstorming session as a workout by encouraging participants into the right frame of mind through some mental limbering-up, as discussed in Chapter 4.

- ✔ **Use a skilled facilitator.** This area is one of the keys to successful brainstorming. Choose a facilitator who's experienced and can handle a lively – or awkward – group with ease. It also helps to have someone transcribe the session as it evolves.

- ✔ **Don't allow the few to dominate the many.** This phenomenon is a function of the way social dynamics typically work. Allowing one or two individuals to dominate often overwhelms those less skilled at social interaction. (Indeed, the visible discomfort of the less forceful as they lose control often goads dominant players to greater excesses.) Experienced facilitators with the skills required for pacing, structuring, stimulating, and regulating the creative process in groups can handle issues like this.

- ✔ **Overcome conformity.** In group sessions of all kinds, participants seek, often unconsciously, to align themselves with their peers. Colloquially this behaviour is called *groupthink* and *social matching*. If you see this trend in a session, interrupt the pattern by switching to a different task, calling a break, or physically moving the participants around by getting them to work individually, in pairs or break-out teams for a while.

✔ **Stay in focus.** Many brainstorming sessions begin to drift after a short time, and participants follow random trains of thought as they would during a chat in the pub. After drifting starts, only an experienced and skilful facilitator can put the session back on track. Here, prevention is better than cure, and a good facilitator will begin by establishing clear rules and boundaries – prominently displayed – and remain alert to nip any infractions in the bud.

✔ **Prevent judging.** Much of your daily chit-chat may be mildly adversarial – 'Yes, but . . .' 'Don't be daft.' 'That would never work.' Letting go of this habit may be difficult, but in a brainstorming session it's essential that everyone feels free to express any idea without fear of others seeing them as stupid or wrong. Many ideas will never be voiced if participants think they'll be judged.

The facilitator should clearly state and rigorously enforce from the outset an injunction not to judge ideas. Adopting a silent strategy or ensuring that early idea generation is conducted individually can prevent this negative pattern from gaining hold. I explain these refinements in the upcoming section 'Making refinements for better brainstorming'.

✔ **Set the right amount of time for your session.** Brainstorming sessions can actually be both too long and too short. Studies have found that most ideas are generated within the first five minutes, on average, followed by a rapid drop-off in productivity (and quality). Many groups continue long after they've ceased to be productive, for the mundane reason that the room has been booked and five minutes doesn't look like a serious meeting.

At the same time, other research has shown that many ideas require a period of gestation outside the time limits of the typical brainstorming session. For this reason, many experienced creative thinking specialists often advocate extended workshops.

Consider the topic, its level of challenge, its complexity, and any other relevant factors, and then schedule your brainstorming session accordingly. Some problems are inherently simple (a single issue building on an existing foundation, such as thinking up a new flavour for a food product, for example) and may require a relatively short session. More complex problems involving many factors or going into new territory, such as dreaming up a totally new product for a new market, need a major allocation of time and resources. In fact, when issues are very complex, brainstorming may be only a starting point before employing more suitable techniques like Synectics or TRIZ. (I cover Synectics later in this chapter and look at TRIZ in Chapter 8.) Bring sessions to a close by saying 'last two minutes' to generate a last-minute energy burst and a flurry of ideas.

✔ **Change the format.** Having a range of resources at your disposal is always helpful. Don't get locked into the brainstorm mindset and miss the opportunity to deploy different cognitive tools that may be better suited to the topic.

Even the best-run session is subject to the vagaries of the situation, and sometimes even a well-planned brainstorming session can fall flat. Instead of trying to analyse the problem (best done at another time), the best solution is to reinvigorate the group with a different approach:

- Consider a drawing task if the process has been verbal or written, because a change of modality can instigate a change of mood.

- Split a large group into triads, pairs or individuals, because physical change is another signal for change of mood and pace. The largest natural size for a group is around eight. Beyond this, groups start to fragment. So if you're working with a large group, consider subdividing it into two or more smaller groups from the outset. You can always rotate individuals as the session evolves.

- Use natural breaks as an opportunity to regroup, rearrange and, if necessary, rethink the next phase.

- Encourage participants to move around, stand up, and write on a flip chart or whiteboard. Standing up can often encourage the generation of more ideas.

- Depending on the situation, playing some background music can aid the generation of ideas. Classical music, ideally without distracting vocals, is beneficial.

Above all, remember that brainstorming is just one of many tools in the creative thinking box.

Making refinements for better brainstorming

In recent years, experts in creative thinking have developed an impressive array of tools to address all aspects of the creative process, many of them informed by significant advances in knowledge of the brain and human behaviour. In this increasingly sophisticated environment, classic brainstorming – now a 70-year-old veteran – is showing its age. So are better brainstorming techniques available?

A number of experts have responded to the perceived limitations of classic brainstorming by creating practical refinements which often produce more engaging and productive sessions. I explain them in the following sections.

Preserving your ideas now

Great ideas don't just happen in organised sessions. You'll never know how many great inventions, ideas and masterpieces have been lost because their originator missed the chance to record the moment. One notorious example is the poet Samuel Taylor Coleridge, of *Kubla Khan* fame, whose reveries were interrupted by the mysterious 'man from Porlock', as he wrote afterwards, causing his crowning achievement (as he described it ruefully) to be lost to us forever.

Always seize the moment. Just as Boy Scouts were advised to 'be prepared' and always carry a pen-knife, the intrepid creator should always be ready for the fleeting instant when inspiration comes, and carry a means of recording those precious moments. Nowadays the choice is much wider than the back of an old envelope or a cheap notepad and pencil stub. Most smartphones come with a recording facility, and lots of recording apps are also available.

Always keep a notepad or recording device with you so that you can write down your thoughts as they happen. Don't censor your notes yourself. Some may be rubbish, but others may be gold. If you've captured them, you can do the judging later. But if you haven't, you may just find you've missed a nugget!

Each of these alternatives is designed to overcome some of the more common objections to brainstorming, such as the loudest voice or most senior group member dominating proceedings, and the destruction of fragile new ideas before they've had a chance to flourish.

You can devise an approach combining some or all of the methods described, and as a starting point you may want to consider mixing:

- Silent sessions
- Individual generation of ideas
- A pool or gallery showing the best ideas, with points awarded to 'winners'

The other factor not to be underestimated is the importance of a strong, experienced facilitator to guide the session and keep it within the agreed boundaries.

All these alternatives are easy to use, especially if you adhere to the original brainstorming guidelines (see the 'Processing the rules' section earlier in this chapter). Whether you want to generate ideas in a group at work, at home alone, or with a colleague, these processes will help get the creative engine running.

Going solo with individual brainstorming

Research shows that individuals consistently outperform group output in both quantity and quality of ideas. A basic aim of brainstorming is to produce *a lot* of ideas based on the principle that, as one creativity expert eloquently put it, 'There is nothing more dangerous than an idea – if it's the only one you have'.

An abundance of ideas isn't a solution in itself, but it can create an excellent starting point, especially if those raw ideas aren't censored at the early stages. Solo idea generation allows this process to flourish.

If you have a team working on a common project, one approach to individual brainstorming is to brief everyone as a group before separating the individual team members. Idea generation tends to work fast, with many ideas being produced immediately, so monitor activity as closely as you would in a group session. As for the outcome, you can keep the individuals apart and conduct a third-party appraisal, or bring the group together to evaluate everyone's outcomes.

There are no hard and fast rules, and if you're conducting several sessions, vary the approaches and explore what works best for your team.

Switching on to electronic brainstorming

Software now exists to assist the brainstorming process, and given the extraordinary proliferation of computer power in the form of smartphones, iPads and other tablets, along with a vast range of apps to support them, technology provides a useful alternative to traditional routes. A good starting point is to try some of the many apps based on mind mapping.

One advantage of going electronic is that, as well as suiting the way many people prefer to work nowadays, you have an immediate and permanent record of the process. And it's easy to use networks to link several participants at the same time. (Some businesses and individuals are experimenting with international idea generation sessions in the shrinking global village where everyone is 'next door'.) The rapid rise of social networking is another factor encouraging people to work together, wherever they happen to be geographically.

Working in pairs

Whereas groups of participants can inhibit the creative process, especially when not under the guidance of an experienced facilitator, research shows that people working in pairs somehow avoid the trap of premature criticism of each other and the limitations of self-censorship to a large degree. Pairs of people can also be very productive.

Based on the observation of creative partnerships (for example, while John Lennon and Paul McCartney wrote 17 number-one hits individually, they had 49 as a pair), this is an option worth exploring.

Scheduling silent sessions

Anyone who's been in a brainstorming session knows how noisy, chaotic and emotionally charged they can be. At the other extreme, they can be very negative, with sullen, resistant participants and hostile verbal and non-verbal reactions to any attempt at generating new ideas. Obviously, neither of these scenarios is satisfactory.

Silent sessions, in which the participants follow the classic brainstorming rules but work silently as they generate their individual ideas, have been shown to overcome some of these potential problem areas. Here, the participants begin by writing their ideas down (preferably on 3-x-5-inch index cards – one idea per card).

After the initial idea generation period (preferably to a pre-agreed time limit), several options are available:

- ✔ Have everyone pass their sheets or index cards to the person on their left, so that each participant gets a colleague's ideas to work with. Participants can then add their own (positive!) comments, and continue this 'pass the parcel' sequence for an agreed number of turns.

- ✔ Create either an idea pool or a gallery. For an idea pool, place completed cards in the centre of the main table, so everyone can see and use all the output. The galley approach involves fastening the cards to a wall, so that all the output is on show.

  The moderator can decide whether to invite participants to speak as the silently generated ideas spark additional thoughts.

Silent sessions are fascinating to observe and participate in, because they break the normal patterns of group behaviour. You don't usually sit in a room of people without chatting, so the enforced silence generates a volume of pent-up energy, and when it's released the output can be very exciting. Extra impetus can be added by encouraging the participants to award merits to their preferred ideas (have coloured stars on hand to stick to the cards), and to explore the most promising ideas in different (and perhaps outrageous or unexpected) ways.

Shifting your ground

Recent research at Harvard on more effective methods for generating ideas has shown promising results for what the researchers call *shifting*. In this approach, participants first work individually and then in groups, alternating between the two at five-minute intervals over a pre-defined period.

Shifting is just one of several alternatives that researchers are exploring. No hard and fast rules exist about idea generation, so whether you work alone or with a team, you can conduct your own experiments to discover what works best for you.

Signing Up To Synectics

Unlike some creativity tools, *Synectics* is based on a highly structured approach and can be described as brainstorming for grown-ups. It incorporates brainstorming, particularly at the initial idea generation phase, but with the added ingredient of metaphor. (Take a look at Chapter 6 for more about metaphor and its contribution to creative thinking.)

Synectics is a proprietary process (originally developed at Arthur D Little in the 1950s), and it's now called by the less than snappy name of Synectics World (unkind wags have observed that if they'd used Synectics in the branding development they'd have come up with a better name).

Synectics is designed to be a group process for businesses, and is best conducted in a meeting area well equipped with whiteboards or flip charts, lots of drawing equipment, good work surfaces and plenty of space so participants can stretch their legs and regroup or break off into smaller groups periodically.

The best-run Synectics sessions are conducted by an experienced facilitator who guides and gets the best out of each session. (You can contact professional facilitators at the main Synectics website, www.synecticsworld.com, a site which enables you to connect to all Synectics resources internationally.) However, one principle of creative thinking is that rules are made to be broken, and several Synectics principles can be adapted for different situations if needs be. Several of the individual ingredients can selected for less formal sessions. For example:

- ✔ If you don't have access to a professional facilitator, you can choose one person from your group to become familiar with Synectics principles.

- ✔ If you're working alone, you can use some of the features I describe in this section as tools to stimulate your creative thinking.

- ✔ If you're feeling especially creative, you can take the Synectics model as a catalyst for designing your own unique system!

You can find lots of valuable insights in the Synectics model, and they are worth examining, however you decide to apply them. The choice, as ever, is yours.

One concern mentioned by some critics of Synectics is that, if done properly, it takes a long time to go through the processes. At the root of this timescale issue is the question of matching the technique to the scale of the problem. Like TRIZ, which I describe in Chapter 8, Synectics comes into its own with large-scale or complex issues that deserve a great deal of careful attention. Applied to relatively simple and straightforward issues, it can certainly seem like overkill.

Synectics has been defined as a way to approach creativity and problem-solving in a rational way. Co-creator WJJ Gordon observed that, 'Traditionally, the creative process has been considered after the fact. The Synectics study has attempted to research creative process in vivo, while it is going on.' Gordon coined the phrase 'making the strange familiar and the familiar strange', which is the shorthand description of what's actually a sophisticated and subtle process.

Inventing a prototype for brainstorming

The team that created Synectics would have been familiar with the principles of brainstorming as I describe in the 'Brainstorming the right way' section, earlier in this chapter. The team's aim was to build a better model for creative thinking and problem-solving. What they came up with can be described as a prototype for brainstorming, bringing a sense of structure and direction to a process that was often chaotic.

The team's starting point was that creativity isn't a mystery, but that it can be taught like other skills. Synectics is based on three main assumptions:

- ✔ The creative process can be described and taught.
- ✔ The invention processes in the arts and in science are similar and driven by the same psychic processes.
- ✔ Individual and group creativity processes are comparable.

Working with these assumptions, Synectics teaches that people can be better at being creative if they understand how creativity works.

Synectics builds on the notion that apparently irrelevant material can be important for creative thinking. It emphasises emotion over intellect, and irrational thinking over rational thinking. Encouraging both the emotional and the irrational can provoke creative ideas and solutions to seemingly intractable problems.

Referring, reflecting and reconstructing

The Synectics process takes the topic at hand and uses it as a starting point for a thorough analytical procedure involving three core processes, conducted in a logical sequence:

✔ **Referring:** Defining the problem and gathering information about it

✔ **Reflecting:** Deploying a wide range of techniques chosen by participants

✔ **Reconstructing:** Merging the referring and reflecting phases into a solution

The next sections cover each phase in more detail.

Referring

Think of the referring process as laying the foundations for the project by following these three key steps:

1. **Precisely defining the problem.**

   Here, the emphasis is on *precision*, otherwise you may begin with a structure built on sand! When embarking on creative problem-solving, rushing your fences and getting straight into the exciting process of playing with ideas is always tempting. However, precision is important, because understanding your problem in every possible way from the outset is essential. Get curious about it; ask questions; don't take anything for granted; don't be afraid to ask questions that seem obvious or stupid. The Polaroid camera, for example, was invented after a little girl asked her father why she couldn't see the photos on her camera instantly.

2. **Comprehensively researching the factors surrounding the problem.**

   Many creativity experts believe that this is the stage most often skimped, because it's boring and everyone wants to get to the exciting problem-solving part. But poor foundations here are likely to lead to poor solutions.

3. **Reviewing and understanding the solutions already tried.**

   Research is essential, because it's all too easy to discard some promising routes in the rush to try a new approach.

The referring phase is all about rigour – taking the time and making the effort to work through these three steps thoroughly and in depth. Conducted properly, this phase is a powerful and robust creative thinking tool.

Reflecting

The reflecting phase is the fun part of Synectics, when you use your creativity and imagination to address the problem.

As with other open-ended processes, it's important to conduct the reflecting phase in a positive, relaxed frame of mind, with your critical faculties turned down! This isn't the time for editing, censorship or negative thinking.

Inevitably, users of creativity tools see some comparisons between this phase and classic brainstorming, because the guidelines (including positivity and prohibition of critiquing) and the emphasis on a rich flow of ideas resemble brainstorming to a degree. However, purists argue that what differentiates Synectics here is the focus on *associative thinking* – actively finding links between ideas.

You can certainly start this phase with a brainstorming-type session, but the heart of the reflecting process is deploying the various triggers, which I describe in the next section.

The 22 Synectics triggers

You don't need to use the *Synectics triggers* – specific actions to help you locate the links between ideas – in the following list in order, because Synectics is an exercise in freeing your creativity and using your imagination. Keep the emphasis on positive exploration of each theme you try, and refrain from the natural tendency to be critical or rational until the task is completed. Loosen up!

The Synectics triggers are:

- **Subtract:** Take an element away or simplify it. If the problem concerns a car, take away the engine. If the car has four wheels, what about three or two? Or even one? If it's about a drink, take away the liquid. What might happen then? How could the product still work? (Red Bull and other energy products now come in inhaler form; Lemsip is now in a capsule as well as a drink.)

- **Repeat:** Duplicate elements, or add more and more resources. What might happen as a result? (Smartphones consist of many elements added to a basic mobile phone.)

- **Combine:** Mix ingredients from other situations, a bit like trying a new recipe. (The beauty market offers many examples of combining different functions in a single product.)

- **Add:** Increase the number, size or strength of various elements. Explore the possible consequences. (Mobile phones and music players go through phases of miniaturisation, and size increases according to prevailing trends.)

✔ **Transfer:** Create new situations or locations for the elements of the problem. How might they have to change? (Consider the myriad products based on the simple electric motor.)

✔ **Empathise:** Become the customer for your problem and look at it from that perspective. Or become the problem itself. Does this make you think differently? (The Sony Walkman was the result of its inventor wanting personal music on long flights and using technology that had not until then had an obvious purpose.)

✔ **Animate:** Wave a magic wand and bring the problem to life. What is it like as a living thing? (Pixar was the result of a software designer realising the potential of a simple landscape program to transform the animation industry.)

✔ **Superimpose:** Add other layers, like a collage, dropping in new meanings, fresh ideas, even random ingredients. How does the picture change? (The original *Sunday Times Magazine* revolutionised what a magazine was supposed to look like.)

✔ **Change scale:** Increase or decrease the size dramatically like in *Alice in Wonderland*. What happens to the problem? (Considering the extremes of microscopic nanotechnology and giant Cray computers, computing has never been smaller – or bigger.)

✔ **Substitute:** Cut and paste different elements of your problem, adding in elements from outside it. (Legend has it that the first hot dog was created when its inventor ran out of paper wrappers for his frankfurters and used his baker brother's bread rolls instead.)

✔ **Fragment:** Take your problem to pieces. Try different ways of doing this: explode it, disassemble it. (Budget airlines were a result of asking what elements were essential for relatively short flights.)

✔ **Isolate:** Look at the parts of your problem in isolation. Examine them in their own right then and as parts of the whole. What do they contribute? (*Auto Trader*, which revolutionised second-hand car selling, simplified the link between seller and buyer with a stripped-down product with just the one aim.)

✔ **Distort:** Put on your (metaphorical) distorting spectacles. Bend it, stretch it, every way you want it! (Imagine vacationing not as Joe Public but as a celebrity – that's the thinking behind Virgin's Rockstar Service holiday packages.)

✔ **Disguise:** Camouflage your problem. Hide it. Dress it up as something else. Look for unexpected consequences. (In order to compete with the American gas-guzzlers of the 1960s, Volkswagen made a virtue of its Beetle being a unique, small, rear-engined car, ignoring its German heritage in a country recovering from the Second World War in which Germany had been the enemy.)

✓ **Contradict:** Instead of just thinking of a solution, be perverse and try to make the problem worse. Test the problem to destruction. Then reverse the process. (This contrarian thinking contributed to the iconic Avis 'We try harder' campaign, making a virtue of being second in its market. And more recently Comparethemarket.com has built its success on potential consumer confusion about its brand name.)

✓ **Parody:** Ridicule can be a powerful tool. Mock your problem. Be merciless. (*Private Eye* began as a response to the conventional press refusing to publish critical or satirical political comment. The more risks it took, the more successful it became.)

✓ **Procrastinate:** Take time to dream or fantasise about your problem: no hurry, no pressure. See what happens to your problem. (Richard Branson largely built his business empire by dreaming the questions: 'What if . . .?' and 'Why not . . .?')

✓ **Analogise:** Create analogies for your problem, both close and remote, logical and wild. (See 'The Synectics springboards' section later in this chapter.)

✓ **Hybridise:** Try cross-breeding your problem with another one – the more unlikely the better. (Soft, cheap, disposable contact lenses were the result of Johnson & Johnson combining its experience in different fields of expertise to create a totally new product category.)

✓ **Metamorphose:** Think about how your problem may change over time. What if current trends continue? What if they don't? (Early entrants to the online news market are taking the gamble that the desire for news will survive the continuing decline of paper-based products.)

✓ **Symbolise:** Create a symbol of your problem. Make it as simple as possible, while embodying the essence of it. (Many luxury brands have become their own symbols, with the logo symbolising fashion, wealth and status.)

✓ **Mythologise:** Taking the symbol further, turn it into an icon or even mythologise it. (Guinness did so with wild horses emerging from the raging sea in its award-winning advert of 1999.)

Write the 22 triggers on 3-x-5-inch cards so that you can shuffle and use them randomly to stimulate your thinking when you get stuck.

Another factor that differentiates Synectics from other techniques is the stress placed on the power of language in the form of narrative, metaphor, symbols and myth. This reflects a keen interest in tapping into the subconscious mind, a practice increasingly seen as a central component of all creative thinking.

One of the UK's creative gurus, Robin Wight, was fond of telling his clients, 'We interrogate the product until it confesses.' In the same way, the test of whether you have conducted this stage successfully is to continue to ask tough questions to establish that the objectives have been achieved. Classic questions here are, 'What else . . .?' as in 'What else would I have to have to give my product iconic status?', and 'What would happen if . . .?' as in 'What would happen if my main competitor knew about this now?'

The Synectics springboards

The final step in this phase is to introduce the springboards. Here, associative thinking comes into its own by using analogies at various levels. These analogies may be based on similarities (similar products, markets and functions), differences (different kinds of events and phenomena) and *stretches* (such as symbols or emotions).

An easy way to generate analogies is to ask questions about resemblance, such as 'What does this remind me of?', 'What else looks like this?', 'What else behaves like this/does this job?', and so on.

Analogies can also be *close* (based on material similar to the subject) or *remote* (at the outer limits where no obvious link exists between the topic and the chosen analogy).

Using the table in Figure 7-1, draw a matrix of categories of analogies, and then choose two or three routes and see where they lead you.

Similarities:	Differences:
Close:	Remote:
Stretch:	

Figure 7-1:
An analogies grid.

Reconstructing

In this final phase, you take the material from the referring and reflecting phases and examine what you've achieved. Having analysed your problem thoroughly and taken it apart, you now have a fresh perspective to work from as you reassemble the whole picture.

Sometimes the outcome is startlingly clear, and your analysis will have pointed you in a new direction. More frequently, your work will have yielded fresh insights, which will move your thinking forward. At this stage, you may decide that you've achieved your aims or you may want to go around the block again for a second round.

Tooling Up with SCAMPER

The SCAMPER model is one of several list-based idea-generation processes, using an easy-to-remember acronym. One of the reasons for its enduring popularity among creativity specialists is that it offers a down-to-earth set of options designed to trigger the imagination.

The seven elements are a reminder of different ways to view any given subject matter. You can deploy the elements individually or in any combination to achieve a fresh perspective.

Before using SCAMPER, bear in mind these two important points:

- ✔ SCAMPER works best when the subject is specific and clear. It's most useful in addressing a single product or service. So isolate the topic or challenge you want to address. (If you have an imprecise or complex creative challenge, use a different technique.)

- ✔ SCAMPER is an interrogative technique. It works best when you take the stance of an inquisitive child, relentlessly asking questions, probing every aspect, taking nothing for granted and not being put off by brush-offs.

Working with a handy toolbox

Working with SCAMPER is very straightforward. It can be useful to think of SCAMPER as a toolbox, where you can use one or more individual tools to tackle a challenge. Just as a hammer has a particular role, one SCAMPER element will suit one situation, and a different one may be more appropriate for another. The more you use the elements, the easier it becomes to pick the right ones for the job.

The seven elements of SCAMPER are:

- ✔ **S**ubstitute: Put one thing in place of another. You can choose a component, materials the item is made of, users of the product (or service), or any other factor involved in the product or with the people who use it. This need not be logical, and it can be productive to consider unlikely or even apparently silly substitutions. For example, what if a component normally made of metal was made of jelly instead?

- ✔ **C**ombine: This is stirring the pot, and just as in cooking, you can get unexpected results by mixing, integrating or placing items together. This does not have to be logical or even plausible – always bear in mind that your imagination is at work here and anything is possible. The ice cream cornet was, according to legend, created by combining the need for a holder for ice cream with another product that was also edible.

✔ **A**dapt: Here, you can play with all the variables. Try altering an aspect of the product, changing its function or using another element instead. Can one part of the product perform a different function? The deceptively simple one-button operation of the iPod comes from adapting a single button to perform many functions. As an exercise, take your TV remote control and consider how many of the essential functions a single button may be made to control. Do you really need all those buttons? (My remote has a fairly typical 47 buttons!)

✔ **M**odify: Move the product on by increasing or reducing a feature. Consider its scale, shape or any aspect that grabs your attention. The fashion industry uses this process frequently, not always with great results (consider the bell-bottom trousers, wide ties and extra-long shirt collars that were a feature of the 1970s).

✔ **P**ut to another use: In the 1950s, a number of retailers, including McDonald's, realised that their premises had another use: they had intrinsic value as properties in their own right. This fact became an important part of McDonald's product portfolio. When Ray Kroc, the businessman who built the success of McDonald's, discovered this angle he immediately set about buying back properties he'd franchised, in anticipation of their long-term value.

✔ **E**liminate: This is a way of exploring what's essential in a product. You can try removing, simplifying or reducing a product element and seeing what happens. Does the product still work? Does this action suggest an alternative route? The budget airlines are experts at testing how much can be removed from a product (cheap flights) while remaining viable. This already includes removing the hold-luggage allowance, in-flight food and drink and allocated seats – and even more options are now under consideration, if rumours are to be believed!

✔ **R**everse: Here, you take the product and stand it on its head, perhaps literally. What happens if you turn the problem upside down, inside out or sideways? An ingenious example comes from Sir Alec Issigonis, designer of the original Mini, who had the revolutionary idea of turning the car's engine sideways, thereby increasing the leg room of the interior and shortening the exterior dimensions at a stroke.

When using the SCAMPER model within a team, you can follow some of the principles of brainstorming, although SCAMPER can work very effectively for individuals, too.

Displaying the individual SCAMPER elements prominently during the session is good practice. If one route seems promising, what might happen if you combine it with another one? Alternatively, if you're getting stuck, starting from a different place may be productive. What happens if you allocate a time limit and run through all seven elements in sequence (forwards or backwards)? You may find that some elements simply *demand* more time while others fall by the wayside.

In Table 7-1, I've subjected a humble chocolate bar to SCAMPER. See if you can fill out the matrix with other possibilities. And remember, don't be constrained in your thinking – go for some improbable or outrageous ideas!

Table 7-1	Subjecting a Chocolate Bar to SCAMPER					
Current Features of Product or Service	**S**	**C**	**A**	**M**	**P**	**E**	**R**
Size	Bite size and party size bags	Multi-pack; different flavours	Mini or king size				
Shape				Triangle; circle			
Type of chocolate			White, dark, milk, and so on		Laxative		Chocolate on the inside, nuts on the outside
Number of calories per bar					High calorie energy bar	Low calorie version	
Flavours		Crazy combinations		Add a variety of flavours			
200g bar					Cook with it; make it into ice cream		

Using Thinkertoys – a bigger toolbox

Michael Michalko has worked for many years in the field of creative thinking. With his Thinkertoys process, he uses the SCAMPER elements to form the basis for an exploration of dozens of creative tips and tricks to stimulate the imagination, supported by real-life examples and a liberal sprinkling of optical illusions to loosen up the brain.

If you get stuck in the thinking process, a random dip into the Thinkertoys compendium will give you a shot of creative caffeine.

In addition to the seven core SCAMPER elements, Thinkertoys adds two more:

- **Magnify:** Make the product bigger. Coca-Cola and McDonald's both realised the potential of super-sizing and created bumper versions of their best-selling lines. They anticipated – accurately, as it happens – that customers already buying their products could easily be persuaded to buy more.

- **Rearrange:** Adjust the product ingredients. A classic example comes from the yogurt market, where a recent innovation, breaking with convention, has been to take the various ingredients apart and put them in separate compartments of the packaging, so consumers can combine flavours and textures to their individual taste.

Thinking Laterally

If you ask a professional what creative thinking is about, the term lateral thinking is likely to come up quite soon. *Lateral thinking*, also described as *sideways thinking*, is a term originally coined by Edward de Bono in 1967 to describe an alternative process to conventional linear thinking – one that breaks out of the habitual cognitive patterns learned at school. Lateral thinking is based on the view that traditional critical or analytical thinking (exemplified by the Greek philosophers Plato, Socrates and Aristotle) is actually a limitation to thinking rather than just a structural framework.

Lateral thinking is neither vertical (logical, analytical, compliant) nor horizontal (unstructured, daydream-like, directionless). Instead, lateral thinking encourages you to change the direction of your thinking, to look at things from a different perspective or to permit yourself to reinvent what you see in fresh, original or humorous ways. A simple way to get into a lateral thinking frame of mind is to use a model like SCAMPER (see 'Tooling Up with SCAMPER' earlier in this chapter) to twist, turn and stretch your problem in a number of different directions, so you can gain a different perspective.

Introducing Parallel Thinking

A variation on the lateral theme is *Parallel Thinking*. In this trademarked process, you're encouraged to link two opposite viewpoints by progressing towards a common aim. So instead of adopting the all-too-common adversarial approach in which you argue that you're right and the other party must give in, both parties explore routes to get to where they both want to end up. In this case, the dialogue assists the ultimate purpose rather than being used to score points.

The Parallel Thinking process is pretty simple to master. You can expand upon each of the steps as your creative thinking challenge or problem demands. The essential steps of the process are:

1. **Identify the different viewpoints.**

2. **Zoom in on the similarities rather than the differences between the viewpoints, and search for any common ground that exists.**

3. **Search for ways to move forward from the points of common ground.**

   To help you think up ideas for moving forward, techniques such as brainstorming are useful. Aim for ways forward that enable both parties to make compromises on the areas of difference they can live with or be happy with.

4. **Reach agreement.**

This technique is best suited to problems where the arguments on each side are equally powerful. Examples are the perennial debate between conflicting investment strategies, and union or management negotiations.

This technique is also useful away from work, in the home. You can, for example, use Parallel Thinking to decide which of two schools to send your children to or whether to spend a windfall on a holiday or home improvements.

Say you've received such a windfall, and you feel in need of a holiday. Your partner, however, believes your home is in urgent need of redecoration. Both arguments are strong and emotional, and both are valid. In the normal course of events, this difference of opinion may result in an argument as each party defends his or her choice while attempting to weaken the other's case. (You can imagine it: 'I'm exhausted at work and need a break, but you just want to keep up with the neighbours!' versus 'You laze around at weekends, and our home is shabby!')

Parallel Thinking removes the emotion by considering the strengths and weaknesses of each case, and evaluating the desired outcomes:

- ✔ Party A is exhausted and feels that a holiday would recharge the batteries. The windfall must be spent wisely.

- ✔ Party B is ashamed of the home and feels that redecoration would restore pride in it. The windfall must be spent wisely.

The key to Parallel Thinking is looking at whether a way exists to satisfy both parties, and then exploring where to go from there. Both parties agree that the money should be spent wisely, so that is the area where common ground exists between them.

Having identified the common ground, the parties can ask questions such as 'Perhaps the windfall can be split?' and 'Is there a third way?' to help them to look for a way forward. Think about it: with the benefit of a break, Party A may then have the energy and desire to redecorate. If Party B enjoys the holiday, creative ideas about how to redecorate cheaply may begin to flow. Party A may then concede the holiday doesn't have to be an expensive one.

Now both parties are Parallel Thinking instead of bickering.

Debating with yourself

You can use the principles of Parallel Thinking as an individual. The easiest way to do this when you're undecided about a problem is to draw a vertical line down the middle of a sheet of paper, and write the opposing arguments on each side of the line (bullet points work best). Now work through each argument in turn, putting the case as strongly as possible and noting how you respond. Typically, the outcome is either that you see how you can create an all-win outcome or that one argument emerges as much stronger than the other. Prepare to surprise yourself!

Keeping it simple

Another core concept for Parallel Thinking is *simplicity*. Simplicity is more an approach than a technique. Based on his strongly held belief that much creative failure is rooted in unnecessary complexity, de Bono assembled a series of processes to activate the route to simplicity. These include

- ✔ **Shedding:** Dropping ideas and concepts that aren't useful.

- ✔ **Reframing:** Distorting and manipulating concepts and suppositions in order to yield fresh perspectives. Reframing is also popular in neurolinguistic programming.

Whether in a workshop setting, as a couple problem-solving at home, or as an individual, a major theme for achieving simplicity is *challenge*, which exhorts participants to confront existing beliefs and behaviours at many levels, resulting in a much clearer view of the situation.

Provoking Provocative Operation

A tool developed to encourage lateral thinking and the path to simplicity is based on *Provocation*, a process also used by Einstein to test the limits of his imagination. Provocation is the process of taking an idea to its limits, beyond what may be considered reasonable or rational. For example, Einstein knew he couldn't ride on a wave of light, but he tried to imagine what it would be like if he did.

Provocative Operation, or PO, was created by de Bono to signal that a sequence of thoughts was about to introduce a different way of looking at a problem, and should be taken seriously, however odd it may appear at first glance.

As an illustration, consider the following problem which arose at Amsterdam's Schiphol Airport. Men were being insufficiently careful when urinating in the public lavatories, raising issues of hygiene, high cleaning costs and related problems. The PO solution was to provide the men with something to aim at. And so, if you visit the men's lavatories at Schiphol Airport, you'll see a decal of a fly sitting in the urinal bowls.

The PO technique uses a number of different starting points to kick-start the creative process, such as:

- ✔ Escape, where you 'get outside' the issue and see it from a fresh perspective.
- ✔ New stimuli, where you introduce other elements and explore the consequences.
- ✔ Reversal, where you turn the problem on its head or twist it around to see it from another viewpoint.

Of course, you can also borrow freely from the tools in SCAMPER to widen your approach.

Wearing the Six Thinking Hats

Among the wide range of tools de Bono has created over his long career, a favourite of mine is the Six Thinking Hats. This method is a practical, user-friendly way for groups and individuals to work creatively and effectively in many different problem scenarios.

The hats symbolise six different states of mind (rather than the number of participants – you can have just one participant or as many as eight), and you can use them in many different ways. Depending on the composition and mood of the group, the hats of this technique can be metaphorical or real, displayed or actually worn. While wearing the hats and passing them around can be an amusing way to proceed, many teams settle for visual depictions of the hats, perhaps with brief descriptions of their purpose to remind participants of their role.

A typical Six Thinking Hats session draws on the processes I look at in the earlier 'Introducing Parallel Thinking' and 'Provoking Provocative Operation' sections to enrich the experience.

The key strength of this system, apart from the fact that it's fun to participate in, is that it's results-orientated and a time-saver. Using the Six Thinking Hats, industrial giant ABB reduced the length of international project team discussions from 30 days to just two!

The Six Thinking Hats method works like this:

1. **The scope and scale of the problem are agreed in advance, and as in all creative processes, the group signs up to the rules of the game.**

2. **The facilitator describes the six hats and their functions.**

   The facilitator can be a trained individual, and there are benefits in such expertise. However, the process is designed to be simple to use, and a little preparation and familiarisation before the event can ensure a successful session, provided you follow the basic guidelines.

   In a group, the facilitator assigns individual hats in a sequence chosen as the session evolves. The facilitator also decides how long to remain in one mode, and when the time has come to move on to the next one. The remaining steps that follow are only a typical scenario in which hats are assigned.

   If you're planning to use this technique with a group for the first time, don't allow individual participants to adopt a favourite hat. The hats are there to help the whole group explore different frames of mind.

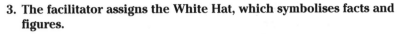

3. The facilitator assigns the White Hat, which symbolises facts and figures.

Starting with the White Hat isn't essential, but it's a fail-safe option and the White Hat is the one that most sessions begin with. With this hat, you investigate the structure of the problem and deal unemotionally with all the factual material. The purpose here is to gain a deeper understanding of the whole picture and the details that comprise it.

At its heart, this process deals with two levels of facts: the first being hard, incontrovertible facts; the second being less tangible information, which may be facts or beliefs.

The White Hat phase is the chance to interrogate the facts, to separate fact from belief and to create a proper map of the territory. In the course of a typical Six Hats exercise, returning to White Hat mode after using some of the other hats can reveal fresh insights into old perceptions.

4. The facilitator moves everyone to the Red Hat, which symbolises emotions and feelings.

Making the Red Hat your next stop isn't essential, but in a typical scenario the Red Hat is great for getting things moving.

This usually isn't the first hat to be deployed, but when it's used, it can release a great deal of energy. The Red Hat is the signal for sharing the feelings that give power to the issue. The Red Hat gives permission to explore the limits.

Of course, these feelings can be both negative and positive. It's good to release negative emotions that may be causing blockages to progress. Once articulated, these emotions are open to inspection, and consequently can be dealt with.

Positive emotions, too, can be exposed to light, and the group can address questions such as: 'Are we being distracted, tempted by the magic?' 'Are we doing this because it makes us feel good?' 'What if we took it even higher?'

Many of the best real and fictional detectives place great faith in the hunch. Essentially, Red Hat is hunch mode, where you follow your intuitions, wherever they go, even into unknown and potentially dangerous territory.

5. The facilitator moves everyone to the Black Hat, which symbolises caution and care.

The Black Hat isn't intended to signify anything negative, and the Western association between a black hat and the villain is unfortunate. That said, the Black Hat is concerned with the very ingredients that are the kiss of death for many creative thinking scenarios.

The Black Hat is about being cautious with your precious idea. Black Hat is primarily about fit. Does this fit with past experience? With *our* way of doing things? With what *should* happen? The Black Hat signifies the need to keep your feet on the ground, even if your intention is to fly to the moon.

For many creatively disposed individuals, criticism is the hardest pill to swallow, even if it comes from the best of motives. Clearly, the Black Hat has to be worn with care, but the design of the overall Six Hats model allows for the Black Hat to work in context, so as not to affect the outcome disproportionately. And because the model is about ease of switching, uncomfortable moments can segue into more congenial territory at the change of a hat.

6. **The facilitator moves everyone to the Yellow Hat, which symbolises speculation and positive thought.**

When you adopt the Yellow Hat, you're opening up new perspectives. This is the place for all the positive 'What if . . .?' questions. Where can you go with this? Are there limits to this? How can we get beyond the limits? A mantra of Steve Jobs, a creator of Apple products, was 'Dare to be great.' Never interested in the adequate, Jobs always sought the exceptional. The Yellow Hat is the place to go beyond the limits of your thinking.

In Six Hats sessions, I sometimes find it useful to point out that the sunshine balloon of the yellow scenario has a string dangling from it – although not yet tethered to the ground. It can be useful to bear in mind that even the grandest ideas have to relate to the ground sooner or later, and they'll need a context.

7. **The facilitator moves everyone to the Green Hat, which symbolises creative thinking.**

Imagine a lush, growing green field of possibility. The Green Hat is the space where you run free across the landscape. In the Six Hats model, this is where you deploy any and all of the tools of creative thinking. Depending on the shape of the issue you're dealing with, this is the place to explore and extend the fruits of your imagination.

Here, you use tools such as lateral thinking and Provocative Operation, and of course this is an ideal context for applying any creative thinking tool that takes your fancy. In short, the Green Hat is for alternatives and choices.

Often, this step is used in conjunction with the Yellow Hat, perhaps flipping from one to the other to see where and how a concept may evolve.

8. **The facilitator moves everyone to the Blue Hat, which symbolises controlled thinking.**

The Blue Hat is often the concluding hat, brought into play when the other hats have done their work. Wherever it's used, the purpose of the Blue Hat is to introduce focus and order. De Bono has a nice term to describe the Blue Hat's role: choreography. Like all the hats, however, the Blue Hat can be deployed whenever it's deemed appropriate for the task. For example, an ill-defined issue may need to start with some Blue Hat control, or a drifting session may need to be brought back on track with some Blue Hat thinking.

Sequencing the hats

The sequence in the preceding section, from white to blue, is a common scenario, starting with tangible facts, opening up emotions, coming back to earth for a while, before speculating and imagining creative possibilities, then wrapping up by pulling all the strands together.

However, you can use the hats in any sequence, and the emphasis is on the direction of thought they encourage, which is why they're effective in getting participants to change mood or thinking framework at – well – the drop of a hat! A common approach is to think of the hats in three pairs:

- ✓ **White and red:** Facts and figures paired with emotions and feelings

- ✓ **Black and yellow:** Caution and care together with speculation and positive thought

- ✓ **Green and blue:** Creative thinking and controlled thinking

However, other pairings such as yellow and green can be equally interesting. It really depends on context and where you want to go with your ideas.

A frequent misuse of the model is to give individuals one hat for the duration of the session, either on the assumption that the hat fits – 'You're argumentative, Mary, so you wear the Black Hat' – or because it goes against (perceived) type – 'You're in accounts, Paul, so you get the Yellow Hat for a change.' The hats aren't for individuals but thinking modes, and flexibility is central to the integrity of the model.

Imagine you've been in Black Hat mode, considering where you may need to be cautious about a situation and careful to avoid potential dangers. You can say, 'Let's do some Red Hat thinking' to encourage a quick shift to exploring emotions and intuitions about the topic. Or from a Blue Hat phase, where you have been focusing on the task, you may leap to the Yellow Hat to hitchhike onto a flight of imagination.

Realising that six hats are better than one

I believe that one of the reasons for the continuing success of Six Thinking Hats is that it's rooted in the basic tenet of *simplicity*. Too much of our thinking in many walks of life is needlessly complex and fuzzy. With the Six Hats, you have a technique that takes minutes to learn and apply, with the power to achieve a rapid solution to even the most seemingly intractable problems.

The second reason – the secret of Six Hats' success, if you like – is that it encourages *switching*, so emotion can be eliminated from an issue, negativity can be replaced by positive thinking, and a firm opinion can be relaxed very rapidly by using the hats.

Try Six Hats on an everyday problem that's been nagging you for some time. An intriguing outcome frequently reported by users of this process is that decisions seem to make themselves. Strange as it may seem, solutions just emerge from the session without special effort on the part of the contributors.

Chapter 8

Closing In on the Answer: Creative Problem-Solving

. . . .

In This Chapter

▶ Finding solutions through creativity

▶ Being in character with the Disney model

▶ Taking Young's Five Steps

▶ Dividing your brain with Herrmann's model

. . . .

*O*ne of the key areas of creative thinking is problem-solving. I talk about the first step, opening up, where the main purpose of the activity is generating ideas, in Chapter 7. This chapter focuses on the closing-in phase in which you aim to find a solution or perhaps make sense of a complex problem. If opening up is the imaginative phase of creative thinking, you can consider closing in to be the practical phase where you turn ideas into reality.

Many different techniques exist for helping you close in on solutions to a problem, so in this chapter I serve up several of the most effective. Some originated in the commercial world, but they're equally effective when you're working on a problem at home or in your personal life. So, whether you're part of an international conglomerate driving towards the solution to a critical problem, or sitting at the kitchen table working out how to accomplish a task, the need to have a process for closing in on the solution is the same.

Working Creatively to Find a Solution

The process of working towards a solution can take many forms. Some systems are highly systematic and structured – step-by-step sequences of actions that follow specific routes. Others involve a looser, more flexible approach. There is no single right or wrong answer here. Both approaches have their merits in the right context, and both are more suited to some situations than others.

Both types of approach have common themes:

- ✔ **Preparation:** What makes creative thinking so exciting for many is the electric charge of having the original idea. However good an idea, though, it only works if it becomes reality. Each of the methods described in this chapter places a premium on thorough preparation, analysis and research. Unless you really know your subject and have immersed yourself in it, you may find that the gap between idea and reality remains wide.

- ✔ **Exposure to criticism:** Criticism is almost inevitable, so prepare yourself for it. Seeing criticism as part of the process that helps deliver your idea, and not just as a negative, is the best approach. Exposing your ideas to the cold light of day ultimately makes the surviving solution that much stronger.

Many professional thinkers spent their lives devising methods to find ways of focusing on their problems and delivering solutions. Among the contributions to this issue, some of the processes can seem simple. But it's worth bearing in mind that in many cases the originators spent years evolving the effective strategies described here.

Using the Disney Model – Being in Character

A good starting point for looking at the problem-solving process is the model devised by Walt Disney, one of the creative giants of the twentieth century. He overcame several early failures and bankruptcy before creating the entertainment empire that bears his name.

Disney was a prolific creator who played a significant role in American culture. From humble beginnings, he steadily built an empire step by step. He had a single-minded determination to make his vision work, and as well as being a first-rate idea generator, he was an unrelenting critic of his own work. His success wasn't just about his ideas but how he nursed them into life through self-criticism and a constant search for better ways to do things.

Disney's creative legacy survives not only in the artistic side of his operations – such as film production, theme parks, television shows and networks, and even Broadway shows that bear his name – but also in the more commercial side of his work, such as hotels, resorts, studios and the organisation of the Walt Disney company itself.

So how did Disney generate so many innovative ideas and deliver them to the world? Disney himself described his unique style, now known as the Disney model. Apparently, Walt Disney had a rare ability to come at a situation from several different perspectives, summarised as:

- ✔ **The dreamer:** This is the first step in the process, where you are in the realm of unlimited possibilities. Anything is possible here, and there are no limits. This is the classic 'What if . . .?' scenario.

- ✔ **The realist:** In this second phase, feet are back on solid ground. What is feasible? This is where you explore the practical limitations in depth.

- ✔ **The critic:** The third phase is also the toughest, because this is where you ruthlessly test the dreams and practical solutions to destruction.

Disney himself and those who worked with him (many of whom did so through long careers) said that no one knew which Walt would turn up on any given day. Walt would stay in his chosen role until he was satisfied with the outcome, however long it took.

When doing this exercise yourself, you may find it helps to immerse yourself in the character of each role, as many participants do. Your dreamer should embody freedom of imagination, throwing caution to the wind and letting ideas really fly; the realist is hard-headed and focused; the critic is stern and unforgiving, taking no nonsense and leaving no stone unturned in the search for hidden faults. Apparently Disney himself inhabited his roles so convincingly his staff never thought he was play-acting.

To use the Disney model yourself, work through each phase in sequence, starting with the dreamer. In groups, everyone stays in one phase until they all agree that the phase is completed. After one complete cycle, you can revisit the process, or key parts of it, as often as necessary.

If you're working alone, you'll probably discover that one of the phases is more difficult than the others. For example, natural dreamers can find it hard to be their own critic, whereas natural critics may find it difficult to dream. Don't worry: this is perfectly natural. Just persevere and you'll discover it gets easier with practice!

If you're exploring your imagination, the dreamer makes a good starting point, because you can float ideas or even vague possibilities without criticism. This is, in fact, the recommended way to begin the creative process according to Disney and his successors. If you consider the logic of the sequence, it would be more inhibiting or even impossible to start with the realist or the critic, unless of course you work in an environment where the aim is to limit creative thinking!

Dreaming, realising, and surviving critics – Richard Branson's journey into space

When the young Richard Branson decided to enter the travel market, he started with the idea of air travel. Despite industry experts telling him that his ambition was impossible, he sought the advice of Sir Freddie Laker, founder of the UK's first cheap airline, and started his airline anyway. (He also fell out with his own bankers, Coutts, who wouldn't underwrite his investment in the early days. They too thought it would never work.)

He then endured a massive struggle with British Airways over landing slots and spoiling tactics, and a vigorous personal campaign against him by the then-heads of that airline.

Every step of Branson's journey in building Virgin Atlantic was dogged by critics who said he was over-reaching himself or that it 'just couldn't be done'. Nevertheless, Branson overcame the doubters and Virgin Atlantic has established itself as a major player on the world stage.

The idea of Virgin Galactic, offering intrepid travellers a trip into space using NASA-type space shuttles, was also slammed by critics who thought it was just pie in the sky or a publicity stunt. Sales passed the 500 mark in 2011 (at $200,000 a time, with a $20,000 deposit) and continue to rise, even before the launch of the first flight. Branson has the advice of NASA supporting his venture.

Branson's journey into space exemplifies the Disney model at work: the dreamer conjuring up the 'impossible dream' regardless; the realist using the best available expertise to test the viability of the concept; and the critics' voices heard but overcome.

If you're planning to use the Disney model, set up your workspace accordingly. You need four separate areas: one for each of the three phases, and a neutral space for breaks, refreshments and briefings. Use each area in turn as you work through the phases.

If you have a large area, you can divide it using curtains or screens. If your space is limited, perhaps a single average room in your home, you can still arrange the space appropriately. Use a different colour for each area, so participants can identify each sector with a phase. Collate the output generated and pin it on the walls as you go, to retain a sense of dynamism.

Disney brought many small innovations to his work environment, including storyboards. Now commonplace in creative work environments such as design consultancies, film studios and advertising agencies, storyboards are a valuable tool which Disney created as a response to the increasing complexity of his animations. In order to keep track of changes in plot and story sequences, he had his animation teams pin the individual cells (animation drawing frames) to a wall, so that all thedrawings were visible at once. Like many really good ideas, it seems obvious once you've done it!

The Disney model has stood the test of time and is widely used today. Its many advocates include Robert Dilts, who has written extensively on the subject of genius (see Chapter 16). Using the model may not make you a genius, but you'll find it an energising and deceptively simple way of tackling even the biggest problems!

The dreamer

This phase is full of imagination, a place where you're capable of taking ideas to their limits. 'If we had no constraints, what would we love to do next?' was a favourite Disney question. This kind of unrestrained speculation is precisely what appeals to those of a creative disposition, so the outcomes are often very exciting.

As you embark on this phase, think about how best to generate a positive atmosphere and a sense of excitement. Some of the techniques from Chapter 7 are excellent for facilitating this part of the process.

At the outset of the dreamer phase:

- ✔ Identify the key features of your problem or idea
- ✔ Begin to imagine where you could go on the journey to the solution

You have no limits to constrain you, and anything you can conceive is possible.

You can explore the dreamer phase alone or as part of a team. If you use a team approach, it can be helpful to have a designated team leader whose role is to keep the session on track and to gather and collate the material generated. Creative sessions of all kinds can easily get out of control unless monitored, so it's important to have this element of structure, even if it's handled with a light touch.

Some individuals are natural dreamers; others are more comfortable as realists or critics. However, it's good to encourage people to play against type and pitch themselves into less familiar roles.

As exciting as the dreamer phase can be, bear in mind that this is only one of three phases, so while everyone can enjoy the fun part, the other two phases are essential to create the whole picture.

The realist

The realist phase is essential because it marks your transition from vision to reality. The key question for the realist is, 'How do we do this?' However ambitious the original idea, you need to keep both feet on the ground and test feasibility. In Disney's words: 'Our work must have a foundation of fact. . . . We cannot do fantastic things unless we know what is real and what is not. . . . When we consider a subject, we must really study it. We must know everything about it.'

His ground-breaking movies, from the early short black-and-white cartoons into talkies, colour and then full-length films, were all meticulously analysed, with Disney seeking the best technical advice at every step and monitoring developments in the industry to gauge trends. Again, his own words say it best: 'Our business will grow with technical advances. Should technical advance come to a halt, prepare our funeral. We need new tools and refinements.'

Using this aspect of his model, Disney was one of the first to spot the potential of television, then in its infancy, and he used this insight to wait for the companies to come to him, as he knew they would, in the search for material to satisfy this new medium.

From the dreamer phase, you already have the idea in your imagination. When you move into realist mode, start to consider what has to happen for that idea to become reality. In other words, begin the rigorous, analytical process of assembling the ingredients that must be in place for your idea to work in the real world. Ask yourself questions such as:

- Is anyone else in the marketplace doing anything similar?
- Does a proven customer base exist?
- Is it technologically feasible?
- Where can I get expert advice?
- Can I fund my idea?
- Where will I make my idea come to fruition?
- What resources do I require?
- What team do I need?

The realist phase is where you break your concept down into its component parts so you can see clearly what you need to do, where the gaps in your knowledge or ability are, and what the sequence of events should be. Disney's own comment eloquently captures his forensic approach:

Our success was built by hard work and enthusiasm, clarity of purpose, a devotion to our art, confidence in the future, and above all by a steady day-by-day growth. We all studied our trade and learned everything we could.

This is a perfect description of how to approach the realist phase of your project.

The critic

In Disney's time, this phase was called the spoiler, perhaps as a reflection of his ability to deliver withering critiques of even the best ideas. As creative individuals often have thin skins and tend not to respond well to criticism, this is probably where Disney gained the reputation of being difficult to work with and something of an ogre among some ex-employees. However, many of his colleagues remained loyal to him and his vision throughout his life.

When in critic mode, Disney was not being a prima donna. He saw the critic as essential to the delivery of products that worked. As a colleague commented: 'We had to become perfectionists. . . . Our studio became more like a school than a business. Walt developed a philosophy that anyone who wants more success would do well to adopt.'

Disney described the critic as being like the audience who would see his films or visit his theme parks. Unless he spotted the weaknesses and ironed them out before launch, he was certain the audience would, and he knew that audiences can be very unforgiving. Disney felt that however harsh, the critic ultimately contributed to growth and success.

When you adopt the critic mode, you're not out to destroy your own idea but to expose it to real-life considerations. When you do so, consider:

- ✔ What isn't working yet?
- ✔ What's missing here?
- ✔ What would someone who encountered this for the first time think?
- ✔ What would my competitors say about this?
- ✔ How would my competitors improve on this?

The appropriate mindset here is that of the customer or competitor. The role of the critic is not to kill the idea but to identify and deal with any and every weakness. Your questions should be forensic, probing every aspect of the topic. Here, you are the awkward customer or the confident competitor. The aim of this phase is to identify necessary adaptations and survive.

Disney withstood battering from critics at every stage in his career. He was told that talking cartoons wouldn't appeal, colour was expensive and irrelevant, no one would sit through a full-length cartoon, and so on. The reason he had the confidence to pursue his goals was because he had already anticipated every possible objection and come to a satisfactory decision.

No one will ever know how many ideas Disney and others like him quietly dropped because they didn't survive this process, but the ones that did survive – and succeeded – had all been tested to destruction in the early stages.

Trusting Young's Five-Step Technique

James Webb Young was an advertising copywriter when he published a short but influential book modestly entitled *A Technique for Producing Ideas*. In it, he describes five essential steps in the creative process which are a timeless reminder of how to go about thinking creatively in the search for solutions.

Many how-to books on the creative process have been published since Young's in 1965, but his spare and elegant monograph seems to encapsulate the essence of working through the phases of creative thinking. And perhaps because he was a professional engaged in this activity with his colleagues on a daily basis, his observations have the ring of truth for everyone who's struggled along the journey from problem to solution.

I think the reason his book is still in print to this day is that Young managed somehow to distil the essence of the creative process in a way that anyone can adopt.

The five-step process has some superficial similarities to other processes, including SCAMPER (which I describe in Chapter 7), but what marks it out is that instead of prescribing a series of elements to work from, Young's technique focuses on the states of mind that come into play at various stages during the process of coming up with ideas.

What Young describes aren't tricks or mental games but is an orientation that encourages the creative juices to flow. His approach is remarkably effective and will find favour with anyone who's familiar with neuro-linguistic programming (NLP) methods, as well as anyone who's suffered on the journey from problem to solution. And of course you can use it with opening-up processes like those I describe in Chapter 7.

You can conduct Young's process alone or in a team. If you're working as a team, limit the number of people involved to those directly relevant to your project (as a rule of thumb, around half a dozen participants is the maximum number you should consider, simply because groups start fragmenting when they have too many participants). One individual should be team leader, defining the progress of the exercise (such as when to move from one step to the next) and acting as final arbiter. Keeping a record of your or the group's progress is helpful.

Here are the five steps in Young's technique:

1. **Research what you already know.**

   The first step is thoroughly researching what you already know, or what Young called combining the old elements of your problem, to gain an understanding of the subject in as much depth as possible. He held the view that all so-called new ideas are essentially re-combinations of existing ones. This wasn't a negative or cynical point of view but a starting point for thinking about things afresh.

   As an advertising man, Young characterised this step as knowing both the product and the customer. This understanding, he felt, was the foundation for all creative thinking. Robin Wight, who created one the UK's most successful advertising agencies, worked on the principle that you 'interrogate the product until it confesses'.

   Of course, you can apply this perspective in many situations other than advertising. Both a world-changing idea and a mundane family problem can share similar elements – it doesn't matter whether you're creating the strategy for a major conglomerate or planning the family holiday. Whether you want to sell your holographic television to a world marketplace or convince your kids that Center Parcs is a better destination than Disneyland, in both situations you have a product, a communication issue, and a target audience. The quality of your research helps your case immeasurably.

   Experience shows that the more thorough your research, the richer the outcome. If you really understand your problem in depth and you've taken the time to learn everything possible about it, then the next steps become much easier.

   Having run and observed many creative sessions and workshops, I can confirm that not only is research a crucial first step, but it's also the one most likely to be skimped, because it's regarded by many people as the boring bit before the excitement of 'real' creative thinking.

2. **Digest the information.**

The second step is to digest the information gleaned through the research from the first step. The first research step, if conducted properly, generates a great deal of material; this step is about how you process and assimilate it.

Living in an age before computers were commonplace, Young advocated using a deck of 3-x-5-inch cards and writing a single statement on each card to build a filing system for study and review. Nowadays, technology offers many solutions for capturing information, and dozens of apps are available for collecting files of information, most of which work very efficiently. In this way, you can review the subject at leisure while new ideas gestate.

Giving this traditional card method a trial is worthwhile, because there's still something special about capturing key facts in your own handwriting and building a deck of cards you can shuffle and refer to, similarly to the way in which you may have used revision cards at school. As you build your card collection, be sure to refer to it regularly. Shuffle your cards so you don't always start at the same place or go through them in the same order. It can be surprising how this simple process can often provide you with new insights into your topic.

Time is an important ingredient in this step. Just as digestion after a meal takes time if you want to avoid indigestion, new facts are best absorbed when you allow them to bed in, despite the urge to rush to creativity. So, as with the first step, take your time with this process.

3. **Drop it!**

The third step is perhaps the most surprising and counterintuitive. Having researched the issue and thoroughly digested it so you understand all aspects of it, you now walk away from it completely. In fact, during this step, you tap in to the power of the unconscious mind. You give your brain time to do its job of sifting and sorting information, away from the attention of the conscious self.

If you're exploring this stage, it can be helpful to play with some of the techniques that weren't available to Young, but which are commonplace now, such as visualisation, meditation and self-hypnosis. They can help you de-focus and change your perspective, so that the problem doesn't dominate your thinking.

Alternatively, you can just do as Young originally suggested and park your problem for a while until the fourth step materialises.

4. **Wait for an idea to come.**

This fourth step, when an idea comes, often happens suddenly and unexpectedly. Many people report the surprising moment when an idea or solution pops up full-grown, apparently out of nowhere. If this has happened to you, you'll know it's something you don't forget in a hurry – a unique mix of shock and exhilaration! No wonder so many people find the creative process addictive, despite its frequent frustrations.

If you immerse yourself in your problem, allow time for gestation, and then walk away from it for a while, you provide fertile ground for the flowering of the solution.

5. **Reassess your idea.**

In the fifth step, you hold up what you think is your fantastic idea to the cold light of day. Some creative types call this the *overnight test* – finding out whether what seemed like a great idea yesterday still shines as brightly the next morning.

This is the real moment of truth for your idea.

If you've experienced the thrill of suddenly realising the solution to a knotty problem, chances are that you've also known the disappointment of acknowledging that what looked so right yesterday evening just doesn't stand up this morning. It's a bitter pill to swallow. However, this is all part and parcel of the creative thinking process. And one female creative of my acquaintance noted that, as in childbirth, the joy of the arrival of the baby makes you forget all the pain along the way!

You need to follow each of the five steps in sequence and give each proper time and attention. For example, if you don't thoroughly combine the old elements in the first step, you don't have a full meal to digest in the second, and so on. The first and second steps are essential to your ultimate success, so fight the natural inclination to rush ahead. The third step you can think of as a pivot, where you absorb what you've learned before moving to the solution. The fourth step comes when it's ready, but if you've followed the first three you'll have created the best conditions for the fourth. Finally, it's important not to treat the solution as the final step, because that moment of truth in the fifth step is when you know for certain what you've achieved.

Using the Whole Brain with Herrmann's Model

The notion of *lateralisation* (that's a fancy way of saying that the human brain has two halves – left and right – each with different functions), is now widely established in popular thinking. The notion is based on the premise that humans are symmetrical: you have two eyes, two ears, two arms, two legs, and so on. And because you're symmetrical, you develop *dominance* in one side of your body.

Most people are dominant on the right side (right-eyed, right-handed, right-footed, and so on), but many people are dominant on the left. You can also be mixed, so some people – like me – write and eat with their left hands but are right-handed when it comes to playing certain sports and doing other activities.

TIP

Counting up brains

How many brains do you have? The ability to analyse our brains and their functions has always been closely related to the available technology of the time. Once, the prevailing ideas about brain function were based on what could be seen with the naked eye. In ancient times, it seemed obvious that our bodies were the seat of all our powers, with the heart as the great driver. The brain might be the home of the soul perhaps, but it obviously didn't contribute much else of value. Then, it was thought that big heads had to house cleverer brains than small heads. Unfortunately, this notion was easily disproved by dissection.

As anatomical understanding and dissection skills improved, medics used the effects of illness and injury to try to work out which parts of the brain governed particular activities. One famous example was Phineas Gage, a railway construction foreman whose forehead was pierced by a metal spike, changing his personality from placid and friendly to verbally abusive and aggressive. This was considered evidence that the frontal region of the brain was responsible for civilised behaviour. However, it is worth noting that the case attracted much publicity, and many stories about him may owe more to myth than reality.

Technological access to the brain improved dramatically with the invention of the electroencephalogram, or EEG, which generated a vast body of research on the functions of the brain in both humans and animals. For many years, the EEG was the primary tool for investigation of brain activity. However, the EEG is designed to provide most information on the cortex – the top and outside of the brain. Until recent years, electrodes were needed to look more deeply into the brain.

The biggest revolution in examining the brain was facilitated by the invention of the magnetic resonance imaging (MRI) scanner, which won its developer the Nobel Prize for Medicine in 2003. Magnetic resonance imaging allows detailed examination of the living brain and has become the leading tool for research, giving rise to a whole new generation of neuroscientific thinking that has exploded many old myths, including the idea that 'we only use 10 per cent of our brains', and that specific functions are tied to single regions of the brain.

As it's now possible to investigate our other brains – the limbic system and reptilian brain – understanding of the interaction between these brains is now improving, and attention is even extending to the influence of the enteric, or stomach, brain that appears to control many of our regularly performed activities. (It's distributed throughout the body's central nervous system, but if gathered together would be about the size of a cat's brain.) With ongoing research, the boundaries keep shifting, so for every argument that one single 'whole brain' exists, counter-arguments suggest that the functions indicate several different semi-autonomous brains.

So how many brains *do* we have? It seems the jury's still out.

Of course, this is only a metaphor to help us grasp the hugely complex structure of the brain, but at an everyday level it has its uses as a model for how we receive, process and use information.

However, the brain consists of more than just the left and right cortex, and over the years, many clinicians, academics and business people came to regard the two-brain model as too simple, and searched for a metaphor that described brain function more accurately. In the 1970s, Ned Herrmann, then head of management education at GE, created a different metaphor for the brain, which he called the Whole Brain Model. He started with the premise that the basic left–right notion was inadequate to describe how people think and behave. He also devised the Herrmann Brain Dominance Instrument (HBDI), which is the standard tool for assessing the patterns of brain dominance in individuals, and which I describe later in this chapter.

Herrmann's model is based on four quadrants:

- **Right:** This side of the brain processes incoming information, which is then rapidly moved to the left side, where it is processed and stored.
- **Left:** You can be consider this side the filing cabinet of the brain, where information is stored.
- **Higher (cortical):** This upper region (the familiar wrinkled bulge in most brain diagrams) has a wide variety of roles in consciousness, conscience, processing information from the senses, language and more.
- **Lower (limbic):** About the size of a baby's fist, the top of the spine has a complex structure that controls the basic drives for survival, the urge to reproduce, and movement.

Hermann's system identifies people according to which of these quadrants acts as their dominant centre of operation. His model has become the most widely used in business, with more than a million users. It's still only a metaphor, but as a model it provides a robust and practical tool for developing creative thinking skills with individuals and teams, which is why it's remained so popular for so long.

Listing dominant types

Herrmann's system identifies people as one of four main types by their dominant mode of operation. Some people even have two of these dominant characteristics; very few have three, and hardly any have a balance of all four:

- **Analyser (quadrant A):** A natural decision-maker, comfortable with a leadership role
- **Organiser (quadrant B):** A data organiser, likely found working alone on spreadsheets
- **Personaliser (quadrant C):** A people person
- **Strategiser (quadrant D):** At home with ideas and imagination

Analysers (As) and strategisers (Ds) operate mainly in the upper (cortical) region of their brains, using rational processes like reasoning and analysis, whereas organisers (Bs) and personalisers (Cs) operate mainly in the lower (limbic) area, and use more emotional processes like intuition and gut feel. Think of these as natural states or default positions, because of course rational people can operate emotionally, and vice versa.

When considering how the different types fit into various roles, the phrase 'square peg in a round hole' comes to mind as you consider what happens when people have to work in areas outside their comfort zone. Personalisers, for example, like working with other people and are likely to be uncomfortable in a solitary work environment.

When it comes to getting the best out of teams and individuals, Herrmann's system proves a powerful tool for understanding and using everyone's strengths and appreciating the limitations experienced by others.

You can get insights into your own profile from the short version of the HBDI in this chapter. As you become familiar with the various characteristics, you'll begin to recognise them in the people around you.

Using the information in these sections to determine the dominant quadrant of you, your colleagues and loved ones can help you figure out how to communicate effectively to improve your creative thinking and creative abilities.

Seeing HBDI in action

Most of the time, you don't work in groups comprising only people like yourself, but when the four main types are tasked with solving a complex problem alongside others of the same type as themselves, the following list presents the typical outcomes:

- **Analysers (As):** They're organised and, as you'd expect, analytical in their approach, getting straight to the point and tending to reject anything they regard as 'fluffy' thinking. They examine the problem carefully, do some research, analyse the components and embark on a linear approach to solving the problem.

    Analysers are likely to work rapidly and decisively, quickly dropping ideas that look weak, and being openly critical of poor input and enthusiastic about breakthroughs. Their approach will have a sense of pace about it, and they're probably going to be first to complete the task.

    Within the group, they're likely to defer to a naturally emerging leader, and to work within a hierarchical structure.

✔ **Organisers (Bs):** They tend to focus on facts: numbers, measurements – things they can get hold of. They'll look for the structure of the problem and construct a sequence of stages to solve it.

Organisers prefer to work alone or in small groups on specific aspects of the problem, delivering details of their progress back to the group.

Organisers will appear purposeful, and little chatter or conversation away from the topic in hand will occur.

✔ **Personalisers (Cs):** They're emotionally driven and *feel* the experience. They may be bothered by how difficult the problem seems and whether they're worthy. If they do crack it, they'll be euphoric.

Not to put too fine a point on it, their approach may not seem as organised as that of the As and Bs, and it will be highly interactive. A lot of initial to-ing and fro-ing, much paper-shuffling, and considerable noise and movement will take place. Their group dynamic will be very informal, in contrast to the purposeful approach of others.

Experience suggests that Cs will almost always finish last, probably beyond any time limit that may have been set. They're almost certain to be full of praise and appreciation for the As and Bs and their problem-solving powers. And they're likely to defend the creative abilities of Ds and their unique way of doing things, even though they may not understand them.

✔ **Strategisers (Ds):** In contrast to the others, Ds live in their imagination and can be highly creative, but are often less adept at sticking to plans and delivering the goods.

Ds may appear not to be doing anything in particular, just doodling, looking out of the window, perhaps even appearing to doze briefly if the task is a long one. They may work individually or drift in and out of interaction, depending on what catches their attention at any given moment. Then they may have an 'aha!' moment and the thrill of grasping the solution. However, explaining it to the As and Bs in the session will be a different matter.

These behaviour patterns are, of course, just illustrations of common characteristics, but it's surprising how often workshop participants demonstrate their dominant traits, just like those summarised here, in very clear ways.

In the typical work or family environment, you live alongside different kinds of people. The true value of the Herrmann model comes into its own here. The better you understand your own thinking and behavioural style, the better you see how and why others think and behave as they do. In teams and group situations, if you notice one dominant type missing, it may be beneficial to imagine stepping into the shoes of the missing type to ensure these elements are still covered. And if you're working alone, trying the other types on for size is a good practice to get into. So, if you're naturally a focused A (analyser), try being a creative D or a chatty C for a while – you may surprise yourself!

Here's a slightly tongue-in-cheek description of how each of the profiles tends to see others in stereotypical ways:

- ✔ A-dominant people, being purposeful and decisive, tend to regard all the others as slow. They're tolerant of Bs, because they provide useful material and keep everything organised, but can be patronising about them. They regard the people-orientated Cs as disorganised and more worried about people than the task in hand, and as for Ds, what planet are they on? (Although sometimes they do seem to get lucky.)

- ✔ B-dominant people, getting on with the job, like to help As run the project. They want to help the Cs tidy their desks and files, but they like them for their warmth and positive attitude. Ds are a bit of a mystery, but their work is often very good once it's been put in order.

- ✔ C-dominant people are busy, busy, busy, and there's never enough time. Everyone's very good at what they do, but As don't usually have the time to discuss things. Bs are very efficient, and it's best to chat with them in breaks, when they're not so busy. Those Ds seem happiest left to their own devices – they can be very funny, but seem to sit apart from the others.

- ✔ D-dominant people want to dream. The As want to run everything, which doesn't suit at all, and they always want to get things done, as though it's a race. Bs keep their heads down, but they're invaluable when you want to know something. Cs are always rushing about and can be very distracting.

Although these are obviously caricatures, you'll probably recognise some of your own perceptions in relation to others here.

In terms of creative thinking, appreciating the interaction of these four profiles can markedly improve problem-solving ability: Ds will be most overtly creative, and will probably solve the problem; As and Bs will provide the analysis and validation that underpins the solution; and the Cs will enthusiastically sell it, ensuring that everyone is involved in the process and buys in to the idea.

Having the benefit of the insights provided by Herrmann's model, it becomes easier to see why others do what they do, and to value their contributions on their own merits.

Putting the Whole Brain Model to work

The ideal scenario for working with this model as a group is to work with an experienced HBDI practitioner who can guide and use the session to educate the team on the finer points. A professional practitioner can help you to identify your own dominant type and that of your colleagues, and then advise you on how best to put those character types you identify to work for you or your organisation.

However, in real life this isn't always possible, in which case it's best for one or more individuals to take responsibility for running the session(s), and to conduct preparatory work.

Discovering your own HBDI profile (and those of other people)

If you're running an HBDI session, read this whole section beforehand so that you know how to proceed. Then encourage the team to complete the short version of the HBDI assessment in Figure 8-1 to identify the types in the group.

This version provides a quick checklist to give a pen portrait of individual profiles. Of course it can't take the place of the full HBDI, but it will give you a flavour of the model.

Take a look at the four boxes in the figure and tick the ones you regard as 'most like me'. Place a cross against those you deem 'least like me'.

A – Rational Self	D – Experimental Self
Analyses	Infers
Quantifies	Imagines
Is logical	Speculates
Is critical	Takes risks
Is realistic	Is impetuous
Likes numbers	Breaks rules
Knows about money	Likes surprises
Knows how things work	Is curious/plays
B – Safekeeping Self	**C – Feeling Self**
Takes preventative action	Is sensitive to others
Establishes procedures	Likes to teach
Gets things done	Touches a lot
Is reliable	Is supportive
Organises	Is expressive
Is neat	Is emotional
Timely	Talks a lot
Plans	Feels

Figure 8-1: Characteristics of the four main HBDI profiles.

Bringing out the big guns with the TRIZ model

TRIZ is a great creative thinking tool, but it most definitely isn't for lightweight problems – or for lightweight thinking. However, if you have a monster problem and need some heavy-lifting equipment in the creative thinking department, take a look at what TRIZ has to offer.

The starting point for TRIZ is the notion that you can treat creativity systematically. The inventor of TRIZ, Russian engineer GS Altshuller, believed that new ideas were based on re-combinations of existing ideas, and that devising a system for creativity based on logic rather than intuition was therefore possible. He gives an indication of his philosophy in the title of one of his books: *Creativity as an Exact Science*. He analysed many thousands of patents (because, by definition, a patent records a new invention), and used this data as the basis of his TRIZ model.

You can best understand TRIZ not as a single process but as a substantial toolbox containing a variety of analytical methods and a series of prescriptive tools. Such a complex model leaves a lot of room for possible error, especially when applied by inexperienced practitioners, so TRIZ isn't the sort of process you engage in if your problem is simple or small in scale. Altshuller designed TRIZ specifically to address complex engineering issues, and that's where it excels.

An accessible part of the TRIZ model is the 40 principles of problem-solving, which describe 40 ways of analytically exploring a situation, such as *segmentation* (dividing an object into independent parts), *merge* (bringing closer together or merging similar or identical objects), and *universality* (making a part or object perform multiple functions or eliminating the need for other parts). The book includes examples of situations where each principle has been applied effectively to solve a problem. TRIZ practitioners use this catalogue to aid their creative thinking.

The second basic driver of TRIZ is the concept of *contradiction*. Put simply, contradiction reflects the fact that every time you improve something, something else has to give. To understand this idea, picture the air in an inner tube: if you squeeze the tube in one place, it pops up somewhere else. Similarly, if you want to get more power out of an engine, you may have to pay in increased fuel consumption or greater wear and tear. TRIZ works with two kinds of contradictions:

- ✔ **Technical:** One thing is improved at the cost of something else getting worse. So you can make an aeroplane's wing stronger, but the plane will weigh more.

- ✔ **Physical:** Also called *inherent*, this principle is evident when a product benefit is delivered against contradictory requirements. For example, a computer must be complex in order to perform all the tasks required of it, yet simple so users can operate it successfully.

The natural home of TRIZ is within specialist teams working on complex problems, but individuals can and do use it. To illustrate how, here are examples of three friends of mine who incorporate it as a tool in their personal areas of interest and expertise:

- ✔ The restorer – a car fanatic whose hobby is bringing vintage cars back to life. He uses TRIZ principles he learned as an engineer to reconstruct cars.

- ✔ The musician – a professional composer using TRIZ tools for work in film and television which demands innovative compositions combining orchestral and computer-based skills and tied into tightly defined storylines.

- ✔ The designer – a friend who uses TRIZ tools for three-dimensional product design.

TRIZ places strong emphasis on training and practical experience, and isn't for the faint-hearted. However, many of the general principles that underpin TRIZ provide useful ways of looking at problems and are worth considering. The most useful introduction to TRIZ is through the official website of the TRIZ organisation (www.aitriz.org).

You'll probably find that most of your ticks cluster in one or two of the quadrants, and most of the crosses are in different quadrants.

Some of the phrases may provoke a flash of recognition, and many people find that even using this abbreviated version of the instrument enables them to see characteristics of friends, family and work colleagues.

To discover a dominant quadrant with the full HBDI assessment, you need to fill in a 120-question survey form. (You can do this online at `www.hbdi.co.uk`.) The detailed analysis of your individual profile provides you with a range of information you can use personally, in relation to your work or as part of a group assessment. A comprehensive HBDI report provides feedback on your own profile and a wide range of supplementary information concerning interaction with other profiles, work and lifestyles, and areas for development. The model also extends into recommendations about how people in each quadrant can develop their creative thinking abilities.

Putting HBDI profiles to work: Stimulating creative thinking

Whether you're working in groups or by yourself, you can use your knowledge of HBDI profiles to help you generate creative ideas or solve problems. In a group, you can quickly spot its composition of types and their patterns of interaction. If you're a C, for example, it helps to know that any As (diagonally opposite you) in your group are the ones most likely to antagonise you or cut idea-generation time short in their quest for quick decisions. Your allies are most likely to be the adjacent Bs, who will provide solid underpinning for the ideas and any research necessary, while the adjacent Ds seem able to conjure smart ideas out of thin air!

To put this knowledge into action in a group situation, and get the creative juices flowing, follow these steps:

1. **Establish your type, using the short version of the HBDI in Figure 8-1 (or use the full version available at www.hbdi.co.uk).**

   Don't be surprised if your profile shows up across more than one quadrant – individuals are commonly a combination of two types.

2. **Spend some time reflecting on how you do what you do, in the context of your natural type.**

   So if your profile is an A type, do you find you naturally focus on tasks, prioritising, and working to deadlines? And if you're a C, do you prefer to start a task with a cup of coffee and a chat, and maybe a couple of phone calls, before getting down to it? And is that the time already?

3. **Think of friends or colleagues who conform to the other types, then consider how you interact with them.**

   Notice the patterns that start to emerge. (Here is when you realise that someone 'always talks too much', 'never seems to be part of the team' or 'always kills off ideas', for example.)

4. Consider how others' patterns can contribute most usefully to the task in hand.

Ask whether you could benefit from some solid research (that's a B strength), whether you really need a decision (As excel at this) or just a great idea (select a D for this), and whether you need the group to be stronger as a team (a good role for Cs).

If you're working alone, you can apply the HBDI principles by considering your own natural type and putting yourself in the shoes of the others to approach your problem from those different angles. If you're an A, for example, you may want to slow down your inclination to search for 'quick fixes' and try some B-type research and planning. Or just relax and give yourself permission to dream like a D for a while. You may even attempt to be more of a C, and spend time dealing with all the odds and ends and general 'stuff' that you'd normally avoid when you focus on an issue. Whatever your natural type, this kind of role playing can produce genuinely unexpected results and insights.

Chapter 9

Playing Creatively

Somewhere between childhood and adulthood, many people lose the ability to play as part of their everyday activity. The unwritten rule is that you should conform, and this means taking things, especially work, seriously. However, many practitioners of creative thinking believe that creativity should be fun.

For many people, work is inextricably associated with serious, focused activity to the exclusion of anything else. For many, the only opportunity for playfulness of any kind is during breaks. The photocopier, kitchen, water-cooler or drinks dispenser are always the focus for gossip, jokes and general levity. To take advantage of these unplanned get-togethers, Pixar Animation Studios ensured that the company loos were in the middle of the workspace so that employees would have an opportunity to bump into each other several times a day and disrupt the serious work pattern.

Along with this serious attitude, the dominant mode of most work is based on the written and spoken word, even though it's estimated that more than half, and perhaps as much as three-quarters, of the human brain is devoted to vision. Developing your capacity for visual expression in all forms, and exploring how your whole body can contribute to a productive experience, is one of the most positive things you can do to enhance creative thinking in everyday life. And if you add the ingredient of play, you have a recipe for some very productive creative thinking indeed.

Provoking New Ideas with Thought Experiments

To get into a creative frame of mind, sometimes you need a trigger or jolt to get things started. A technique called provocation can help you rise to a challenge or take the bait from someone who's trying to start an argument. *Provocation* – the process of testing a thought to its limits – isn't always comfortable, but it can have the effect of energising you. The idea of provocation is an old one, described by many individuals, including Albert Einstein, who used to goad himself to the limits of his imagination by asking impossible questions.

Provoking yourself (or your team if you're working as a group) is a powerful way of getting to the limits of your thinking. Key questions to ask are:

- ✔ 'What if . . .?'
- ✔ 'Why couldn't I . . .?'
- ✔ 'What would have to happen if . . .?'

These and similar questions help you test the outer edges of your thinking. At the outset they may seem deceptively simple, but these questions are your starting point for a potentially infinite journey of your mind. The art of this process is being relentlessly curious and not stopping at the first hurdle. Using this process, scientists and the best science fiction writers have the ability 'to boldly go' wherever their flights of fancy take them. And after all, what could possibly go wrong?

Einstein said he thought mainly in pictures, and his powerful and provocative images included riding on a beam of light, meeting himself coming back on a trip around the universe, and speculating on the relative speeds of two trains passing at impossible speeds.

Thinking experimentally is a useful technique for limbering up before or during any creative thinking activity. The umbrella term *thought experiments* is used to describe a range of conundrums and parables designed to stretch thinking skills. In a thought experiment, you contemplate paradoxical or 'impossible' concepts.

Ancient Greek philosopher Zeno's paradoxes form one of the oldest collections of thought experiments. Apparently, Zeno created 40 paradoxes, but only a few are known today – somewhere between three and nine, depending on how you count them, because some cover the same topic in different guises. Examples of Zeno's paradoxes include:

- ✔ **Achilles and the tortoise:** Considered the main paradox, this problem describes a principle that occurs in many other contexts. If Achilles gives the tortoise a head start in a race, Achilles can never overtake the tortoise, because whenever he reaches where the tortoise was, the tortoise has moved on. In another version, a frog jumping across a pond half-way with each leap can never reach the other side, as the gap diminishes to an infinitely small degree but is never eliminated.

- ✔ **The ship of Theseus:** Another ancient thought experiment, this poses the question: 'If all of the original timbers and sails of a ship have been replaced over time, is it still the same ship?' This question is known as the pocket watch in modern versions: you consider whether a watch is the same watch after all its parts have been replaced.

Modern philosophers, scientists (especially quantum physicists) and mathematicians have continued the tradition of devising thought experiments, and today there are many to stretch your brain cells. Here are just a few:

- ✔ **Hawking's tortoises:** Stephen Hawking delighted in the following question: if, as in some myths, the earth stands on tortoises, then what do the tortoises stand on? The answer, 'tortoises all the way down', was used by Hawking to warn of the danger of building theories on top of other theories, similar to a house of cards.

- ✔ **Schrödinger's cat:** This is the scenario of a cat in a radioactive box with a phial of poison that's released if the box is opened. If the cat stays in the box, it dies; if the box is opened, the cat dies. Is the cat both dead and alive at the same time? This scenario is somewhat similar to the image of the man in the forest – if he yells and no one can hear him, has he actually yelled?

- ✔ **Infinite monkeys:** The classic question is: if an infinite number of monkeys tap at an infinite number of typewriters, will they eventually produce the complete works of Shakespeare?

In terms of creative thinking, many consider these intellectual games useful, because they question your assumptions (surely Achilles would just run straight past that tortoise!) by playing with rules of logic in ways deliberately designed to provoke and frustrate. Einstein, along with many other exceptionally creative scientists, attributed some of his greatest breakthroughs to wrestling with problems like these.

One way to kick-start your own imagination with thought experiments is simply to ask questions outside the normal rules. The author Robert Harris had the idea for his novel *Archangel* after his young son suddenly asked about Stalin's son. ('Stalin didn't have a son,' said Harris. 'Yes, but what if he *did*?' persisted the boy, launching Harris on a thought experiment that became a best-seller.) Whatever your personal or professional creative interests, once you launch yourself on a thought experiment with a paradox, a conundrum or a speculation, you never know where your imagination might take you!

Drawing and Doodling

As far back in time as you can imagine, people drew and doodled. In 1940, schoolboys discovered more than 2,000 images, mainly hunting scenes, in caves at Lascaux in Southern France. Scientists dated the paintings at around 17,400 years old. For many years, the Lascaux cave paintings were thought to be the oldest drawings on record. However, more recently, cave paintings dated at around twice that age – more than 30,000 years old – were discovered in another cave in France, called Chauvet. And cave art can be found all around the world. It appears, then, that the urge to draw has existed as long as humankind.

In more recent years, focus on the visual aspects of creative thinking has grown substantially. Many practitioners have devised ways of teaching and developing visual thinking in the workplace as well as in the classroom.

Getting started with the visual side of creative thinking isn't difficult, and you don't need to be an artist to make simple images to capture your thoughts. In fact, the more basic your drawing style, the quicker and easier it is to work. As you start to play with this approach, you'll quickly find that you lose your reservations and begin to enter into the spirit of the activity.

Drawing on the right side of the brain

If you ask a roomful of people whether they can draw, typically three-quarters will say they can't (or won't) draw, and only a quarter will declare they can. The inescapable conclusion is that most people are not using one of the brain's most important functions to anything like its full potential.

Unless you're fortunate enough to have been born with a natural gift or have been taught by a professional, it's likely that your attempts to draw are limited by your deep-seated belief that you just can't do it. A common reason is that, when drawing, you're still actually in verbal mode. If you believe that you can't draw, then instead of observing what is actually there you're likely to think in terms of verbal descriptions. So if asked to draw a face, you think 'Well, the head is round, the eyes are at the top, the nose is in the middle, and the mouth is at the bottom' rather than noticing how the spatial relationships actually work.

Try to draw copies of photographs of several faces. Look carefully as you do so, noticing where the features actually are – not where you thought they were. Draw guidelines from the forehead through the nose to the jaw and across from ear to ear through the eyes to help you see spatial relationships and patterns. You'll notice that the head, which you may have thought of as a circle, is more like an inverted egg with the broad bit at the top; the eyes aren't at the top but around the mid-point, and the nose and mouth occupy the bottom half.

The Gorilla You Missed

One of the most surprising, and amusing, demonstrations of the limitations of conventional seeing was given in an experiment in which the subjects were asked to watch a film showing two teams, one wearing black tops and one wearing white tops, throwing a ball back and forth for a few minutes. The experimental subjects were asked to count which team, black or white, passed the ball most times. Most of the subjects came up with reasonably accurate answers.

Then the subjects were asked whether they saw the gorilla. Most were shocked by this unexpected question because they had certainly not noticed a gorilla! When the scene was played back to them, they saw that, while they were busy counting balls, a person in a gorilla suit had crossed the stage, pausing to wave at them on the way.

This experiment has been repeated many times since, and the result is always the same – most people just don't spot the gorilla.

This is a perfect example of the difference between looking and seeing. Most of the time, we see only what we expect to see. Active looking involves being alert to what's really happening and noticing the unexpected.

After you master the basic geography of the face, you open the door to a whole new world! Looking at the whole body, you start noticing that hands and feet are bigger than you probably thought in relation to the body, as is the head. The top of the head to the navel is about half the body's height, with the navel to the feet making up the other half.

Drawing, painting and other creative artistry should be something to enjoy, not a chore. The more playful you are, the better your skills get, because you're taking risks and learning – consciously and unconsciously – similarly to how children do unconsciously. Children don't think it's wrong to paint the sky yellow or to make the cat bigger than its owner. Many of the most exciting works by modern artists such as Paul Klee, Marc Chagall and Pablo Picasso are the result of experiments testing the limits of expression. How do you depict happiness or crying; how do you show the feeling of being in love; what does a summer's day feel like?

If you're interested in developing your innate drawing ability as you explore your creativity, pick up a copy of Betty Edwards' breakthrough book, *Drawing on the Right Side of the Brain*. With her open and accessible style, Edwards has encouraged millions to overcome their inhibitions about drawing and painting. Her work continues to stand out amid many imitators, because it's rooted in a whole-brain approach to how we see, rather than just focusing on making prettier pictures.

Seeing passively and actively looking

When you begin to think visually, it's important to distinguish between just seeing and actively looking. Many people are in the habit of merely seeing what's around them passively, without question. *Active looking*, however, involves tuning in to all your senses and looking beyond what you think you can see. It provides clearer understanding, enhancing colours and details and giving a real feel of what's actually there. Like many aspects of creative thinking, active looking improves with practice – the more you look, the better you get at looking!

You can break down *active looking* into three aspects:

✔ **Your eyes:** The first aspect of active looking is to use your eyes actively. Examine what you see, run your eyes over surfaces, notice colours and the relative positions of objects in your sightline. A simple way to break your normal pattern of seeing is to look twice. Normally, you just glance, especially when the scene is familiar. Next time something interests you visually, make a deliberate effort to look at it again and notice those surfaces, colours and shapes.

✔ **Your mind's eye:** The second aspect is using your mind's eye. Question what you see. Is it what it looks like? A quick way to develop the ability to question what you see is to look at a scene then photograph it and compare your personal image with the photo. You'll be surprised at the discrepancies. Your brain gets used to filtering patterns and encoding the enormous amount of visual material it processes. Activating your mind's eye requires effort, but if you do it frequently, your brain begins to adjust.

✔ **Your hand and eye:** Thirdly, develop your hand-to-eye co-ordination. Art students are taught not only to look actively but also to match their visual experiences to drawing actions. If you watch a typical life class (the exercise in which a group of students spend a long session drawing or painting a model in a single static pose), you'll see the students minutely examining the model, and the small marks they make to build the overall picture. They're taught to move their eyes rapidly between the model and their easel, to capture details and check continuously, and to constantly focus and refocus – even defocus periodically – in a continual analysis of what's in front of them. You don't need to become an art student, but playing with exercises like this can deliver remarkable results very quickly as you teach your hand to help you see.

The same principle of active looking applies to drawing objects. You don't need to know the rules of perspective (which can be quite complex) to draw a house, the animals in a farmyard, or a car. Even toddlers draw these images as they start to depict the world around them.

Excel-ling at visual thinking

Dan Roam, the visual thinker whose work informs much of the background here, worked with the head financial honcho of Microsoft, who wanted a way to make his own department's Excel spreadsheets more accessible in presentations and analysis of day-to-day performance. Together they came up with a solution that decoded the mysteries of spreadsheets in a user-friendly way. Breaking the overall spreadsheet into a number of smaller stand-alone topics, Dan provided navigation tools and a series of 'visualisers' so that interested parties could look at the data in different ways.

Using the simple diagrammatic approach that I outline in this chapter, Dan showed Microsoft how to present complicated spreadsheet data in a format that people can easily understand and absorb. Unusually for an organisation that normally closely guards its commercial workings, Microsoft gave Dan permission to include the whole journey in his book, warts and all. So, if the inventor of Excel values visual thinking, I believe that's not a bad endorsement of the principle!

You can find the full story of how Dan and the Microsoft team cracked this complex problem in Dan's excellent book *Unfolding the Napkin*, published by Portfolio.

Building a visual vocabulary by asking questions

Visual thinking is based on the use of a visual vocabulary. Mastering a new visual language may sound a bit daunting, but it's actually where the fun begins, because you recognise the pleasure in literally playing with pictures.

Creating a visual vocabulary is easy if you break it down into the main questions you ask when you address a problem. In the next sections I describe the scenarios as problems, but the process works just as effectively for generating ideas and other types of creative thinking.

Spend some time getting used to the images you use to depict the six sides of a problem, each of which I look at in the following sections. Try attaching images to each element, but don't just follow these illustrations; make the images your own and play freely with them.

No single right approach exists, and in fact being outrageous or off the wall can actually help. Our brains respond to the unusual, and it's easier to remember things that are exciting, even if they are silly or off-colour. The more you use and adapt the images, the more they become unique to you. If you're working in a team, the idiosyncrasies of your imagery, and those of your colleagues' imagery, will help you personalise each problem, which then generates energy as you work towards a solution.

Who/what?

Ask who and/or what is at the heart of the problem. The problem may be a person or a group of people: your customers or your competitors; your boss or a colleague; someone you're experiencing conflict with in your personal life; or maybe even you yourself (for example: 'Am I the right person to be dealing with this?').

You can represent any person or group of people with a simple face or stick figure drawing, as I've done in Figure 9-1. Adding individual features and even exaggerating them, as in a cartoon, can be helpful.

Figure 9-1:
Represent-
ing who
or what
is at the
centre of a
problem.

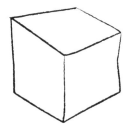

 One getting-started exercise involves drawing a version of yourself and the people you work with, rather like creating avatars in a video game. Exaggerate characteristics to dramatise or make the images more amusing. (Be careful who you share your images with if they're not flattering!)

Note: If the problem is a thing rather than a person, create a simple box or other shape to hold the problem.

 If you're dealing with a problem that's a big issue, draw a large crate; if it's a major obstacle, consider sketching a brick wall; if the problem is something you can't quite grasp, make it a balloon flying out of reach; if the problem is the elephant in the room – well, you know what to do.

And, as you'd note your own observations in a diary or journal, you can make this material part of your creative identity. If you work with a team, encourage them along similar lines.

If you can stand the pressure, compare notes. Does your image of yourself or your boss correspond with what your colleagues depict? How do you all see yourselves and each other? Does your depiction of the problem match other people's? After all, one man's fish is another man's *poisson*. (I'm exhibiting a little creativity of my own – *poisson* is French for 'fish'.)

Work at making your images personal and relevant. Go for extremes: make your images exaggerated, funny, outrageous or rude. The more extreme they are, the easier they are to hold in your mind.

How much?

Since most problems in the real world have a cost attached, you may want an image that quantifies value (see Figure 9-2 for an example). A universal image for money, business and performance is the graph, so this can be your basic symbol. As you get deeper into the analysis of your problem, you can become more sophisticated about your imagery.

Figure 9-2:
Represent-
ing the
financial
value of a
problem.

Of course, many kinds of graph exist apart from the basic bar chart; as you start working more deeply with your problem, you can begin to introduce other varieties of graph. However, bear in mind that the thinking behind this visual approach is all about simplicity, so resist the temptation to over-complicate, or you can end up back where you started.

Where?

Your problem probably has a location. This may be physical – where the problem is situated (for example, in a building, an office or a factory) – or it may be a less tangible location (such as a goal you're seeking). And here, a ready-made image is the map. You can consider where you are, where you want to be, and outline how you might get there past various obstacles. Your map gives you a sense of place (see Figure 9-3).

Because most people have had a fascination with pirates since childhood, who can resist a treasure map? Creative visuals are about playing with ideas, and a map on which X marks the spot is a lot more fun than a conventional list of objectives.

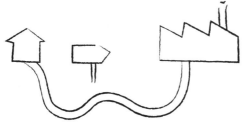

Figure 9-3:
Represent-
ing the
location of a
problem.

When?

Many problems exist in time, so the image of a timeline comes to mind. For example, you can use a series of arrows to depict the problem, each representing a stage in your progress towards a solution (see Figure 9-4). At its simplest, you have the problem now, you spend time exploring options, you discover the solution and then you implement it.

Of course, many real-life problems involve layers of complexity, but a simple starting point and progression helps you stay in control of the sequence of events.

It's important not to over-complicate your timeline, especially in the early stages of your project. As your project evolves, your timeline will inevitably grow, but it's useful to question the need for each stage: does it get you nearer your desired outcome or just add another layer?

Figure 9-4:
Represent-
ing the
timescale of
a problem.

How?

The tools you need to solve your problem may comprise a whole toolbox or a few choice instruments. For your visualisation, a depiction of some basic shapes (circle, square, pentagon, hexagon) can serve the purpose (see Figure 9-5), and as you progress you may prefer to identify each one distinctively.

A feedback loop is also a useful image if your progress from problem to solution follows some kind of sequence. Again, remember that simplicity is the guiding principle. If you've had to sit through presentations based on feedback diagrams, you'll know that their owners love them so much that they don't notice the audience has fallen asleep while they explain them!

Figure 9-5:
Represent-
ing
approaches
to the
problem.

Why?

What is the reason for your problem? In many cases, your problem can be depicted using a basic *X/Y axis* – a horizontal line crossed by a vertical line (see Figure 9-6). Each line describes a single dimension – time, monetary value, market share or any other key dimension you choose. Sometimes, adding a third, *Z*, axis at right angles to the other two, to indicate a third dimension, can be helpful.

Perhaps you need to understand where you are in relation to your competitors. Or you may need to create a new product. Or you may need to achieve an objective within a certain time limit. All these situations can be analysed in *X/Y* (and sometimes *Z*) diagrams.

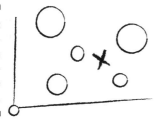

Figure 9-6:
Represent-
ing the main
issues relat-
ing to the
problem.

Working with SQVID

The principles underlying one approach to visual thinking are encapsulated in the slightly awkward (but I think memorable) acronym SQVID, which professional visual thinkers like Dan Roam use as a handy way of covering the elements of a topic with their clients. I break down the components of SQVID in the following list:

Each of the keywords in SQVID is one end of a spectrum, and you can place your problem at either end or somewhere in between – it's simply a device to help you clarify your visual thinking. You then consider various aspects of the problem along each continuum. The keywords are:

✔ **Simple:** You determine whether you're more interested in a simple or elaborate view of your problem. The central notion is that simplicity is at the heart of many great insights. The other end of this spectrum is elaborate. As with all these elements, there's a time and a place for each end of the simple–elaborate spectrum. However, beginning with simplicity is often most useful.

If the problem lies at the elaborate end of the spectrum, break it into its components. Often, this single action will suggest solutions as you define and depict the six elements of SQVID. If you have trouble getting started, a tool like SCAMPER, described in Chapter 7, can be helpful. You can then move along the spectrum to the elaborate dimension, exploring the effects of adding ingredients. This approach can be helpful in changing perspective and seeing where individual elements fit within the problem as a whole.

✔ **Quality:** Are you more interested in quality or quantity? Essentially, this range helps distil the problem by posing a question such as, 'What is the single key quality of this problem?' Often, just asking this kind of question can provide an answer – or at least a clue to the answer.

When you've explored the quality issue, move on to the quantity question. Does the problem have a single, easily defined centre, or is it fuzzy around the edges? What would each end of this spectrum look like if you drew it?

Often, problems are part of a nest of problems, and it can be difficult to decipher and separate one from another, rather like the spaghetti wiring behind your television. Once again, breaking the problems down into their individual components and then treating each one in isolation with the quality measure can be helpful.

✔ **Vision:** Here, you consider the difference between where you want to get to and how you might get there. Vision is the big picture; at the other end is execution. At the vision end of the spectrum you're primarily concerned with the problem as a whole. This isn't the place to look for solutions but to examine the problem in its entirety and explore its dimensions.

Moving to the execution end of the spectrum, you begin to explore how to proceed, and a visual analysis frequently suggests routes you can take.

An advantage of the visual approach is that it often evokes strong images that suggest analogies for your problem(s). For example, if you see your problem as a brick wall, what does that suggest? It may not be possible to climb over it, but can you find a way around it? Can you build a staircase? Can you dismantle the wall brick by brick? Can you just hire a demolition ball to smash right through it?

Winning privacy the smart way

An American billionaire loved his house and wanted to stay in it, but was concerned about his privacy when he became famous, because a neighbour overlooked his house. He constructed a wall for privacy, but a local law prohibited walls above a certain height, and the local authority ordered him to reduce the height of the wall he'd constructed.

The billionaire's had based some of his most successful ideas on extremely simple diagrams and images (one was a sketch with just three images, which became a billion-dollar product). So, unfazed by this problem, he visualised an elegant solution. He demolished the offending wall then built a hill, on top of which he built a regulation-height wall. Everyone was satisfied.

✔ **Individual:** At this point, you consider the single item, as against the whole picture. The other end of the spectrum is concerned with comparison. This dimension, more than some of the others, benefits from being considered as a continuum rather than as an 'either/or' dimension.

At one end of the scale, the individual aspect may be the single distinguishing feature of your problem. Or it may be the differentiator between your problem and that of your competitors. The Wright brothers, accredited with designing and building the first flying machine, apparently succeeded where so many had failed because, as bicycle designers, they were comfortable with the notion of inherent instability, while everyone else had tried unsuccessfully to build stable structures.

Then, at the comparison end, you might look at alternative approaches, competitors or how the topic changes when seen in a group context.

✔ **Doodling:** What's the difference between drawing and doodling? Whether you consider yourself good at drawing or not, you'd probably agree that drawing is something you do deliberately and consciously, whereas doodling is what happens when you're bored or not concentrating.

Apparently, doodling has always had a bad reputation. One advocate of doodling – Sunni Brown, the author of *Gamestorming* – said that in the seventeenth century it was a term for a simpleton, in the eighteenth it meant a swindler and was a term of ridicule, in the nineteenth it referred to a corrupt politician, and today it's frowned upon because it means, among other things 'dawdling, dilly-dallying and doing nothing'. Of course, 'doing nothing' in the workplace is regarded as especially unacceptable, so perhaps it's not surprising that doodling remains beyond the pale in the work environment.

However, doodlers are fighting back, and specialists in visual thinking argue that doodling has a rightful place in the toolbox of creative thinkers. This rehabilitation of doodling is based on the premise that doodling serves a useful function as part of the overall thinking process and deserves to be encouraged rather than inhibited.

Recent evidence that doodling is actually a constructive activity underpins the argument for the value of the activity. Doodling increases attention, meaning that doodlers in a variety of work or study situations (think of those boring meetings or lectures you have to sit through!) recall more information than those who don't doodle. It appears that doodling replaces daydreaming, and daydreaming really does lead to forgetting.

Where creative thinking is concerned, doodling is one of the tools you can use to move away from purely verbal thinking around a problem. If you're working alone or in a sympathetic team, you can feel free to doodle, knowing that it can be useful in helping you retain and process information. Just remember that your boss may not share your enthusiasm!

Do your doodles mean anything? A vogue for analysing all sorts of personal manifestations in the search for access to the subconscious mind occurred in Sigmund Freud's time, from slips of the tongue to dreams; even doodles didn't escape this close scrutiny. Much has been written about the meaning of the symbols found in doodles but, like in dream analysis, there are almost as many interpretations as there are experts. One illustration makes the point: at an international conference of politicians and industry leaders, the press got hold of a page of former Prime Minister Tony Blair's doodles, and an analyst diagnosed him as, among other things, unstable, aggressive and megalomaniacal. Accurate? Maybe or maybe not, but it emerged they'd poached the wrong page, and the doodles were in fact sketched by Bill Gates.

Also part of SQVID, but not included within the acronym itself, is:

✔ **Change:** Change is represented in SQVID by the Greek letter delta (Δ), because it's a common mathematical symbol for change. Change is the area where you can let your imagination run wild and play with ideas.

The other end of this spectrum is 'as is', meaning of course, things as they are at present. The 'as is' end of the spectrum is current reality, which is useful in reminding you of the here and now, as long as you remember that it's *only* the here and now. You may like to consider the present-tense observations of some important figures of their time:

- 'Heavier than air flying machines are impossible.' William Thomson (Lord Kelvin), a physicist who lived from 1824 to 1907, who also observed: 'X-rays will prove to be a hoax.'

- 'Rail travel at high speed is not possible because passengers, unable to breathe, would die of asphyxia.' Dr Dionysius Lardner, a science writer who lived from 1793 to 1859.

- 'I think there is a world market for maybe five computers.' Thomas Watson, president and chairman of IBM from 1937 to 1956.

- 'Stocks have reached what looks like a permanently high plateau.' Economist Irving Fisher, in 1929.

To assist your thinking around these elements, use the six classic questions I describe in the preceding section.

Playing with paint

Play in all its forms is an essential ingredient of creative thinking, and painting provides a great opportunity to be creative and have fun at the same time! Small children love playing with paint. They don't mind making a mess, often getting as much paint on themselves as on their masterpieces, and they use colours, brushes and fingers freely to make their marks.

As they grow, however, children progress through a well-documented sequence of changes in their artistic style, which appears to be universal. If you look at the artwork of children anywhere in the world, you can usually guess ages reasonably accurately through the drawing style. As children's skills increase, painting and drawing become more organised and controlled through several recognisable stages, and the results progressively lose the spontaneity of the early years.

Many artists have explored ways of getting back to the freedom of expression of early childhood painting. Once the Impressionists started using paint in fresh and original ways, some artists pushed the boundaries even further by using looser structure and purer colour in their work. Picasso, who could paint brilliantly in the classic idiom, worked hard to create the childlike styles for which he's best-known, and frequently spoke of the importance of rediscovering childhood.

If you're drawing or painting for work or leisure, loosening up by working with your inner child can be great fun:

- ✔ Try painting without mixing your colours, using only pure rainbow hues.

- ✔ Paint with a single brush instead of using several.

- ✔ Instead of drawing an eye or mouth 'properly', try using a mark that's just close enough.

The nearer you get to spontaneity, the more confident you'll become about painting what *you* want instead of aiming for a result that gets everyone's modest approval. Take a look at Henri Matisse's work during the period in which he led the Fauvists (their name meant 'wild beasts'). Along with his colleague André Derain, he painted in extravagant colours and stretched and bent conventional shapes to their limits. You cannot fail to see the fun they had producing these works! Derain's painting *Charing Cross Bridge*, a much-reproduced example of the period, features the bridge in deep blue, with the Thames beneath in vivid yellows and blues, a mauve sky, green buildings and a red foreground. The painting really shouldn't work but, amazingly, it does.

Throwing soul bombs

When he was stuck, Leonardo da Vinci sometimes soaked a sponge or rag in paint and threw it at the wall. He'd then study the outcome and find inspiration in the forms and shapes he saw in the splashes, dribbles and puddles. Artists have practised variations on this approach ever since. The group known as the abstract expressionists, whose best-known exponent was probably Jackson Pollock, deliberately created works using these free-form techniques.

More recently, the technique of 'soul bombs' has been deployed by some businesses specialising in creative thinking. Dressed in suitably protective clothing, participants hurl bags of paint – soul bombs – at a wall, then augment the results with additional marks and brush strokes. While the purpose is serious, solving a problem or generating ideas, the activity is invariably something of a riot as participants discover that it's virtually impossible to throw paint around without descending into anarchy.

Playing with Role Play

Role play has been used for many years, in many businesses, to provide insights into the ways different disciplines and departments work.

A good example is the advertising industry. Advertising agencies have traditionally been divided between the *suits* – the team that administers the agency's account with the client, and the *creatives* – the team that devises the advertising campaigns you see in the media. Other departments handle the media buying and the planning, or the research and intelligence function that provides information about the client's products and customers.

On the client side, the main roles interfacing with the advertising agency are the brand team, sales and marketing, and the research department.

These are the traditional core roles, but in large agencies and client companies, many other functions are added to each side to increase their range and depth.

In this complex relationship, role play – in which participants act out the jobs of their opposite numbers – has always been seen as a way of learning about the functions and responsibilities of each party. Role play is typically undertaken as part of sessions away from the place of work, often over several days of mixed activities.

Walking a mile in their shoes

Taking the advertising agency example, a classic focus for role play has always been making the creatives role play clients, and vice versa. This is because traditionally, clients and creatives have been perceived as poles apart in terms of their roles, with a predisposition to misunderstand each other. Clients are focused on their business, brand and bottom line, it's said, whereas creatives concentrate on ideas, imagination and innovation.

In principle, this seems like a sound strategy, but in real life the outcomes can be very different from what you might expect. Many role play scenarios end in tears (sometimes literally). This is because a fundamental weakness of the role play concept is that clients and creatives are in those roles precisely because they're where their skills and personalities function best. Few creatives want to be clients; and few clients are inclined towards creativity. The result is that – consciously or unconsciously – each group ends up sabotaging the process, despite the best efforts of the organisers.

However, role playing does have its place in thinking creatively. When both groups stay focused on the exercise and work hard to inhabit their roles, and when the organiser keeps a tight rein on the session, role playing can generate valuable new insights and ideas that might otherwise have remained hidden.

Even if you're working alone, you can apply some of the principles of role play if you like this technique. If you're an author, you have readers; if you're an artist, you have viewers (and hopefully buyers) for your work; if you have a business, you have customers. Try walking in their shoes, and ask yourself these questions:

- ✔ Who am I doing this for?
- ✔ What do I want them to think or experience?
- ✔ What are they seeking from me?
- ✔ How can I improve what I offer?

Evaluating role play

The debate about role play continues. Advocates argue that role play provides insights into the perspectives of other people. Opponents say that role play provides participants with an opportunity to push their own agendas at the expense of the bigger picture.

Role play is very engaging for individuals who like to throw themselves into tasks, and for those who like to explore their inner actor. Like in brainstorming sessions, individuals with more extrovert characters tend to dominate role plays.

If you do decide to engage in role play, it's best to have your session run by an experienced organiser who's alert to the opportunities and risks as the scenario unfolds. At the planning stage, you can work together to agree the overall objectives and select the best scenario for achieving your aims. If you want to solve a problem, you choose a different scenario from one in which you only want to generate ideas.

To give your role play the best chance of success, consider not only the aims of the project, but also the personalities of the participants. By its nature, role play exposes each individual's personal characteristics in sharp focus, and you need to be sensitive to the possible outcomes – winners don't like to lose, followers resist the chance to lead, the shy don't want the limelight.

Over years of organising, observing and participating in role play, I've seen the whole spectrum from true team breakthrough experiences to resignation letters after the weekend. So, in the words of the desk sergeant in the old *Hill Street Blues* cop show: 'Let's be careful out there!'

Keeping and Breaking Rules

In most walks of life, sticking to the rules is a given. We're brought up within boundaries on the assumption that they're in place for good, valid reasons, and part of the game is always to play by the rules.

Many sets of rules have deep cultural roots, and traditions are respected. So you're expected to play with a straight bat and not do anything that isn't cricket. However, many sports stars have learned to play as close to the edge as possible and bend the rules as far as they can.

Tennis is a classic example of a game that's played to the limits of the rules, with shots within millimetres of the dreaded white lines. Without those white lines, the game would lose all meaning, and in the same way rules can enhance rather than limit creative thinking.

In the pursuit of creative thinking, bear in mind that staying within, bending and breaking the rules can all be options:

 ✔ **Stick to the rules:** You and your team devise a set of rules and stick rigidly within them. You might base the rules on requiring participants to submit ideas in rotation, limiting the number of ideas per participant, introducing a voting system, requiring all ideas to include certain criteria, and so on.

The Danish Dogme 95 film group made films based on a strict set of rules that emphasised traditional cinematic values and prohibited special effects and other gimmicks. The results were more entertaining than you might have expected and the group produced some excellent films.

✔ **Bend the rules:** Imagine having John McEnroe on your team, protesting every line call and constantly questioning the judgement of the umpire. In the bending scenario, you agree to a set of operating rules but then systematically test the boundaries you have agreed upon. With every idea generated, you ask questions like: 'Why can't we . . .?' 'But what if we could . . .?' 'What if we dropped that rule . . .?' The outcome is often a lively debate in which questioning the validity of rules opens up fresh territory.

✔ **Break the rules:** This scenario can go either way and is highly unpredictable – greatly enjoyed by the adventurous souls in a group, but not for the faint-hearted. When this approach works, rules are established and then broken selectively in the search for better and more original quality of thought. When this technique doesn't work, the scene can descend into anarchy, and having coffee and doughnuts on hand to massage bruised egos is a good idea.

Creativity is often thought of as a maverick activity, outside normal conventions, and indulged in by outsiders who are not good team players. But those suppositions are mistaken. You can play creatively with rules in a team context. And if you're working alone, you can try each option. Just remember that breaking the rules you decide to set is like cheating at patience – you're only deceiving yourself!

Thinking in and out of the box

A popular phrase when creativity is mentioned is *thinking out of the box*, indicating a move away from conventional thinking into unknown territory. This is one of those phrases that sounds exciting, which is perhaps why it has become something of a rallying cry in meetings about idea generation. But what does thinking out of the box actually mean in the real world?

The creative process is usually a mixture of logic and occasional leaps of imagination. Regardless of the techniques used (many of which I describe in the preceding chapters in this part of the book), new thinking comes from all sorts of places, and it's often difficult to recall exactly where a great idea originated. So to ask a team to 'think outside the box' is a laudable aim in principle, but not always possible to achieve in practice.

By all means try to extend yourself, or encourage your team to extend themselves, and put best efforts into every exercise, but don't expect creativity to come at the flick of a switch.

Walt Disney and the origins of 'thinking outside the box'

The true origins of the phrase 'thinking outside the box' and its usage are lost in the mists of time, but two of the more persistent stories are that:

✔ Walt Disney's staff used the 'nine-dot test' as a way of measuring the creative ability of applicants. (The nine-dot test is a 3 x 3 matrix of nine dots, and the challenge is to draw a single line through all nine dots.) This test is still used by some management consultancies and other businesses to illustrate lateral thinking processes, but whether it originated at Disney is a matter of conjecture.

✔ A science fiction author (who shall remain nameless, to spare his blushes) was invited to give an inspiring talk to some of Disney's 'imagineers', as the idea teams were called. Having celebrated a little too much the night before, he was unprepared and at a loss for what to say to these highly creative individuals the next morning. Casting around the room for inspiration, he set his eyes on a carton in a corner, and he found himself saying 'so we have to learn to think . . . out of the BOX!' and a phrase was born. Allegedly.

Encountering blue skies, clouds and storms

Another phrase that is inextricably associated with creativity is *blue sky thinking*, which is intended to address the notion of freeing yourself from existing thoughts. Of course, this is easier said than done, because patterns of thinking are ingrained over long periods of time, and change can't usually be introduced simply at the press of a button.

Like other thinking processes, blue sky thinking is a skill. Often defined as the generation of idealistic or visionary ideas, although not always with practical applications, blue sky thinking can be useful. In many ways, having such thinking as an aim is admirable. However, like many mantras, blue sky thinking doesn't happen just because you say it, because the term describes an aspiration rather than a specific technique.

If you want to come up with something genuinely fresh and original, here's a simple three-step process to get you started. You can use the steps sequentially or switch between them as you discover what 'clicks' for you today:

✔ **Relax.** Getting excited about generating insanely great ideas is easy, as is becoming disillusioned when the ideas don't happen immediately. Your unconscious mind plays a big part in generating ideas, but it doesn't work at the same pace as your conscious mind. So, to give your unconscious mind a chance, sit comfortably (Richard Branson favours a hammock!), close your eyes for a while, and don't try. Just relax and see what happens.

✔ **Doodle.** Take a blank sheet of paper and start sketching randomly. Ask yourself (and your team if you have one) deliberately vague questions, even silly or provocative ones. If your task is to invent a new ice cream, for example, visualise unlikely ingredients or clashing colours. Consider what the best and worst shapes for an ice cream would be. (The chef Heston Blumenthal, for example, has built a successful career on 'crazy' culinary ideas using unusual ingredients, creating provocative meals like snail porridge, parsnip cereal and, of course, bacon and egg ice cream.)

✔ **Stretch.** Whenever you think you've reached the limits of your imagination, go the extra distance. You can either redouble your efforts (say, by pushing yourself into an idea sprint), or walk away for a while (maybe make a drink or go for a walk). Although these approaches are very different, both can help you generate interesting solutions, simply because they help to switch your mind rapidly into a different state.

At worst, exhortations to achieve a state of blue sky thinking can be counter-productive, especially for individuals who don't consider themselves especially creative to begin with. Creativity thrives in a positive atmosphere, and the oxygen for this is laughter and having a good time. Avoiding language that could be stress-inducing or cringe-making is always best.

If you're tempted to use a phrase as a motivator, consider whether it would pass a test based on the TV sitcom *The Office*: would David Brent say it? If he would, you're probably better off without it.

Choosing chance

Creativity has always been associated with chance. At the turn of the twentieth century, many professional thinkers imported practices from the East. Among them was psychologist Carl Jung, who was fascinated by the I Ching. The I Ching uses a simple system based on selecting sticks or tossing coins to direct users to one of 64 *hexagrams* (Chinese characters); each hexagram is a short description of actions appropriate for a variety of situations.

So if, for example, you toss your coins and the result is hexagram 24, the title of which is 'turning point', you have a description of 'success after a period of decay' (very appropriate for an idea generation session). Of course, the interpretation is entirely in your hands. As with many such systems, the I Ching is based on the belief that this random activity gives access to the subconscious mind. So, depending on your situation here, you might find yourself focusing on 'turning point' if you feel you're in transition, 'success' if you anticipate a good outcome, or 'decay' if you think you've been off form recently. No right or wrong answers exist, and the system is deliberately ambiguous. Your response depends entirely on your situation at the time.

Numerous books exist about the I Ching and how to use it. The I Ching doesn't appeal to everyone, but its fans report consistently good results – perhaps because they're open to allowing subconscious influences on their creative thinking.

An extension of the idea of random thinking involves the use of dice, which was popularised in the 1970s novel *The Dice Man*, by Luke Rhinehart. Several films, books and TV programmes have since picked up on this theme. The principle is that, at each decision point, you let the dice decide the outcome. In fiction, of course, doing so gives rise to some pretty hairy situations, and in real life too it can lead you in some very unexpected directions.

Here's how to proceed. Bear in mind that if you're trying to think of a plot for that novel you want to write, for example, your list will be very different from the one you create in relation to a problem with a project at work:

1. **Take a dice.**

2. **Take a piece of paper and write down the numbers 1–6, representing the six numbers on the dice, in a column.**

3. **Dream up and write down, next to these numbers, six possible ways forward for you in dealing with the issue or problem you have at hand.**

   The fun is in the rules you set yourself here. You can be precise or vague, conservative or outrageous. The choice is yours! Whatever you choose, the results may surprise you. For example, you might write:

   1 – Say 'yes' to the next question you're asked.

   2 – Turn left at the next corner, enter the first shop you come to and buy something.

   3 – Say 'no' to the next question you're asked.

   4 – Talk to the person on your left.

   5 – Strike a blow for freedom.

   6 – Start an argument.

4. **Roll the dice.**

5. **Follow the option you've set yourself for the number rolled.**

Using a single dice gives you six options, and of course by using two die you can yield many more.

Even if you don't want to dedicate your life to a throw of the dice, die can still be useful in thinking exercises in which choices are involved. Notice whether you're pleased or disappointed by the outcome of each throw, and always remember – it's only a game!

Having Whole-Body Experiences – Indoors and Out

Some professionals in the creative thinking industry use *whole-body experiences* (which engage the whole body rather than just the brain) as part of their methodology. Sometimes they employ actors and trainers to intensify the process.

Many whole-body activities originated in team-building exercises, and they often retain a sense of pulling together. On the positive side, this pulling together can generate a sense of momentum and achievement as group members work towards a common goal; but creativity is fickle, and some of the best ideas come from being out of step and not part of the gang.

Indoor exercises can be scripted or unscripted. In scripted exercises, the group works through a formally constructed and carefully structured scenario. A typical example is the murder game, in which the team follows a series of clues to unmask the murderer – an actor planted to appear as a regular member of the team, or one of the group selected by lottery. In terms of creative thinking, this and similar scenarios are positioned as techniques to stretch the mind and produce an atmosphere conducive to the creative process. Whether or not this is true, participants generally enjoy the experience.

Unscripted exercises are often conducted as a series, with the intention of lowering inhibitions and stimulating the senses. Three typical examples are:

- ✔ **All change:** The group is divided into pairs. One of each pair turns away while the other changes his or her appearance with a single adjustment. The object is to identify the change.

  Typically, this exercise begins cautiously with the loosening of a tie or the re-buttoning of a jacket. But as the game progresses, it gets more interesting as individuals run out of safe options, and organisers secretly hope that some extravert will not be able to resist the temptation to strip off! Whether this contributes to creative thinking is debatable, but the experience is usually memorable.

- ✔ **Pass the ball:** Participants stand in a circle. The object is to pass a ball to each member within a given time limit, which reduces with each round. No rules or advice are offered. The usual sequence of events is that the participants begin by missing their deadline, and become more frustrated as the time intervals diminish. Then participants gradually realise that there are no rules, and they get closer and closer together, often ending with a noisy melee. Perhaps this activity aids creative thinking, but often participants are too exhausted (or embarrassed) to embark on some humdrum thinking exercises immediately after a session.

✔ **The mat:** A mat consisting of a series of squares is laid out, and the team's task is to get individual members from one end to the other as fast as possible without setting off buzzers embedded in some of the squares. The guinea pig has to decide at each square how to proceed – left, right or forwards – while the others observe in silence. This seems quite straightforward, but in practice this exercise often becomes chaotic as individuals freeze, unable to decide, while the silent team members become increasingly frustrated.

Teams that work well together make careful observations of the patterns and overcome the silence rule through hand gestures and nods or shakes of the head, while poorly co-ordinated teams just get more frustrated with each mistake instead of finding non-verbal ways to communicate. So the mat is certainly a test of team co-ordination and observation (there's a secret pattern, which, once spotted, enables the task to be completed very rapidly), but whether the mat is useful as an aid to creative thinking is debatable.

These and other indoor exercises certainly qualify as whole-body experiences, and their proponents believe they enhance creative thinking by engaging all the senses.

Going outside to get creative also has its origins in team-building, and has been found to generate controversy in some quarters. 'I'll work 24 hours a day for this company, but I'm ******ed if I'll die for it!' This was the response by the straight-talking Australian marketing director of a well-known international corporation to the suggestion he should take a high-wire walk between trees 40 feet above ground level. Outdoor whole-body experiences thus tend to divide opinion, sometimes dramatically.

Other activities, some derived from military exercises, involve bridge-building, river-crossing, paint-balling, abseiling (rapelling), and a variety of orienteering-style treks.

Most of these outdoor experiences involve, by their nature, a great deal of physicality – exposure to the elements, some physical risk, and extensive exercise. For many individuals, such activities are a welcome change from orthodox work and an opportunity to test themselves in unfamiliar ways. Advocates argue that testing yourself is all part of growing the whole person and has beneficial effects on thinking ability and overall resourcefulness.

However, some make a strong counter-argument and raise ethical questions about the rights of employers to make staff undergo potentially risky endeavours in order to prove their commitment to the company vision. Such exercises can also be seen as providing a showcase for the egos of the organisers and the inevitable embarrassment of weaker members of the team. In any event, some opponents of this approach argue that the link between physical activity and thinking ability is tenuous or even non-existent.

Whatever side you come down on, it appears that the outdoor industry will be around for a long time, with an added boost from reality shows that excite public interest in the prospect of watching people struggling through endurance tests.

Creating Movement When You Get Stuck

When you embark on creative activity, being part of that process is exciting and absorbing. Your mind is alive with possibilities, and your imagination takes you to fresh horizons. If only it could be like that every time!

If you've ever attempted to think or play creatively, however, you've probably experienced that awful moment when you realise that you're stuck. If this hasn't happened to you yet, don't worry, it probably will. Like the common cold, getting stuck is something that only happens to other people, until you experience it yourself, when suddenly it's the single most important thing, preventing you from doing anything, requiring all your attention. And of course, as with the common cold, men suffer much more than anyone else (my wife made me put that bit in).

Experiencing getting stuck can take many forms, and it can interrupt your creative play – or any other creative process – at any point, often unexpectedly:

✔ It can be personal, making you doubt your own abilities.

✔ It can be professional, focused on the difficulties presented by the task.

✔ It can happen at the outset, as you try to get to grips with the task.

✔ It can occur during the creative play process.

✔ It can cause you to stumble near the end.

You can experience getting stuck in many different ways: being hazy, unfocused, afraid, out of your depth or feeling an overall sense of disempowerment. If you experience this kind of discomfort, the first step to extricating yourself is to recognise that you're stuck. Then, take steps to remedy the situation.

You can try several courses of action when your creativity gets blocked:

✔ **Disrupt the pattern:** Make a decisive change and carry out a new action. Somebody once said that doing the same thing and expecting a different result is the path to insanity so, whatever you've been doing, do it differently. For example, if you've been deeply immersed in your creative play, make a point of disengaging so you can see things from a different perspective. If you've been engaged in one form of play, try a different one.

✔ **Make a step change:** Often, getting stuck is a result of persisting in seeing an issue from a single point of view. Divide the task into smaller chunks or change your perspective, for example.

✔ **Walk away for a while:** Physically remove yourself from the situation that's causing you to feel stuck. Do whatever feels right until you're ready to re-engage. You may just need to take time out to prepare a drink, or you may need to go for a walk. In extreme cases, it may be best to leave things alone for longer. There are no hard and fast rules here, but trust your instincts. The key is to take that decisive first step.

These and other options allow you to disengage, cool off and (hopefully) reduce your levels of stress or anxiety before returning to the fray.

Getting unstuck is an essential part of the creative thinking process. You can't drive anywhere if your engine doesn't start.

A useful free app exists that help when you're stuck for any reason. It's called 'Unstuck', appropriately enough, and works by walking you through a simple sequence of actions. It's available from the App Store (www.appstore.com) and Unstuck (www.unstuck.com). You don't have to have the app to follow the recommended sequence (you can buy a book of the same title by Keith Yamashita and Sandra Spataro, published by Portfolio), but if you have a smartphone or tablet, Unstuck is a useful addition to your repertoire, especially if creative thinking is part of your everyday life.

The Unstuck app recognises that becoming stuck doesn't only happen during the creative thinking process, and also covers how you can feel stuck in many different ways, both personally and professionally. You can take the Unstuck app seriously or simply play with it. If your stuck issue is procrastination, this is an ideal tool for you to use instead of getting on with the task.

Part IV
Applying Creativity to Your Life

The 5th Wave   By Rich Tennant

"Don't let it bother you. The doctor told my wife it would keep her mind sharp if she learned a new skill."

In this part...

You embed creative thinking in your life. You discover the benefits of living the creative life and explore the role of happiness and humour. You take a look at how children learn creatively. And you take your creative thinking to work and explore how creativity and innovation fit in the commercial world.

Chapter 10

Living the Creative Life

Are creativity and length of life related? This question crops up whenever anyone exceptionally gifted dies.

It's true that, throughout time, some exceptionally creative individuals have died young. In these days when everything has a place on the Internet, you can even find sites commemorating those famous people who died at 27. It's a long list, including a number of musically creative types such as guitar legend Jimi Hendrix, Kurt Cobain of Nirvana and British diva Amy Winehouse. From this evidence, it would be tempting to assume that the good die young.

However, the notion that creative individuals die young is just an urban myth, like the idea that artists starve in garrets and poets die from consumption. Many creative people live to a ripe old age, and an increasing body of evidence supports the view that creativity is very conducive to a long and healthy life. And it seems that a creative life can bestow many other benefits along the way.

Living the Benefits of a Creative Life

Creative thinking isn't just about having good ideas. For many people, creative thinking spills into every corner of life. This may be connected to a heightened level of awareness – described as *being present* – that often comes with continuous creative activity. It boils down to noticing who you are, where you are and what you're doing at any given moment.

One characteristic of being present is curiosity, so many individuals experiencing this trait are predisposed to question everything and to explore even the most mundane aspects of their daily activities. They're likely to examine their diet, lifestyle and attitudes to life a little more closely.

In any event, cultivating the habit of asking questions, even about mundane parts of your life, is good practice.

Next time you have a meal, give yourself a little quiz – nothing too heavy – just some simple questions about what you're eating:

- ✔ Why did I select this? Was it habit or a deliberate choice?
- ✔ Which parts of this meal do I like most?
- ✔ What do I like least?
- ✔ Am I *really* tasting this?
- ✔ What are the textures?
- ✔ How fast am I eating?
- ✔ What's happening around me while I eat?
- ✔ How will I know when I've finished?

Apply this process as you perform a variety of everyday activities – travelling, washing, dressing, or relaxing at the end of the day.

Just asking a few questions can change your perceptions about your daily routines and encourage you to think differently about why you do what you do. From a creative thinking point of view, habit-changers are themselves a good habit!

Curiosity about yourself is a key to enhancing your creativity, and you can apply it to all the main areas of your life. The cumulative effect of this continuous curiosity has positive mental and physical consequences, making you more alert to what's happening cognitively and in your body as you go about your daily business.

Improving your health

Your health is, of course, a major factor in your quality of life. It's difficult to exude wellbeing if you're feeling one degree under.

Evidence suggests that any exercise you take leads to the production of fresh brain cells. Whether you walk or work out, as long as you keep moving you're nourishing your mind as well as your body.

Health is rooted in lifestyle, and the way you choose to live has a direct bearing on how you feel, not just physically, but in terms of your overall attitude.

A recent international survey reported that the healthiest people are those who don't spent money they haven't earned on things they don't need to impress people they don't like.

Managing stress

In recent years, stress has emerged as a major problem, affecting many aspects of personal and professional life. Stress has been identified as a major contributor to a wide variety of illnesses, some of them life-threatening.

Stress isn't a simple subject. Experts have described it as a tautology – a circular situation in which you feel stressed because you have stress, caused by, yes, stress. In other words, stress can be present without any apparent cause outside the experience of stress. If you're fortunate enough not to have lived through stress, this may sound a little strange, but to anyone who's been there, it will be all too familiar.

Chronic stress – the kind that's continuously present – can be extremely debilitating. Sufferers report that it's difficult to perform even simple tasks and every action requires great effort. Inevitably, feeling this way has a direct bearing on your ability to be creative, and under these circumstances creativity is likely to be the last thing on your mind.

Unfortunately, no quick fix for chronic stress appears to be available, because it's very deep-rooted. But you can take some steps to ease it. In the work situation, you may not always have control over your conditions – you probably can't change a boss you don't get on with, an annoying colleague, or your workload, much as you'd like to – but it's worth examining your routines.

To reduce stress in your daily work activities, try these tips:

✔ Start Mondays slowly. Monday is the worst day for stress-related illness, and most heart attacks take place on Monday mornings.

✔ Do one thing at a time to avoid getting overwhelmed.

- ✔ Do the worst tasks first. It makes the other tasks seem easier.

- ✔ Decide when to access your emails. Deal with them in batches – get rid of the ones that just distract you, so you can deal with the more urgent issues.

- ✔ Show appreciation. People like people who like them; practise random acts of kindness.

- ✔ Be mindful. Notice what's happening around you and adjust accordingly.

- ✔ Aim to have your biggest workload in the middle of the week. Then appreciate the fact that you're on the way to the weekend.

- ✔ Don't rush your breaks. Take time to appreciate them, even if you're busy. You can be more productive in the long run if you take short breaks throughout the day.

As you develop these habits, monitor the impact they have on how you feel about yourself and your job. Cultivate the habits that work best for you.

Floating uncomfortably

Closely allied to stress is *free-floating anxiety*, that awful feeling of impending doom, where your stomach is in knots and you have a kind of gnawing feeling, even a sense that you may be sick at any moment.

Most people experience anxiety, even if only briefly under extreme circumstances. You may have experienced this sensation before having to speak in public, or when you know you're about to get a dressing-down from an authority figure. Whatever the cause, it's bad enough to experience it briefly, let alone when, as in the free-floating version, it can linger for long periods of time, coming and going for no apparent reason.

If you begin feeling anxious, take a few deep breaths, take a quick break, go for a walk around your building – do something to take yourself out of the situation, even for a short while.

Recognising that some stress can be good for you

Stress isn't all bad, and there's growing evidence of *optimum stress* – just the right amount of stress. It appears that too little stress can be just as bad for you as too much.

Harvard Business School is conducting a long-term study of the relationship between stress and creativity. Several years into the project, evidence is accumulating to show that the absence of stress can lead to complacency and disengagement.

Figure 10-1 shows four stress conditions:

✔ **On a mission:** The optimum condition for creativity in the workplace is when high pressure – a deadline, the need to find an immediate solution to a problem, and so on – is coupled with meaningful work. Here, people feel they're on a mission, and are alert, with a sense of urgency.

✔ **On an expedition:** Under conditions of low pressure and meaningful work, people experience themselves as being on an expedition, exploring ideas. Again, this is a situation conducive to creative work.

✔ **On a treadmill:** When the pressure is high, but the work isn't meaningful, people feel they're on a treadmill – busy but just constantly switching gears. You can also think of this situation as treading water – what you're doing isn't getting you anywhere, but you can't stop for fear of sinking. Creativity isn't likely to be a priority in these circumstances!

✔ **On autopilot:** When the pressure is low and the work isn't meaningful, people operate – not surprisingly – on autopilot, with very low engagement. If you've worked on a production line, you'll know the feeling of numbness that clouds your consciousness after a while, making it impossible to think.

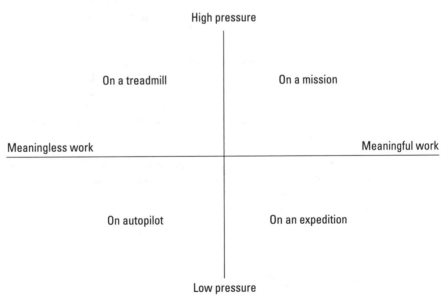

Figure 10-1:
Four different stress conditions.

Just doing your job

The level of evaluation you're subjected to can have a major impact on your creativity. When you're able to get on with the job under low levels of supervision, the result is higher levels of creativity. But when your work is closely supervised, the outcome is lower creativity.

Living a long life

By itself, creativity doesn't guarantee that you'll die old or young. However, the contribution a creative attitude can make to a longer and healthier life is generating a lot of interest. It appears, for example, that people who use a wider vocabulary and longer sentences in early life tend to retain their faculties to a higher degree as they age. And mounting evidence supports a correlation between education and longevity, although the research is still in its early stages.

Someone with a personal interest in the relationship between creativity and longevity is Howard Gardner, a professor at Harvard University. Now approaching his seventies, he's still actively lecturing, writing and conducting research on creativity and intelligence. Gardner developed the theory of multiple intelligences that helps explain the results of MRI scans of brain activity.

Gardner's favourite recommendation for living to a healthy old age is what he calls *neoteny* – which the dictionary defines as the retention of juvenile features in an adult. He suggests being around younger people when possible (one reason he still teaches), and thinking young – a trait that many creative thinkers would recognise. *Thinking young* is about retaining a sense of innocence, curiosity and playfulness about the world.

Richard Feynman, was a Nobel-prize-winning physicist (see Chapter 15) who achieved many significant breakthroughs as a result of his endless curiosity and willingness to ask simple, almost child-like, questions that challenged orthodox science. Feynman was also passionate about jazz, bongo-playing and frisbees. That's thinking young.

Getting good sleep

Sleep is hugely important, not only because it occupies a large proportion of your life, but also because it contributes directly to your quality of thought. Sleep is a very complex subject; despite a great deal of research, many aspects and mechanisms of sleep still remain unclear. Nevertheless, the quality of your sleep is known to have a direct effect on the quality of your thinking. Overall, sleep in all its forms makes a substantial contribution to healthy mental activity, and a bit of shut-eye can often open your mind.

Replenishing your mind

One of the roles of sleep is physical and mental replenishment – both of which are relevant for creative thinking. It's difficult, if not impossible, to think effectively if you're sleep-deprived, and you may have personal experience of trying to work or study when you were over-tired. In these circumstances even the simplest bits of information just won't lodge in the brain. And your body feels uncharacteristically weak.

Sleeping at different levels

Sleep usually follows a predictable pattern. When you fall asleep, you typically follow a cycle of different levels of shallower and deeper sleep, with corresponding mental activity. The major basic distinction in sleep phases is between rapid eye movement (REM) and non-rapid eye movement (NREM) cycles.

Most dreaming occurs during REM sleep, which comprises around a quarter of your sleeping time on average. One interesting characteristic of REM sleep is that your muscles relax, which researchers believe prevents you physically acting out your dreams. If you're woken up during a REM phase, you usually know you've just been dreaming.

NREM is a deeper sleep phase during which you do little or no dreaming. The exception is that some of the scarier stuff like night terrors and sleepwalking take place during the NREM phase.

If you wake someone who's in an NREM stage, apart from being confused and unable to describe their state of mind, they're likely to be very grumpy!

Keep a dream diary. Keep a notepad and pen by your bed and record your dreams as soon as you wake up. At first, your efforts may be a bit hit or miss, but developing the habit of writing down your dreams while they're fresh assists the process of recall, and you'll soon find that you can recollect more of your dreams and in more detail.

Taking the overnight test

Many professional creative thinkers use sleep as a creative resource. This overnight test is useful in at least two ways:

✔ It can be useful in solving a problem. When you can't see a solution despite a great deal of effort, a good night's sleep can sometimes deliver the desired result in the morning. As you go to bed, think of an issue you're trying to resolve and then allow your unconscious brain to work on it while you sleep.

✔ It can be an effective process for evaluating the quality of an idea. Before you decide whether to pursue your idea further, sleep on it. If your idea still seems like a winner in the morning, you may have the solution you need.

The idea of sleeping while you have unfinished business can seem counter-intuitive. However, if you give yourself permission (and, of course, if time permits), sleeping can be a valuable way of exploring your creative horizons.

Power napping and the creative siesta

Whereas the idea of dozing during the day was once considered unacceptable, increasingly evidence points to the fact that napping can be beneficial in a number of ways. Apart from recent research indicating a significant positive effect on health, including on cardiac conditions, napping or taking a siesta appears to aid creative thinking.

When you next have a problem and are having difficulty resolving it, take a few minutes out for a nap. For most people, a nap works out at between five and ten minutes. Some people, including President John F Kennedy, found power napping easy, even in the midst of a crisis, and Sir Richard Branson is an advocate of the hammock. You may find it easy to drop off, or power napping may take a little getting used to. Either way, power napping is worth trying. If you feel a bit guilty about it, just tell yourself it's a legitimate creative thinking technique, not just a nap!

Daydreaming

People who score highly on creativity scales often fit a profile whereby disengagement is part of their cognitive style. These individuals tend to get caught looking out of the window or showing other signs of not being part of the group, whether in a classroom, workshop or meeting. This inattention doesn't necessarily mean they're bored. In fact, it can be just the opposite – they're actually immersing themselves in the topic. If you're one of these people, you know that when something intellectually challenging is presented to you, daydreaming is an entirely natural response.

Daydreaming can get you into trouble in the wrong situations. The classroom and office are both places where daydreaming is usually frowned on. In a world in which you're expected to be wide-awake all day, signs of dozing, drowsiness or drifting are usually interpreted as a breach of acceptable behaviour: you must be hung-over, ill or burning the candle at both ends. So before you try daydreaming as a creative tool, make sure that you won't get into trouble for it!

Next time you're confronted with an intellectual challenge, instead of automatically focusing on it, take a mental step back and choose to do nothing for a while, except perhaps gaze out of the window. Wait and see what happens. This technique doesn't work for everyone, so don't be concerned if nothing happens for you. But you may find you surprise yourself.

Measuring wealth

How do you measure wealth? For some, wealth is how much money you have. For others, it's whether you can live off the interest on your savings. And for others, it's whether you can live off the interest on the interest.

Another measure of wealth is well worth considering: wealth is what you have left when all your money is gone.

Thinking creatively helps you to be smarter not only about your attitudes towards wealth, but also how you acquire what you require, how you retain it and how you grow it. A positive belief system around wealth allows you to let go of old associations and encourage a new perspective aligned to your own intentions.

Thinking about wealth

Many individuals persist in having negative views about wealth and wealth creation. Often these views are caused by thinking habits formed early in life and left unchallenged since then. Attitudes to wealth are rooted in belief systems, so if your beliefs are negative your attitude to wealth is affected. Typical negative beliefs include:

- ✔ I'm not worthy; wealth is not for me.
- ✔ Wealth is wrong; only bad people are wealthy.
- ✔ Wealth corrupts; I'm glad I'm not wealthy.
- ✔ Wealthy people are snobs; I want people to like me.

Don't let beliefs like these affect you. Negative beliefs inhibit your ability to be creative, as creative thinking flourishes in a positive atmosphere, free of doubts and distractions.

Avoiding negative news

One of the most pervasive and damaging influences on your perceptions of wealth emanates from the media. Try to get out of the habit of reading about the state of the world's finances (unless, of course, it's part of your job!). If you're limbering up for exercise or a sports activity, you want to have positive images of your participation and the outcome. If you're preparing for a race, you wouldn't dream of letting images of failure enter your head. Yet, consider how easy it is to pick up a newspaper or television report warning of dire events that will end in catastrophe. So if you're limbering up for some creative thinking, apply the same principles as an athlete and clear your mind of negative clutter.

Don't become a newsaholic! Addiction to news about the financial and business world can be as destructive as any other type of dependency. The media always makes a drama out of a crisis, because that's what sells. However, it can have a negative effect on your health and your pocket.

Using visualisation and other techniques

If your beliefs about money – or anything else – are positive, and you believe that you deserve wealth (however you define it), try using the following visualisation technique:

1. **Close your eyes and picture yourself in your ideal scenario.**

   This could be a tropical beach, a magnificent mountain landscape, or any other setting that truly inspires you.

2. **Gently start to tell yourself that you're going to achieve the wealth you want, and as you do, gradually intensify the image.**

   Turn up the colour and transform it into 3D. Make the image larger until it fills your entire field of vision. Add sounds that amplify the experience (music, sound effects, supportive voices).

3. **Continue this process as long as it feels right, and then gradually return to your scenario and relax until you're ready to return to the real world.**

   Repeat as often as you like.

You can add to this visualisation by making a collage or even a mind-movie of it. I describe a short version here; there's more on visualisation in Chapter 6.

No one would claim that creative thinking automatically leads to wellbeing, nor that it's a sure path to wealth, but in both cases intelligent application of creative thinking can enhance your life and contribute to a genuine sense of abundance.

You can apply the other creative thinking tools and techniques described in these pages to the topic of wealth, just as you can to any other mental challenge. For example, you can apply SCAMPER (described in Chapter 7) to many situations in which you may want to evaluate issues associated with wealth; and Six Hats (also Chapter 7) is ideal for the decision-making process.

Celebrating the Creative Power of Happiness

Only a few years ago, the idea that happiness was a legitimate concern of science and business would have met with incredulity, if not derision.

For many years, psychologists and social scientists found some of the less tangible human emotional experiences difficult to study, because they lacked effective measurement instruments, so they tended to steer clear of them. There was also a sense that emotions were somehow not worthy subjects for serious study. And businesses were primarily driven by performance and the bottom line, so the consensus was that happiness wasn't really their concern.

However, in recent years, psychologists have become more interested in the subtleties of emotional drivers. This interest is assisted by great strides in understanding brain activity through technological tools like MRI scanners and advances in biochemistry which provide insights into the role of our bodies and physiological states in cognitive and emotional behaviour. Scientists now have equipment that enables much more sophisticated study of the interaction between body and brain during the experience of different feelings and emotions. What this means in practice is that subjects such as creativity, wellbeing and happiness are now seen as legitimate fields for study.

Searching for happiness

In a rapidly changing world, an increasing number of businesses are searching for better ways to manage and motivate their staff, along with striving for smarter solutions to business issues. This climate is very conducive to the introduction of a subject like happiness in the workplace. It becomes all the more relevant when you consider that, according to recent research, more than half of British workers are unhappy at work, and many of them consider leaving their jobs.

Introducing the virtuous circle

A well-established correlation exists between happiness and creativity. This is especially true in the context of empowerment. A virtuous circle appears to occur, as shown in Figure 10-2.

Figure 10-2: The virtuous circle.

Happy
Empowered
Creative

As Figure 10-2 shows, the happier you are, the more creative you're likely to be, and the more creative you are, the happier you're likely to be. This is a circle of empowerment, where feeling good is inextricably bound up with doing good work.

Expecting the unexpected

Happiness allows the unexpected to make an appearance. In rigid structures, where work follows clear rules, the unexpected is often seen as an inconvenience, if not a destructive force. A happy state of mind tends to engender a greater sense of flexibility.

When people are happy, a more flexible state of mind means they're more:

- **Productive:** Willing to go the extra mile to achieve goals
- **Creative:** Confident about thinking smart in the face of problems
- **Motivated:** Individually engaged and interactive with colleagues

Failing happily for success

Happy work environments are not only more tolerant of mistakes and failure but may also actually welcome them – within certain limits.

Some companies have a no-tolerance attitude to mistakes and failures, although substantial evidence now exists that these companies are most likely to fail in the long run. A no-failure kind of intolerance can create a climate of fear, stress and disempowerment. Indeed, the marketing guru Robert Heller is on record as saying that employers should have the courage to fire all those employees who never fail. His reasoning is that they'll always avoid risk, and so never make a difference. Employees who never fail can also inhibit co-workers, creating a negative atmosphere.

Being afraid to fail can provoke some counterproductive behaviours:

- Reluctance to report problems
- Showing no early warning signs of danger
- Working for self, not for the business
- Sabotage, through actions deliberately designed to harm the business

Some companies actually make a point of celebrating failure, with a monthly confession session at which staff air and share failures. These companies tend to have a higher than average happiness quotient, because they share the knowledge that it's acceptable to fail sometimes, that decision-making always involves risks and that a failure is an opportunity for (shared) learning experience.

Happiness in tribes

Everyone is in a tribe (and in this society you're inevitably a member of several tribes). And the tribe you're in, and your position in the tribe, has a major bearing on your happiness.

Following extensive research over a period of years, social psychologist David Logan and his team have explored the way people naturally form into five basic tribes in any social group. These tribes appear in similar proportions and with similar characteristics wherever they occur.

This list summarises each contingent, its dominant attitude, and its proportion in a social population:

- **Me – 'Life sucks' – 2 per cent:** This group is relatively small in number but disproportionately dominant in the dysfunctional areas of society, with many members of a criminal or disruptive disposition. They're usually unhappy and hostile loners or gang members, with a belief system rooted in the notion that life's unpleasant, so they have to look out for number one regardless of the consequences.

- **Me versus the world – 'My life sucks' – 25 per cent:** This group, a quarter of the population, is made up of people who believe themselves to be on the wrong end of the stick. For them, life is basically unfair and does them few favours. They are, inevitably, not very happy.

- **Me versus you – 'I'm great, you're not' – 48 per cent:** Almost half the population in any group lives in a world where feeling okay comes at a cost – to someone else. Logan has a nice illustration of three hospital staff members ascending in a lift together. The first one says, 'Did you see my article in the medical journal' (unstated meaning: and you haven't had one published). The second says, 'I've just done more surgery than anyone else in the department' (and you haven't). And the third one says, 'I'm the new medical director, so I'm going to the top floor' (and you're not). For people in this group, life is made up of these little victories, but they can only be happy as long as they're winning.

- **Me and you – 'We are great' – 22 per cent:** This group, a little over a fifth, is in a much more positive place, and here the happiness is palpable. At this level, fun and creativity come into the equation too. People in this group relate easily to others and share experiences, especially when a common goal exists.

- **World and me – 'Life's great!' – 2 per cent:** This group, whose percentage corresponds roughly to Maslow's self-actualisers (I talk about Maslow's hierarchy in the 'Ascending Maslow's hierarchy of needs' section, later in this chapter), is made of those who really feel a positive connection with the world at large, and are totally empowered. This is where you find great leaders and visionaries, and their happiness is rooted in communication that changes the world.

Joining the club – happiness is catching on

More and more businesses are learning the value of happiness in the workplace. Two practical areas where happiness delivers results straight to the bottom line are reduced absenteeism and greater employee retention. Happy employees are less likely to call in sick or to take days off, it seems. And if they're happy, they're less likely to decide to leave the company.

Alexander Kjerulf, one of the pioneers in the field of happiness at work, describes his role as 'chief happiness officer'. He operates on the principle that happiness is a prerequisite for productive work in most situations. He poses the question: 'Would you rather work in a happy or a crappy place?'

In Kjerulf's view, and that of other experts on the topic, the benefits of a happy workplace aren't abstract, they're tangible. He points to the substantial evidence that happy people are more productive, less likely to leave the company, and more likely to make co-workers happy.

The feeling of positivity in a workplace is linked to what Professor Teresa Amabile of Harvard Business School calls the *progress principle* – the high correlation that seems to exist between the experience of making progress and feeling good at work. Professor Amabile's research shows that the opposite is true, too. Having had the opportunity to study the quality of work life both in good companies and what she calls their evil twins over several years, she observes that perceived lack of progress is a major de-motivator.

This observation about the de-motivating effect of feeling thwarted and not being taken seriously clearly makes good sense. If you don't feel you're making progress, it's hard to feel happy in your work. And this feeling is likely to contaminate the quality of your thinking, inhibiting creativity.

But if you feel valued, and your contribution is noticed, it puts a spring in your step. In these circumstances, your ability to think creatively is likely to be greatly enhanced.

Getting a Sense of Humour

Just as happiness was once a taboo subject in the workplace, humour can still raise eyebrows. You wouldn't dream of telling a joke during a top management meeting about finance, and the sad office clown who seeks attention through loud clothes and pathetic jokes is no one's idea of funny. However, in the right context, humour can be a powerful tool for creativity in the workplace.

Laughing all the way to the bank?

A continuing debate in the advertising industry is about whether humour sells. Many humorous commercials exist, some of them very memorable, but does the laughter convert into sales?

Those supporting the pro side point to commercials that have entered folk memory and have remained in the public mind many years after they were last aired: Cadbury's Smash, featuring the Martians mocking earthlings who used old-fashioned potatoes, Manikin cigars saw the unfortunate comb-over victim in the photo booth lifting his spirits. And now insurance is 'seemples' according to comparethemarket.com. In each case, the campaigns were linked to substantial rises in sales.

Those against humour in advertising take the view that it's the joke that's memorable, not the product. They cite examples like Joan Collins having Cinzano – or was it Martini? – poured over her in a long-running series of ads. While everyone remembered poor Joan, critics suggested that the campaign did at least as much for Martini as it did for Cinzano.

No easy answer pops up here, but it would be a shame if commercials ceased to make us laugh while selling their wares.

Taking humour seriously

Humour is often a manifestation of confidence. In creative sessions, the amount of humour can be an index of success. If the session is going well, the tendency is for the mood to be light and enthusiastic rather than earnest. And humour can also act as a bonding agent, indicating that group members are on the same wavelength.

If you have a culturally mixed audience, testing any planned jokes on different people beforehand is a good idea. For example, executives in some parts of Europe don't approve of levity at work, although they may laugh uproariously at the meal afterwards. The British habit of self-deprecation can misfire in some Asian cultures, where it may be interpreted as an admission of incompetence. And irony isn't perceived as humour in some parts of the world.

A classic application of humour in an otherwise serious situation is when it's used as an ice-breaker. In psychological terms, this kind of humour acts as a rapid frame change, moving participants from one mood to another.

Laughing at an important subject – deflating the balloon

Sometimes, things need to be taken seriously. However, it can be just as important – and productive creatively – to take the opposite line. As professional humorists know, many a true word is spoken in jest, and deep truths can be revealed through a little wit.

Laughter, especially at an ostensibly serious subject, can reveal a fresh perspective – an unexpected angle.

The court jester of medieval days wasn't just a funny man, although one of his functions was to provide entertainment. One of the principal roles of the jester was to remind the king and his advisors that they were just fallible mortals, like the ordinary folk.

Anyone who's had a creative thought knows how easy it is for that thought to become precious – that's my baby! – and beyond reproach. Some balloon-pricking can be called for at exactly this moment. The story of the Emperor's new clothes, in which a conniving tailor convinces the emperor that the non-existent clothing he provides is raiment so fine that only the most discerning eye can behold it, provides a perfect illustration of how even the most absurd ideas can gain currency if no one has the courage to tell it like it is. In the story, it took a small boy to point out that the emperor wasn't wearing any clothes. If a direct hit is out of the question (when it's the boss's idea, for instance), humour can be used as an admirable deflection.

It's worth remembering that many jesters of old lost their heads when the king got bored with their insights, so don't overdo it!

Enjoying humour and creativity together

In many contexts, humour and creativity are happy bedfellows, and hearing a lot of laughter in creative workplaces and workshops is common.

However, a prevailing sense exists in many places that work and humour are incompatible – that if you're having fun, you're not getting on with the job. This situation is unfortunate, because humour is considered an effective antidote to stress, and it's widely known that stress can have a major negative impact, not only on the individual suffering from it, but also on the workplace as a whole.

Exploring the consequences of treating the topic of humour differently and regarding it as a creative tool is worthwhile. Along with several other cognitive processes, humour can instigate an instant frame change, and with it a moment of insight or enlightenment.

Humour can be especially useful if you've reached an impasse and are stuck with a problem. It seems that sometimes your subconscious mind is waiting for an opportunity to alert you to a fresh way of looking at the situation. It's a bit like the times when you decide to pack up because you aren't making progress, and out of nowhere comes a new insight.

Experiencing Wellbeing

If you had a choice, would you rather be in a happy, friendly place, or an unhappy, unfriendly one? Put like that, the question has an obvious answer. So why would you work or study under adverse conditions?

A strong correlation exists between the fundamentals of social status and the experience of wellbeing. If you're homeless and wondering where to eat or sleep, or even how to survive, you're not likely to be flush with a sense of wellbeing. And if you're reading this on a terrace overlooking a beautiful coral reef at sunset, your feelings of wellbeing are likely to register somewhat more highly.

Numerous people have researched what it takes for a person to have a sense of wellbeing, including Abraham Maslow.

Ascending Maslow's hierarchy of needs

When Abraham Maslow created his famous hierarchy of needs in the 1950s, he was searching for a meaningful way to understand the human experience and how it affects perception. At the time, this was ground-breaking work.

Since that time, Maslow's hierarchy has not only survived but has also entered popular culture and been applied everywhere from education to the highest echelons of business. The hierarchy is usually expressed in the form of a pyramid, with the most basic needs at the base and the highest aspirations at the top, as shown in Figure 10-3.

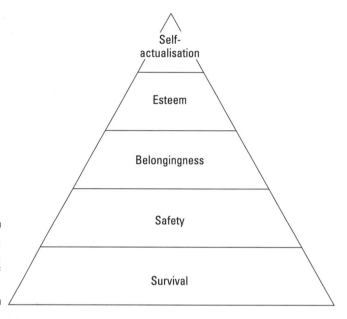

Figure 10-3:
Maslow's
hierarchy of
needs.

Considering the levels in order of ascendance:

- ✔ **Survival:** The most basic needs you must have met in order to live. Air, food, drink, warmth, sex and sleep are the primary concerns here.

- ✔ **Safety and security:** Stability, protection, law and order.

- ✔ **Belonging and love:** Social factors including family, work, community and relationships.

- ✔ **Self-esteem:** Achievement of status, reputation and responsibility. This is where creativity can become a feature of life.

- ✔ **Self-actualisation:** Fulfilment resulting from personal growth. This represents the peak of achievement and is the optimum state for creative expression.

In this hierarchy, designed to describe the progression from basic survival to self-fulfilment, it's usually assumed that individuals inhabit one level at any given time, and move up (or down) one level at a time.

Feeling good about yourself

At the heart of wellbeing is the experience of feeling good about yourself. This means that regardless of external events, the ups and downs of every-day life, you're in a comfortable zone and aware of the unique qualities that make you who you are.

If you want to have the ability to think and act creatively on tap, you can take practical steps to enhance your feelings about yourself. I explore some of these steps in the following sections.

Switching off self-talk

A substantial contributor to the way you interact with the world around you is the process known as *self-talk*, the perpetual running commentary on all your thoughts and actions. Switching self-talk off is notoriously difficult, but techniques like self-remembering and mindfulness, which I talk about in Chapter 13, can be very effective in moderating it.

Regardless of your control over self-talk, however, it's important in the context of creative thinking that you feel good about yourself when working creatively. The reason for this is very simple: if you don't feel good about yourself, it's hard (if not impossible) to generate good, creative thoughts.

In coaching, whether for sport, business or personal development, a great deal of emphasis is placed on being focused, being centred, or even hitting the sweet spot. The terminology itself doesn't matter, but the thinking behind it does. A by-product of effective coaching is that this all-too-human tendency to self-talk is toned down, if not eliminated.

If you want to live and work creatively, feeling good is a good place to start.

Using affirmative action

Affirmations work for many people, and they're a good way to jump-start your feelings of wellbeing. An *affirmation* is simply a method of telling your-self some positive truths, and being sincere about it. Affirmation is related to what happens when you practise creative visualisation, and is a process for embedding new patterns of thought.

Here's how to perform simple affirmations:

1. **Get into a comfortable position, sitting or lying down, close your eyes, and relax each part of your body.**

   It's best if you're in a symmetrical posture, with hands and feet uncrossed.

   The first steps are similar to those of meditation or creative visualisation:

   - Notice your head – it feels comfortable there on top of your body. (If necessary, flex your neck muscles gently to ensure you're relaxing.)

   - Notice your eyes – they're comfortably closed.

   - Notice your shoulders – they're relaxed. (Again, you may want to flex your shoulders a little to make sure.)

   - Notice your arms – they're relaxed.

   - Continue down to your hands. Notice how relaxed they feel, and just flex your fingers and thumbs a little. Now touch the tip of your thumb and middle finger together lightly, and keep them like that for the rest of the exercise.

   - Now notice your trunk and how relaxed your stomach is.

   - Continue down your legs, noticing as you reach your thighs, knees and ankles how relaxed and comfortable they feel.

   - Give your toes a little wiggle, just as you did with your hands.

2. **Now repeat your affirmations quietly to yourself.**

   Keep your affirmations short and simple, one thought at a time. And stick to one theme at a time – don't overload yourself with affirmations about every aspect of your life. Use between three and five affirmations on a single theme per session. You can create your own affirmations tailored to your individual interests and needs or use them to enhance your creativity:

   - 'I am a creative individual.'

   - 'I have all the resources I need.'

   - 'I feel good about myself.'

If you intend to repeat this exercise, recording it so you can run it at any time when you want to perform some affirmations is useful. Speak in a soft, slow voice, as though you're trying to soothe someone to sleep. And keep it natural – this is you talking to you, remember.

As you get used to using affirmations, you won't need to go through the complete relaxation exercise, although doing so is always conducive to producing a positive, resourceful frame of mind. Wherever you are, if it's possible to shut your eyes and sit comfortably, you can run through some affirmations.

Creating a healthy brain

Much of the brain's activity remains a mystery, despite the huge advances in recent years. But experts generally agree that you can do several things to create the conditions for long and active use of this precious and unique instrument.

 Not so long ago, neuroscientists thought that brains were fixed and incapable of change in adulthood. However, scientists are rapidly changing their view as they learn more about how the brain really works. It appears that, as you age, your brain starts to evolve in new ways. The term that neuroscientists use for this phenomenon is *scaffolding*. Just as real scaffolding is used to allow adjustments to a building, your brain apparently has the facility to cope with change by reorganising the location and function of various regions.

Getting physical

The brain's fuel is oxygen, and a healthy supply is essential for survival. On a practical level, this means that physical activity has an important role in maintaining a healthy brain. Ideally, physical activity means exercise, although it appears that any kind of movement nourishes the brain, particularly as you get older.

Recognising that you are what you eat

Few subjects provoke as much debate and contradiction as what we eat and drink. It often seems that last month's poison is this month's manna from heaven: cholesterol kills you, now there's a good version; alcohol is lethal, now drink wine every day for a longer life; count your calories, now calorie-counting is irrelevant. The pendulum swings back and forth, and sometimes it's hard not to feel like Woody Allen waking up in the future and being offered a healthy snack – of doughnuts!

Regardless of all the contradictory advice out there about diet, a few basic guidelines can contribute to a healthier and longer creative life:

- ✔ Consume a wide variety of foods and drinks to ensure a diet rich in vitamins and minerals.

- ✔ Eat only what you need. Listen to your body and stop when you're no longer hungry. (Ignore your mum, who wants you to finish everything on your plate.)

- ✔ Keep only those foods that you like and are good for you. Throw out all the junk food, so you won't be tempted.

- ✔ Don't bother with diets, and just be conscious of the ingredients in your food and drink. And remember that fresh beats processed every time.

Playing brain games

Do brain games work? As with so many topics concerning the brain and cognitive activity, the jury's still out. But increasing evidence suggests that cognitive activities that exercise the whole brain are instrumental in promoting cell growth along the neural pathways.

The surprising Sister Bernadette

Neuroscience is full of surprises and events that defy expectations. Because groups of nuns live similar pure lives, psychologists are fond of assessing them, it seems. One long-term study of 678 nuns in Kentucky gathered a mass of data while tracking personal information and cognitive activity (memory, calculation and reasoning) on a regular basis. The project team examined the nuns' brains after death in order to evaluate the effects of aging.

The autopsy of Sister Bernadette, who died from a heart attack at age 85, revealed fascinating results. Her brain was of normal weight, but further study showed that it was riddled with evidence of Alzheimer's at the highest level.

The remarkable thing is that Sister Bernadette was the star of the research group and performed exceptionally well in all the cognitive tests throughout her life.

Her case isn't isolated – examples are accumulating of individuals who seem somehow to re-wire their brains so they remain fully functional despite substantial brain deterioration. In the scientific community, these individuals are known as *escapees*.

Sister Bernadette's case is part of the growing evidence of the brain's capability for *neuroplasticity* – essentially adjusting itself to overcome strokes, disease and injury.

Chapter 11

Children and Creativity

. . . .

. . . .

*W*ill your children be creative? The answer is that they already are! Babies are born with all the resources they need to make sense of the world, and it only takes them a short time to assimilate the information and skills necessary for a rich and fascinating, sometimes world-changing, life.

The childhood years are a period of unparalleled learning, during which information is absorbed at an extraordinary rate. This is also a time of exceptional creative self-expression.

Much childhood creativity happens regardless of circumstances – even in poverty, children improvise in order to create play scenarios – indicating just how deep-rooted the creative urge is.

As children grow, creativity evolves in predictable patterns. Around puberty, children decide whether to be actively creative. This doesn't mean that children stop being creative, just that their interests and forms of expression are changing.

Looking Inside Children's Creative Minds

As they progress from early to mid-childhood, from around ages three to 11, children are at a creative peak. They assimilate new knowledge at an extraordinary rate and are eager to exploit it. They often get obsessed with themes that capture their imaginations – themes from dinosaurs to ballerinas to fire fighters. And they tend to be avid collectors, with astonishingly detailed knowledge of their pet subjects. Above all, children are usually constantly busy.

Childhood is a time of exploration, with so much to find out, so much to do. The speed of learning in the early months impresses everyone who observes it, not just the proud parents. And so it should, because this phase of learning represents a peak accomplishment of creative thinking.

Children adopt a range of strategies, which I talk about in the next sections, to help them gain new information and skills. By mid-childhood children are very sophisticated at managing their strategies. Adults often miss these processes because many of them take place under the cover of play activities. Surprising as it may seem, children rarely just play – they usually have an agenda involving learning or self-expression.

Blooming buzzing confusion

What is it like to be a baby? If you started babyhood as an adult, you'd probably want some guidebooks to help you get to grips with the situation. You'd want to learn the language as quickly as possible and meanwhile find ways to communicate and help you get about. But that wouldn't be all you'd have to deal with.

When the psychologist William James was asked what he thought the lives of babies were like, he gave the memorable answer that they lived in a 'blooming, buzzing confusion'. James was referring to the fact that humans are constantly bombarded with information via all their senses. The organised world you experience is the result of your having learned from babyhood to *filter* out the vast majority of raw information that your senses receive.

At birth, babies see in black and white and shades of grey. They can't focus beyond about the length of their arms and they have to turn their whole head to look left or right. A couple of months on, they learn eye movement, begin to recognise faces and see brightly coloured objects. Then they begin to co-ordinate hand and eye. This stage is when they learn to distinguish the things that matter and to ignore what's not relevant. This filtering process continues as babies begin to master their world.

Filtering to get the information you need

As a baby, you learn to see, and all the other sensory motor skills, from scratch. You perceive the world by systematically filtering input from your senses, so the world can make sense. Filtering is a learned skill, and in the early stages of life infants are hypersensitive to many sensations that the rest of the population takes for granted. Loud noises, rough clothing, bright lights and strong tastes and smells can all be unbearable for the very young.

To regain a sense of what you're filtering out, get yourself into a relaxed state and close your eyes as if preparing to doze. Instead, start to notice what's around you. Run through all your senses in turn so you *really* perceive what you're smelling, touching, tasting and hearing. Now try to be alert to all your senses – except sight – simultaneously. Then open your eyes and add sight to your sensory experience. Don't look at just one thing, but attempt to take in what's on the periphery of your vision as well. You'll probably find it difficult to sustain this activity for any length of time, because you've taught yourself to use your filters precisely so you don't get blasted with all that extra information.

Piecing the world together

One of the many activities infants have to master is piecing together how the world works: food comes when you scream; some things come back when you throw them away. Each tiny response to a behaviour contributes to a growing repertoire of knowledge that expands at a phenomenal rate.

As an adult, how long would it take to learn, say, a foreign language? What assistance would you need? Maybe some books about the phrases and grammar, audio and video tracks, and mingling with native speakers would help. If you've ever learned another language from scratch as an adult, you'll appreciate the feat of learning that children accomplish in their earliest years, all the time handicapped by not being able to resort to adult aids like conversation and the ability to read.

If you're learning a new skill, spend some time without any aids and then assess which ones you find indispensable. Could you learn without them? What new strategies would you have to adopt? This process is how young children learn everything.

Modelling mastery

Children don't know they can't do something, they only know they haven't done it yet. A universal learning skill exhibited by children is *modelling*, which is acquiring a skill by closely observing someone who has mastered it.

Modelling is one of the building blocks of neuro-linguistic programming (NLP, which I talk about in Chapter 1). Children are very adept at observing others who've mastered a skill and then emulating it until they get it right. Their persistence can be very impressive.

Next time you learn a new skill, perhaps playing a musical instrument or attempting a complex recipe, use the modelling technique to acquire it. Use a competent friend as your mentor, or follow a virtual learning method. In either case, concentrate on emulating your mentor's behaviour down to the finest detail. Notice when your attention wanders, and be prepared to repeat the exercise as often as necessary. Modelling is more than just observing, it's really getting into the experience and *feeling* what your mentor is doing.

If you have children, try the modelling exercise with them. Select an activity in which you have complete mastery, and have them watch as you do what you do. Most children find this a natural way of learning, which differs from conventional teaching because they're absorbing the new skill in a very direct way.

Becoming competent

Another learning method instinctively adopted by children (and also in the NLP repertoire) is moving through competence levels. Of course, children don't know they're using a sophisticated cognitive model, but they enact the steps as though they had been taught them. The process moves through a sequence of four steps:

- ✔ **Unconscious incompetence:** The first step in the process is not knowing you can't do something. Even very young children are attracted to bicycles, and often leap on them not realising they don't yet know how to ride. The same applies to any mobile object, from skates to scooters.

  Adults encounter this first step when they observe something and think 'That looks easy.' Many party games use the embarrassment that comes from this experience, and TV shows exploit failed attempts for amusement.

- ✔ **Conscious incompetence:** The second step in the process is conscious incompetence – the recognition that this skill is yet unmastered. Children quickly learn respect for complex skills, especially if that learning has involved grazed knees.

As an adult, you may well have experienced the frustration that often comes in the early stages of learning a task. Interestingly, it seems that children tend to be better at taking obstacles in their stride, perhaps because they don't expect to be masters of the universe.

✔ **Conscious competence:** The child gradually masters the skill and achieves basic competence, tempered by the knowledge that the skill still requires full attention. Children learning to ride bicycles proceed slowly and cautiously at first. They often resent parents hovering at this stage, because from the child's point of view, an important part of mastery is being able to do it yourself.

✔ **Unconscious competence:** The final stage is the internalisation of the skill to the point where the child can perform it entirely without thinking. After the initial thrill of having mastered another useful activity comes the point at which accidents are most likely to happen, because the child tests the limits of speed and manoeuvrability.

During adulthood, many such skills are internalised, and it's easy to forget how important it is for children to experience each new level of competence as they achieve it.

As an alternative to modelling, when you next learn a new skill, notice the sequence of actions required to assimilate it, and how you feel as you progress through each of the four stages. If you have children, stand back and observe their learning sequence, at each stage refraining from intervening any more than necessary. Endless repetition and refinement is likely to be involved, so notice their concentration and persistence.

Diving for survival

In the early days of flying, most of the learning was by trial and error, because so many experiences were new to the pilots. A cause of many fatal accidents was stalling. This happens when the nose of a plane rises, power drops, and the plane tends to spin before going into a dive.

A crash was thought to be inevitable in these circumstances, until one pilot behaved counter-intuitively. Instead of doing what everyone else had done, which always seemed to worsen the situation, he moved the joy-stick differently (he was going to die anyway, so what difference would it make?). To the pilot's surprise, his plane levelled out and started to climb.

The technique was subsequently taught to all pilots. Unfortunately, however, when under stress many pilots reverted to the incorrect but logical action, and died as a result. Conscious competence can be a life-saver.

Considering what babies do because they don't know better

When babies aren't sleeping (which they do for around 16 hours a day), they're on the move. In fact, they're unstoppable. Every parent knows how much babies wriggle, stretch and reach for anything in sight. Much of this endless movement is finding out what works. Every action is part of a process of gradual refinement, and everything is tried as many times as necessary. At the early stages, when motor skills aren't yet co-ordinated, infants just keep doing everything – all the time.

Over time, co-ordination improves and motor skills are gradually brought under control. One of the early skills that babies assimilate is hand to eye co-ordination, which helps them reach accurately for objects and bring them to their mouths.

Another of the earliest skills acquired is yelling and crying. At first this is undifferentiated, with a cry signalling anything from pain to hunger to boredom. But it doesn't take long for parents to notice that cries quickly take on different emphasis depending on the need. A bored baby makes a very different sound than a hungry baby.

Motor skills also increase at a rapid pace, and increasing co-ordination gives the infant greater command over its world. As children progress to walking and toddlerhood, they absorb each new unit of information both about how the world works and how to get what they want.

Envisage yourself in a giant cot without any of your normal motor skills. Adults appear from time to time but speak in a language you don't understand. And you can't make yourself understood except by yelling. One of the adults feeds you and generally looks after your needs. Objects are around, but some seem to be in reach and others aren't. And your hands don't always work the way you'd like them to. An exciting vision or a nightmare? How do you think you'd cope?

Playing as a learning method

Many adults, whether or not they're parents, believe that young children spend their time playing. To some extent, this is true, but that's not all that children do. The activities of young children are usually described by themselves and adults as play, because this explanation is a convenient way to cover the range of behaviours they explore. However, on closer examination you can see distinctive patterns emerging as children vary their choice of pursuits:

- ✔ **Repetition:** Much play activity is based on repetition. Children do particular sets of physical movement – running, skipping, arm-waving, bouncing on a trampoline – repeatedly. And over time, the movement is refined as the child seeks to get better at the task. Boys tend to draw attention to their efforts and accomplishments: 'Look at me! I did 20 in a row!' Girls, on the other hand, tend to focus on perfecting ever-more complex refinements of a given set of movements.

  Repetition applies equally to static or passive activities. For example, bedtime stories have to be repeated accurately, with no variations or shortcuts permitted.

- ✔ **Rehearsal:** A variation on repetition is rehearsal, in which a child puts a great deal of time into developing sequences of actions, practising many times over to get them 'just right'. For example, arranging dolls into groups in which each one has to be in its rightful place, and applying military precision to carefully rehearsed scenarios, often around dens, stockades or castles. Construction games like LEGO aren't usually spontaneous but are played within sets of rules of children's own devising. Even rough and tumble play may look anarchic but actually tends to follow a ritualised pattern. Similarly, activities such as 'cooking like Grandma' involve elaborate rituals which have to be completed in a precise order.

- ✔ **Play-acting:** Play-acting usually complies with carefully applied rules, even if the rules evolve as the game progresses. In a group, children assign roles to each other, and participants are meant to comply strictly with what's expected of them. Girls can spend long periods on a single game of this nature, whereas boys are more likely to run through a sequence of favourite scenarios.

Each activity shares common characteristics such as operating within sets of rules or parameters. Contrary to what some adults think (perhaps because they've forgotten their own childhoods), children's play is rarely as spontaneous as it looks to outsiders. Usually play follows an established sequence, often involving quite complex details and patterns.

Most people notice how children laugh a lot when they play, but it's interesting to observe just how serious and focused they are at certain points when they want to get something right.

Developing patterns and habits

Children pass through a predictable pattern of changes as they grow. Generations of child psychologists have studied these stages and broadly agree about the overall process, although as usual some experts differ about the details.

Much of the study of children's development was originated by Jean Piaget. As a biologist, he based his technique on close observation and interviews with children old enough to speak.

Piaget observed that, when incorporating new information from the outside world, a child goes through two phases:

- **Assimilation:** Incorporating new information into existing internal structures, similarly to slotting new information into existing files

- **Accommodation:** Expanding existing structures to make room for more information, similarly to creating new files to accommodate new information

He also noticed that children didn't mature in a continuous progression, as had previously been thought, but through a series of definite stages. Each stage signals a fairly sudden spurt of cognitive growth. The stages appeared universal and relatively unaffected by other factors such as intelligence. Each development stage is marked by the child gaining complete understanding of concepts he or she had no grasp of beforehand.

Piaget defined four main developmental stages, which are:

- **Sensorimotor:** In the first couple of years, infants learn that objects are permanent. A common activity of babies is throwing an object out of the pram. At first they don't seem to realise that it still exists somewhere, and they're surprised and delighted when it's returned. Another universal game is 'peekaboo', which has the same element of surprise and can hold a baby's attention during many repeats. During the sensorimotor stage, once the sense of permanence has been established, the concept of ownership is developed, and things become 'mine'.

- **Preoperational:** This stage, from around age two to seven, is egotistical, and the child is acquiring a sense of self. The growing importance of personal identity can lead to tantrums and arguments as children test the limits and boundaries of their behaviour. Much of the world is still unfamiliar, so exploration and testing are constant activities. Children learn to lie – badly at first – and often test this new-found resource to destruction, sometimes enrolling imaginary friends in a cover-up. This is when children make their first real friends and start comparing notes. It's also when schooling begins, so from nursery onwards, another dimension is added.

✔ **Concrete operational:** In the years between seven and eleven, a great deal of conceptual learning occurs, much of it concerned with how the world works. Children learn how much is within or beyond their control. A central event is the mastery of conservation, which applies to many situations. *Conservation* is understanding the equivalence of apparently different objects or concepts. At this stage, a child understands that two different-shaped glasses can hold the same amount of liquid or that different numbers can represent the same quantity ($6 + 6$ and 3×4 both equal 12). This knowledge extends to classification and categorisation of the world – learning where everything has its place. This is the peak period of creative activity, both in terms of learning and self-expression.

Time becomes an important dimension, and many things are measured by reference to age – new things are eagerly anticipated, and old things discarded in equal measure: 'When I'm 11, I'm going to the big school' and 'That toy was for when I was five.'

✔ **Formal operational:** From around age 11, children live more in their heads, and cognitive activity takes precedence. The nature of relationships with both peers and parents changes profoundly. When children reach puberty, parents often start to become marginalised to some degree, while friendships become intensely emotional and intimate. At this time, a marked drop in creative activity can occur.

At each of the stages, children are engaged in a succession of new activities. In the early years, children spend a lot of time in a level of consciousness that makes them especially receptive, which accounts for their ability to absorb huge amounts of information in short periods of time.

Showing acquired skills through drawing

Early childhood years are characterised by rapid assimilation of skills and resources. One of the key measures of children's progress is how their drawing evolves.

If you visit any school in any country, you'll see broadly similar styles and standards of pictures drawn by children according to year. As part of their growth through the ages and stages of development, their pictures form a record of the stages they've achieved.

These universal stages of imagery have distinctive characteristics, so it's possible to estimate children's ages from their drawing styles at any given time:

✔ **Scribbling stage:** Under the age of three, children are in the scribbling phase, making marks for the kinaesthetic pleasure of moving crayons or brushes around and seeing the colours. Efforts at this stage often look something like Figure 11-1.

Gradually these scribbles become more organised, and along with growing command of basic language, children begin to name them ('flower', 'butterfly', 'Mummy'). Adults can't usually make much sense of the scribbles at this stage, but children become confident of what they've produced and recognise their own work, giving it the correct title.

✔ **Preschematic stage:** Around age three, children begin to produce recognisable images. The first image is usually a person represented by a circle (the head) and a couple of down-strokes (legs). This quickly evolves into more elaborate images, with symbols changing as children evolve their thinking and gain mastery of crayons and brushes. By the age of four, children's output can be quite complex.

Figure 11-2 shows the emergence of recognisable people with heads and limbs. These first simple stick figures quickly become more detailed and elaborate during this period.

Figure 11-1: Sample scribbles made by a very young child.

Figure 11-2: Pre-schematic drawings.

✔ **Schematic stage:** This and the preceding stage are named after the schema a child produces by around age six. A *schema* is a definite way of portraying an object. At this stage the child produces confident, recognisable portrayals of people and objects, which include important references, such as 'Mummy's dress'. Drawings show knowledge of space, and objects usually sit on the baseline of the page, as I show in Figure 11-3.

✔ **Gang stage:** This is the dawning of realism. Between the ages of eight and ten, children make great strides as they search for ever-more sophisticated ways of representing the real world. Their output is stylised rather than naturalistic, a horizon replaces the baseline and figures and objects overlap in space. Figure 11-4 shows typically detailed drawings of a tractor and a person, which would've taken considerable time and a great deal of concentration. This is the phase when children begin to compare their work critically and borrow tips from each other.

Figure 11-3:
A schematic drawing with identified objects.

Figure 11-4:
Two examples of 'gang' images, showing preoccupation with detail.

✔ **Pseudo-naturalistic stage:** By age 12, children start to produce drawings that attempt to emulate adult art, and this signals the end of spontaneous output. Work is often painstaking, with attention paid to details such as folds in clothing, shadows and motion. Children make their first attempts at perspective during this stage. The emphasis is on the end product, and children tend to be highly critical of their own and each other's work. Colours are typically subdued, and people in these pictures rarely smile, especially when drawn by boys. Figure 11-5 shows a careful attempt at perspective, painstaking detail and a noticeable absence of people, all typical of this phase.

✔ **Decision period:** In the early teenage years, a young person usually makes an active decision to pursue drawing or leave it alone. This stage is a sensitive one, when teenagers are often painfully aware of their immaturity and are easily deterred. This stage can be bridged by introduction to other art forms like sculpture and non-representational art. Reference points will be adults rather than peers. The drawing in Figure 11-6, probably a self-portrait, demonstrates study of 'grown-up' art, reflected in the attempt at sophisticated shading of the features.

Figure 11-5: An attempt at naturalism, showing fascination with perspective.

Figure 11-6: A typically sombre teenage portrait.

TIP

Regardless of your own estimation of your talents, do a drawing or painting using whatever materials you prefer. Don't try; just do it. Then look at your output with fresh eyes, not to criticise, but to really see what you've produced. Now do another one.

Observing How Education Influences Creativity

Educational experts have contradictory views about the role of education in child development. Education is a subject that evokes strong passions. Some believe that all education is good because it feeds hungry minds, and any teaching is better than no teaching. Others question that model, arguing that education can have a negative impact on unformed minds. One leading figure, Sir Ken Robinson, an ex-education minister in the UK Government, has suggested that the Western education system is designed to produce a narrow form of academic excellence that has limited relevance to today's world.

Whichever direction education takes, it's increasingly felt that it should place greater emphasis on the importance of *innovation* in all its forms.

A steady decline in children's creativity is noticeable through the school years, and some experts blame this on the ways in which children are taught. However, this is a complex issue, and many factors come into play, including:

✔ **Rules and boundaries:** Traditional education places considerable emphasis on the importance of rules. Under this system, conformity of method ensures that children are taught subjects in a consistent way, with clear expectations and measures of performance. At the other end of the spectrum is the view that because children are inherently creative, they should be free to explore and grow at their own pace.

Neither of these extremes is wholly healthy, and it seems apparent that the best option lies somewhere between the two. Children need, and respond positively to, boundaries. Indeed, they incorporate them into their own play from an early age. Without meaningful structure and direction, children find it hard to distinguish appropriate from inappropriate behaviour. This isn't to suggest that a strict regime is beneficial, however, and many of the best teachers work with the lightest of touches.

Most experts agree that the single most important element is consistent application and enforcement of rules and boundaries (which applies equally to parenting).

- **Work and play:** Traditional methods advocate separation of work and play, with an emphasis on enthusiastic participation in each. Another view sees the two as intertwined and merges them into a kind of playful learning with a focus on self-expression.

  Again, a middle position seems to make the most sense. Children have high energy levels and need to let off steam. But equally, they need to be able to concentrate when in a learning environment. It seems only sensible to indicate where each activity is appropriate.

- **Indoors and out:** Here, the traditional approach has a clear division between the classroom (for learning) and outdoors (for play). The other camp sees no need to distinguish the two, because children spend their time both playing and learning, wherever they are.

  Once again, the extremes both seem to operate from ignorance of the way children actually grow and develop. Classrooms can be the home of creative play, and outdoors is a good place in which to learn. Children appreciate clarity about which activity fits where.

Debating the purpose of education

At the heart of the dispute about educational methods are deeply held convictions about the wider social and political purpose of education. It appears that the real interests of children soon get lost in the heat of debate. Fortunately, children are born survivors and very resilient. Generations of children have survived and thrived through poor, sometimes appalling, schooling. The debate is unlikely to be resolved, and it's unfortunate that many educational experts place their own agendas ahead of children's needs.

Balancing rigid and relaxed teaching

Provided they're in a safe and secure environment, children can usually cope with anything thrown at them educationally. If they're in a conventional classroom, children adapt quickly to the norms of the situation. Equally, if they're given the run of the room, they act accordingly.

Good teachers recognise the need for balance and keep their focus on positive learning environments with consistent guidelines. Given their internal resources, children generally thrive when given this balance between structure and freedom of expression. They're less able to cope when given too much of one and not enough of the other.

Applying Creative Thinking Lessons in Daily Life

One of the pleasures of creative thinking is that it's a topic without age limits. Anyone, at any age, can become more creative. Spending time with children is an excellent way to recharge your own creative batteries and also to see raw creative thinking in action. Just as you can benefit from the experience, you can also do much to assist children in their creative development.

Fostering creativity

If you have children in your life, regardless of their age, you can do a great deal to foster their creativity. You already have a head start, because children have many of the attributes of creative thinking in-built. Some of the essential elements for creative thinking that are also childhood attributes include the following:

- **Curiosity:** Children have the gift of a high level of natural curiosity for everything around them. They can't fail to be interested in what's happening, who's doing what, or why something is the way it is. This sense of wonder gradually diminishes over time, but it flourishes for several years, usually until adolescence.

- **Noticing:** Adults may have a somewhat jaundiced eye, but this isn't true of children. Even very young children spend a lot of time noticing things and events around them. Until about age five, they're vocal about their observations, asking a lot of questions. This questioning gradually diminishes, but the noticing continues.

- **Alertness:** One of the most noticeable features of children is their big, bright eyes. This characteristic is partly due to the fact that the eyes are already highly evolved at birth, and also because children are often literally wide-eyed, taking in what's around them. Approximately 80 per cent of children's experience in kindergarten and nursery school is estimated to be visual. Many adults have been surprised or even embarrassed at the amount children observe and guilelessly report back: 'I saw Mummy kissing Santa Claus.'

- **Expression:** Throughout childhood, a strong desire for self-expression through drawing, writing or play-acting exists, and the more it's encouraged, the richer the development. Speech becomes crucial to development from its beginning; by the time children are two or three, they often spend time talking to themselves when alone, especially as they fall asleep or first wake up. And of course physical expression is an integral part of children's lives.

✔ **Awareness:** Normally, children are in close touch with their senses, which makes them very aware of sights, sounds, smells, tastes and touch. Whereas adults tend to stay in one sensory mode for long periods, children switch in a heartbeat to whichever sense is stimulated.

✔ **Agility:** Children believe something until they believe something else. They have no difficulty changing perspective in the face of new information. Whereas adults often cling to fixed ideas despite new evidence, children find it easy to drop old notions when new, improved ones come along.

✔ **Being in the moment:** Children live predominantly in the here and now, so they have no difficulty focusing their full attention. They can concentrate equally on the movements of a ladybird or production of a drawing. Many adults find it difficult to emulate these levels of dedication to a task.

When you next perform a task that requires your full attention, notice how you approach it and what you're doing as you complete it. Be aware of your mood as you embark on the task, whether you can immediately switch on your focus, or whether you need time to ease into it. Does your mood change if you hit an obstacle? Can you stay focused or are you easily distracted? What are your feelings when you complete the task? Afterwards, reflect on whether you were able to sustain being in the moment.

Getting culture into the bloodstream

In creative terms, children can never overdose on culture. Children are not inhibited by notions of elitism and usually take what they're exposed to with equanimity. They can be equally at home with representational paintings or abstract expressionism, especially if a sympathetic adult is on hand to point out aspects that they may not have noticed. Having a focus on reality, children are likely to be more interested in the thickness of the paint and the fact that the artist had to mix his own paints than in when he lived or what movement he belonged to.

In the face of culture, many adults have a tendency to oversimplify or patronise for children. When their attention and imagination are captured, children can prove surprisingly receptive.

Children bring the same principles of non-judgemental curiosity to other art forms, such as music, and to science. Every Christmas, the Science Museum in London runs a series of televised lectures for children, none of which talk down to their audience. Children find these talks, often on highly complex subjects, enthralling.

Partnering with modern technology

Whether technology is good or bad is a question without a simple answer. Once the genie is out of the bottle, you can't put it back in, so the issue becomes how to live with it. Children have always been enthusiasts for technology, and many parents have stories about how their offspring are the ones to consult for any questions concerning the remote control and other devices.

Taking a brief look at some technological products enables you to see just how quick children are to adopt and adapt them for their own use:

- **Mobile phones:** When I suggested at a conference 15 years ago that mobile phones would become universally popular among young children, the notion was ridiculed. Ownership has proliferated across all age groups. Now schools have to examine their policies in relation to mobiles in the classroom. The addition of smartphones has only served to increase the attraction of mobile phones, and young people consider them essential tools for social networking. It's difficult to predict what the future will bring, except that it's a racing certainty that hand-held communication devices will be at the centre of children's lives.

- **Tablets:** Tablet computers were originally designed as handy portable gadgets for people on the move, but they've been adopted enthusiastically even by the youngest children. Some nursery schools, recognising the trend, are supplying their pupils with personal tablets as aids for learning and play. Seeing children as young as two or three playing with them isn't unusual.

- **Games:** The growth of the electronic games industry took many by surprise, and as games gained in sophistication, they became a central part of children's lives. Views on the contribution of games to childhood are mixed, with some experts arguing that they limit children's horizons by keeping them locked into activities for hours on end, while others take the view that they teach a wide variety of cognitive skills which are transferable to many situations.

✔ **Computers:** Computers, especially lightweight laptops, have become a universal accessory, with children treating them as an integral part of daily life. Even in the poorest countries, philanthropists are now putting basic computers in the hands of school-age children.

✔ **The Internet:** It's impossible to conceive of today's children without access to the Internet. Despite claims in some quarters that the Internet dilutes original study and promotes plagiarism, the evidence is that most children use the Internet responsibly, especially if they have supportive parents.

✔ **Social networks:** The growth of social networks has had a huge influence on the lives and relationships of children, and few would dream of living without continuous access to their friends through one or more of these. And children are ahead of the game, being among the first to popularise each new development. It's worth remembering that texting, originally designed for engineers, was first taken up by Finnish children, who spotted its potential as a social networking tool.

Given such pervasive technology, the only conclusion to draw is that it's here to stay and, in all its forms, is a significant part of children's core activities. And children, creative as ever, will always be at the forefront of each innovation.

Learning in all its forms is an integral part of children's creative thinking, and they never tire of the next new thing to discover.

Chapter 12

Working Creatively

. . . .

In This Chapter

▶ Pairing creativity and profitability

▶ Making money with creative ideas

▶ Protecting creativity

▶ Building-in creativity

▶ Realising that resistance is futile

▶ Making your workplace creative

▶ Differentiating between innovation and creativity

. . . .

*Y*ou may be interested in the topic of creative thinking and keen to introduce creative tools and techniques into your personal life, but can you take your creative thinking to work with you? What would your colleagues – and your boss – make of a culture of thinking creatively? And if you're the boss, is your business as creative as it can be?

Fortunately, one of the more encouraging trends of recent years has been the increasing acceptance of creativity in all its forms in the work environment. However, active resistance is still expressed in some quarters where creativity is regarded with suspicion as somehow incompatible with serious business.

Where creative thinking is still frowned on, the task – and it's a creative one – becomes one of overcoming negative beliefs.

Looking at Creative Industries and the Bottom Line

If you're reading about creative thinking, the chances are you're interested in the topic. But does it have a value? The answer is a resounding 'yes!' By any measure, the commercial value of creativity is substantial. Some of the most successful businesses and individuals are in the creative industries, which continue to thrive, even in times of uncertainty.

Understanding the value of creativity, and of the creative thinking that drives it, is a work in progress, and the trend is towards wider and deeper acceptance of the value of creative thinking throughout the commercial sphere.

No single definition of the creative industries exists, although most official sources define them as covering similar disciplines, including:

- Advertising and design (including branding and communication)
- Architecture
- Arts and antiques
- Crafts
- Fashion
- Film (including video and photography)
- Software and applications development
- Games and interactive entertainment
- Publishing (print and electronic)
- Music and the visual and performing arts
- Television and radio

The list continues to grow as many of the core businesses mutate and evolve, reflecting new technologies and new markets. A substantial part of the working population is employed in officially creative business. In addition, several specialists contributing to the core creative businesses include themselves in such a list.

Auditing creative business

The complexity and diversity of the creative industry makes it more difficult to gain an overall estimate of the economic scale of the industry as a whole. It's evident that some sectors are better at measuring their size than others.

Making modern music

The vast music industry once consisted of a few giant labels and a uniform vinyl product. It's now metamorphosed into an entirely different business model with myriad independent performers, composers and labels, and many formats and purchase options, making its profitability much more difficult to track.

Whereas recording music once required dedicated studios with giant mixing decks and acoustically perfect studios, it's now possible to emulate this setup with a laptop. Apple's GarageBand software, for instance, included on every MacBook, is even designed to simulate a full-size studio, with all the equipment necessary to make a studio-quality recording. Musicians and singers have recorded several major hits in makeshift home studios, and a thriving industry of independent composers and artists is now taking advantage of this flexibility.

Music can be marketed virally through social networks, outside the conventional retailing system. None of this would have been feasible a decade ago, and with such a rapid pace of change it's impossible to predict what the music business will look like in another decade.

For example, the global advertising industry is measured by the amount of advertising it buys, and has a current value of $600 billion. From this figure, it's then easy to calculate employee value and other components, because the industry uses recognised commission structures.

However, it's much more difficult to value those sectors that are fragmented by having many small independent operators who contribute at many different levels. *Feeders*, as they're called, assist the creative process by contributing specialist skills essential to the finished product. You can gain an idea of how complex and diverse modern film-making is just by looking at the extensive credits at the end of a *Harry Potter* film or any other production involving special effects and multiple locations.

Driving business through the creative engine

Even in those businesses that define themselves as creative, many have an inner core, or engine, that drives the rest of the business. Advertising agencies, for example, have a creative department that handles the creation and direction of the agency's output for its clients, while other departments such as account handling, planning and media deliver their specific functions. In other words, creatives are free to focus on what they're best at, while dedicated teams handle other aspects of the business.

The creative role is easy to identify in somewhere like an advertising agency, where the discipline is recognised, labelled clearly and valued. But it's not always obvious where the lines are drawn, and in some businesses the boundaries are blurred. This can give rise to problems when various parties want to chip in or claim credit for ideas produced within the group.

If you're in an office environment, examine the dynamics of your business and draw a mind map (I tell you how in Chapter 6) identifying the roles of the team and then identifying the individuals who make the greatest and least contribution creatively. Does their performance correspond to their job description?

Moving creativity from back room to front office

Some organisations are all about their creativity and are proud of the role of creativity in their success. LEGO is a classic example of how creativity can take a centre-stage role in a business environment. The company's headquarters in Billund, Denmark, is more like a university campus than a toy factory, and a major proportion of the space is devoted to research and development of LEGO products.

However, creativity in business isn't always celebrated. In some organisations, creativity still occupies a lowly place in the pecking order. The result is, not surprisingly, that such businesses often deliver second-rate creative output, generating a vicious circle.

In some organisations, creativity is definitely kept in the back room – or below stairs. In extreme cases, it's handled out of house. This situation is fine when it's done for the right reasons, and some superb thinking businesses do exist whose role is to extend the range and depth of a company's creative capabilities. It becomes a cause for concern, however, when creativity is farmed out because those at the top think it doesn't belong in the organisation.

Writing to order

Shabby treatment of the creative artist was brilliantly observed by F Scott Fitzgerald when, having been a lionised author in New York, he was invited to Hollywood as a writer. Instead of the star status he anticipated, he found that writers were on the bottom rung, working from dilapidated offices at the back of the studio lot, and expected to produce endless scripts and re-writes to order, on the whim of a director or executive.

Generating Ideas that Make Money

How do you quantify creativity? If you have a bright idea, how do you put a price on it? This question has vexed creators and inventors since time immemorial.

The first step for many is realising the value of the idea. Nowadays, venture capitalists evaluate ideas using a measure they describe as *disruption*, defined as the potential for a given idea to upset the existing order in a market. A concept like Amazon, for example, had huge disruptive potential because it changed the dynamics of the book market and rapidly extended its new model to other product fields. By the time traditional booksellers caught up with the implications, the upstart Amazon had already achieved market dominance.

Patents, trademarks, copyright and other forms of protection were all established to protect new inventions, but their effectiveness is being tested in a rapidly changing world where many products are quite abstract and exist by virtue of their brand and the software that created them. Also, the complexity of many modern products means that they're not the work of an individual inventor but an interdisciplinary team. In such circumstances, it can be difficult to disentangle who owns what.

Putting a premium on creativity

Once upon a time, brands were simply the labels that identified competing products, but gradually, far-sighted individuals began to see that names like Quaker, Levi's and Coca-Cola had a value in their own right. Then they realised that the value of their brands could exceed the value of the products they sold. The next step was to find ways to put specific values on what a brand may be worth.

Fast-forward to the 1980s, when Rank Hovis McDougall became the first organisation to use the *value* of its popular household food brands like Hovis bread in a defence against a hostile takeover. This event signalled the birth of the modern understanding of brands and brand value, and the rise of specialist agencies such as Interbrand, which are now indispensable advisors to major companies on all aspects of their brand activities.

Inventing invention with Edison

Thomas Edison was not only the smartest and most prolific inventor of his time but, according to many, his real genius was inventing a company that marketed invention. He established an invention laboratory where he engaged promising inventors like himself, including the young Nikola Tesla, and worked alongside them.

Edison's style of working was to move from one project to another continually, constantly re-stimulating himself and encouraging his team. His lab eventually evolved into GE, for many years one of America's most consistently creative businesses.

Other organisations such as 3M, Rubbermaid and Pond's apply a similar philosophy, being companies set up specifically to create and innovate.

Owning ideas that change the world

The many technology companies in Silicon Valley are experiencing the largest lawsuits in history as many of the major players – familiar household names and those that supply them – sue each other for patent infringements (even though they also continue to supply parts to each other).

Winning the right to own your ideas has never been easy, and in a world of less tangible products and algorithms, the complexities of this tangled web are making the legal profession very happy.

Protecting the Creative Franchise

In the twenty-first century, it's more important than ever to protect your ideas. One of the world's fastest-growing businesses in recent years is the social networking site Facebook. The story of its creation and subsequent success has already been turned into a major Hollywood film, *The Social Network*.

Mark Zuckerberg, Facebook's owner, has been the subject of not one but two major lawsuits from people he worked with while still a student at Harvard University developing an early version of Facebook. Both parties claimed that Facebook wasn't original and that they had made substantial contributions to its development.

The difficulty for Zuckerberg was that other primitive friendship sites existed in a number of universities at that time, usually based on the American yearbook. Zuckerberg's position was that he and he alone spotted the true potential of the market; he focused on the key point of differentiation that made Facebook stand out, and he wrote the crucial algorithms that made it work smoothly. And he provided the vision and commitment needed to make it successful. The cases have now been settled.

What this tale highlights is the problem inherent in many computer-age products: their content can't, unlike conventional products, be protected comprehensively, because the idea itself is the product.

Where there's a hit there's a writ

Creativity in all its forms is a fragile flower, and it's easily plucked. Wherever it appears, creativity is at risk of being poached, and plagiarism is a major issue in all the creative industries.

Especially vitriolic is the music industry, which spawned the memorable phrase: 'Where there's a hit there's a writ'. Many artists have been accused of plagiarising the material of others, and arguments can become quite heated, to say the least.

While some artists have been generous with their material, encouraging others to share their work, others have been fiercely protective of their creative output and have even fought over odd lines of melody or fragments of lyrics.

'My Sweet Lord' and the Chiffons' sweet writ

One of the most notorious disputes about the origin of a song was over George Harrison's massive hit 'My Sweet Lord'. A journalist for *Rolling Stone* magazine commented on its similarity to 'He's So Fine' by the Chiffons, and before long a writ was issued. The subsequent court case dragged on for several years.

The action concluded with Harrison being found guilty by virtue of 'subconscious plagiarism', but the case provoked intense debate about the extent to which any pop music can be described as truly original, and more than one artist pointed out that 'Everyone borrows from everyone all the time.'

During the case, the Chiffons recorded their own version of 'My Sweet Lord' (Harrison didn't sue them), and Harrison's ex-manager Allen Klein surreptitiously bought the rights to 'He's So Fine', which resulted in the judge substantially reducing Harrison's penalty (by the amount Klein had paid for the song).

At the end of the case, the judge confided to Harrison's lawyer that he really liked 'both songs'. Harrison's lawyer snapped, 'But you've just ruled it's *one* song!' The judge meekly said he meant he liked both versions, but this episode underlined the difficulty of creative attribution, especially in a field like music.

Engaging in the eternal battle between artist and producer

Why did Prince decide to become The Artist Formerly Known as Prince and paint a symbol and the word 'slave' on his face? What made George Michael so mad he left the record label that had made him famous, muttering unrepeatable obscenities about his one-time mentor? These are just two of the world-class stars who've found it impossible to work with management in recent times. This battle has deep roots.

In the period before recorded music existed, songs were owned by the publishers of song sheets. This was because the music was sold sheet by sheet, much like books. Singers would perform the latest songs at the music hall, and audiences would buy copies so they could learn the words and music. At that time, most homes and public halls had pianos. A variation on this theme was the pianola, which played music imprinted on a revolving drum, so performers could act out an early form of karaoke. Again, this music was sold by publishers.

The first major shift came with primitive forms of recording, first on cylinders, then on vinyl discs. Manufacturers realised that they owned the middle ground between song-writers and the buying public. This led to the establishment of giant record labels which owned the songs, the artists, and the means of production and distribution.

Recorded music allowed the public to hear the voices of performers, and the managers of those performers quickly grasped the opportunity to market their valued artistes. Enrico Caruso, the Italian opera tenor, had a worldwide audience. However Caruso was an exception, and most singers were merely jobbing vocalists providing voices for the songs.

Songwriting to order

The Brill Building in New York was a music factory in which young writers like Neil Sedaka, Gerry Goffin and Carole King churned out many songs each month, to a production deadline – not the most conducive environment for creative thinking.

Nevertheless this treadmill produced many great hits. One day, a bored Neil Sedaka was mindlessly playing a single note on his piano. A frustrated colleague challenged him to write a song with an intro consisting of the same note 12 times in a row. The result was 'Calendar Girl', which shows how creative thinking can flourish even in the most unlikely circumstances.

In the era leading up to the musical explosion of the 1960s, the dynamics began to change yet again, and managers made their artists stars, shifting the balance of power in their favour and away from the once all-powerful labels. This inevitably led to the kinds of tensions seen today as artists struggle to break out of the manager–label straitjacket and regain their independence.

Instilling Creativity in Companies Large and Small

Large corporations often experience problems if they try to instil a culture of creativity where one doesn't already exist. If creative thinking is already valued as a concept, it's easier to create the conditions in which it can be cultivated. But if creativity is being introduced from a standing start, it's much more difficult. Historically, this seems especially true in organisations driven by engineering.

Doing business as usual

It's common to encounter the attitude, 'This is how we do things around here.' Fortunately, this kind of management myopia is diminishing as many companies realise they have to adapt and drop old practices that no longer serve them. However, some businesses continue to adhere to the old ways as though they had some intrinsic virtue.

For many years the automotive industry exemplified this short-sighted attitude, and it was difficult if not impossible to get new thinking past entrenched engineers.

Drawing creativity from the outside in and inside out

Some businesses come to accept – sometimes reluctantly – that they can no longer live without creativity, so they decide they need to get some, and fast. Unfortunately, this is easier said than done. It's a bit like deciding that in order to compete in a marathon, you'd better change the sedentary habits of a lifetime overnight.

Celebrating Saab's cup holder

A perfect illustration of the consequences of myopic thinking is provided by the now-defunct car-maker Saab. Developing a new range of cars, and with an eye on the huge American market, Saab found its ambitious and time-critical venture diverted by a massively expensive and prolonged sideshow. And it was all about a cup holder.

Traditionally, Saabs weren't equipped with cup holders. Even when cup holders became an almost universal accessory in popular rival models, Saab's engineers continued to resist on the grounds that a *proper* Saab driver (note the emphasis) wouldn't want or need such a frivolity, because it would detract from the driving experience. This led to fierce arguments in the boardroom between the inflexible engineers and the pragmatic marketing department.

Then, when the engineers reluctantly bowed to the inevitable and conceded that their masterpiece could have this abomination, they decided that it couldn't be just any cup holder, but a Saab cup holder that would encapsulate Saab's ingenuity. This meant many more months of expensive research and development creating a world-beating cup holder instead of just using one from an existing source.

And all this while the company was fighting a battle for survival through continuing investment from its increasingly reluctant owner, GM.

Saab owners confirm it's a very nice cup holder, as cup holders go.

Bolting on creativity from the outside in is always the most difficult operation – rather like implanting an appendix.

Almost without exception, the best creative businesses are those that start by making creativity intrinsic to how the business operates. Many of these, like good gardeners do, spend their time nurturing the buds and growing their creative skills and resources.

Central to many genuinely creative ventures is the principle of creating a safe space for creative thinking. Such creative companies grant permission to make mistakes, allow time for exploration, and give new thinking a fair hearing.

Overcoming Resistance to Creativity

Creative thinking isn't necessarily about producing new stuff. In the commercial world it can be about being smarter, anticipating trends and noticing what's actually happening – continuously. It's also about being open-minded and willing to examine all the options, including unpalatable ones.

Some businesses seem to have an actual aversion to creativity in all its forms. These are the organisations that take a strict line on risk management as a means of keeping everything under control. If something can't be measured, it can't be trusted. By this logic, creative thinking is dangerous – don't go there! Many businesses have been destroyed by wilful ignorance and a refusal to adapt in the face of reality.

Living by logic – or not

Many organisations focus their energies on what they believe to be logical thinking. For them, the world consists of straight lines. This is the world of charts, graphs and matrices. Unfortunately no straight lines exist in nature, so the logical approach falls foul of reality sooner or later.

One of the dangers of straight-line thinking is that it leads to linear planning. Linear planning is built on the assumption that life will conform to the charts, graphs and matrices set out in business plans, so it will be possible to predict three, five or even ten years ahead. Linear planning isn't designed to allow for the unexpected, and many businesses have fallen foul of the changes and fluctuations of real life.

As an example of linear thinking, anyone who's suffered death by PowerPoint knows that the presenter is usually convinced that the message is sacrosanct because the slides prove the argument. Even in the face of hard evidence to the contrary, the presenter maintains this position.

Being the last best

Management specialists have noted that when a market is in transition, the phenomenon of 'the last buggy whip maker' often comes into play. This is the apparently paradoxical situation whereby the last company in a declining market is the best. This is because even while the world is changing – as in the case of mechanised vehicles replacing horse-drawn transport – traditionalists often gravitate to the last surviving exponent in a given field.

So the last buggy whip maker gets the last loyalists and continues beyond the point of survival, perhaps in the mistaken belief that a market will always exist for its product because its customers are enthusiasts who say so. If the company does survive, it's often as a specialist serving a tiny group of ageing connoisseurs.

Knowing when the end is nigh

In the 1950s, in the light of the considerable paranoia felt in the USA concerning the threat of the atom bomb, several religious cults decided it was the signal for Armageddon – the catastrophe that would end the world. Being privy to this precious information (and pre-selected for immortality), they knew the date and so made their preparations.

At that time, a number of social psychologists thought it might be a good idea to infiltrate one of these groups, wait for the end of time and get a good academic paper out of it (should they survive, of course).

The moment duly came and went, and no one was struck down. The psychologists present were interested in how the cult, and in particular its leader, would handle this unexpected turn of events. When zero hour passed, the leader retired to her room then emerged several hours later with the glad news that being given this date had been a test of their faith, like God in the Old Testament asking Isaac to sacrifice his son, and that they should await further instructions.

This news was reassuring, and no one demurred, but we don't know how many disciples are still in waiting mode.

For another – historical – example of linear thinking, consider communism in Russia and its satellite countries, which provides the most convincing and large-scale demonstration of the absurdity underlying blind obedience to the power of the straight line. Stalin's notorious five-year plans led to failure on a grand scale. For example, massive tractor factories, grain silos and food-production facilities were built on five-year grain harvest forecasts that proved wildly inaccurate from the outset. The tragic result was widespread famine, but because of Stalin's notorious obstinacy, the precious plan could not be adjusted let alone abandoned.

Riding your obsessions into oblivion

One of the by-products of inflexible thinking is the cultivation of obsessions. An obsession may be a preoccupation with past glories instead of present realities. It can also mean that the personal gremlins of those at the top table can overrule common sense.

Conversing with a board of directors in denial who have a shared belief that doesn't correspond to reality can be a salutary experience. One global corporation, for example, was convinced that its fortunes were inextricably linked to a competitor who'd consistently out-manoeuvred it. The directors ignored the fact that in reality the threat emanated from *all* of their competitors, and their real problems were lacklustre product development and a decline in product quality.

Over the years, many otherwise excellent organisations have fallen foul of straight-line thinking, which has taken them into bizarre territory:

- **Cadbury:** Having come to dominate the confectionery market and gained an enviable reputation as Britain's favourite chocolate maker, where should Cadbury go next? An obvious answer may have been to consolidate this hard-won status in the hearts of the nation with a foray into other loved foods.

  But Cadbury's ambitions went much further. In a frantic acquisition spree, it bought businesses in many territories unrelated to sweets – the strangest of which was the purchase of a chain of hotels. Needless to say, management had no experience of any of these new fields, least of all the leisure industry. It wasn't long before Cadbury reversed this spending bender for fear of impending bankruptcy. The hotels were quietly sold and Cadbury refocused on its core business.

- **Heinz:** Beanz meanz Heinz, and Heinz meanz kidz, or so senior management thought when Heinz decided for a brief period that it could become a major international toy maker, like Mattel or Fisher-Price. This curious logic extended into a badly designed voucher scheme to provide the UK's children with sports equipment. The news media had a field day when they discovered anomalies in the scheme that meant individual schools would have to collect vouchers for months to get one football. Amidst this furore, the toy project was quietly dropped.

- **Black & Decker:** Synonymous with DIY, Black & Decker was confident its name could be applied to any aspect of domestic improvement. This was the logic behind the decision to invest in an extensive range of craft activities, the most amusing of which was a felt-gun that allowed hobbyists to cover all their possessions in fuzzy felt. Needless to say, the world didn't beat a path to Black & Decker's door.

Each of these hare-brained ventures was based on the application of straight-line thinking: 'We are successful in this business, so we will be successful in that one.'

If you can, picture the hapless Cadbury executive pitching to the board: 'People like chocolate; chocolate is on the pillows at hotels; therefore we should buy hotels.' Or the Heinz executive: 'Our focus groups show that kids love our beans and they love toys, therefore . . .' Or, and this one is *really* difficult: 'Black & Decker is covering the world with DIY; now we intend to cover it with our felt.' Absurd maybe, but at the time, senior, experienced decision-makers controlling large budgets authorised each of these projects.

The application of more rounded creative thinking, considering the whole picture, should have killed those schemes at an early stage.

Planning in a straight line

For many years, management thinking was predicated on what would now be called straight-line thinking, and MBA study courses focused on rigid, logical, analytic models of the way organisations should work. If you follow this plan, the model predicted, you'll have a successful business. Countless students went through this process and tried to apply the lessons to their own activities. This was the orthodox way to conduct business.

Many of the components of this management model were based on military metaphors and relied on descriptions of motivating the troops, beating the enemy, and winning the victory. Unfortunately, in a much more fluid world, these epithets seem increasingly anachronistic.

The first cracks started to appear in the last quarter of the twentieth century, when many so-called failsafe businesses began to decline and even fail and a new generation of post-war management experts began to emerge. They questioned many of the basic assumptions, introduced models which factored in the uncertainty of changing circumstances and challenged the orthodoxies. Business gurus like Tom Peters and Peter Senge saw new kinds of businesses and methods rising to address unprecedented changes in economic, technological and consumer conditions. Systems thinking (described in Senge's series of books, *The Fifth Discipline*), for example, uses flexible practices rooted in fluid feedback loops in its models to allow for unexpected events. No straight lines there. Organisations that had seemed unassailable suddenly appeared vulnerable to these new kids on the block.

Another major factor in this new generation of thinking is a strong focus on the individual people (both employees and customers) as opposed to rigid business models. Tom Peters, one of the authors of the influential book *In Search of Excellence*, has become an enthusiastic advocate of putting people first in any business model. And a major factor in this is his emphasis on creative thinking as a tool for success.

Resisting vision

Despite overwhelming evidence to the contrary, some organisations remain in denial and claim, like George HW Bush, that 'We don't do the vision thing.' As vision and creativity are inextricably linked, not doing the vision thing puts a person or a business at a distinct disadvantage. Vision is, after all, a dream that may become reality.

Margaret Mead, an anthropologist, observed that every idea that changed the world began with one individual's dream.

The old adage 'If you fail to plan, you plan to fail' is especially true in relation to delivering against a clear vision backed with a purposeful mission and the commitment to follow it through.

Creating (and Maintaining) a Creative Workplace

The first rule about any creative space is that it must be yours – you must feel at home there. This is true whether the space is yours individually or you work as part of a team (if it's a team worth being in, they'll understand and accept your need for self-expression).

Choosing a space

Assuming you have a choice, why do you work where you do? Is it beautiful? Is it energising? Is it intellectually and spiritually stimulating?

It's always surprising to see the working environments of those in the creative professions. Often, very creative people tolerate conditions that resemble the worst kind of student bed-sit. This seems especially true of design studios, although exceptions do exist. Often, when the scruffiness of their surroundings is pointed out to them, people realise they've become inured to this state of affairs and are blind to it. (One business owner adopted a policy of direct action and threw out every unwashed mug and plate in protest, which proved an effective wake-up call for the people who worked there.)

One of the best examples of a creative workplace was the atelier, instances of which first appeared in the Middle Ages. The *atelier* was a large studio for a master artist and his apprentices, which was kept quite clean and tidy so that the environment didn't interfere with the work in hand.

This principle is also to be found in the homes of many creatives, where a balance is struck between the needs of day-to-day living and a setting conducive to inspiration. Creating such a workspace is well worth the effort.

Where not to live

Peter York, the social commentator, has written a delightfully anarchic book on the homes of dictators. It works as both satire and psychological insight.

Unlike the lairs of James Bond's villains – where evil was able to flourish amid Cézannes, stables of thoroughbred Arab horses and all the latest gadgetry – many of dictators' homes seem expensive but hollow, utterly lacking the creative spark of humanity. Hitler's mountain retreat, it transpires, was full of rather twee porcelain, silverware and chintz, not unlike the home of a suburban Edwardian grandmother. One reviewer of York's book invited readers to imagine Hitler plotting world domination in his wicker armchair underneath his aspidistra.

Saddam Hussein, like many of his contemporaries in the dictator community, apparently took his cues from the worst excesses of Las Vegas hotels, with vast rooms stocked with deep shag-pile carpets and over-sized, over-blown furniture, solid gold bathroom fittings and bland landscape paintings (the paintings that weren't of the man himself, that is).

The question, according to the TV programme *Through the Keyhole*, is, of course, 'Who would live in a house like this?'

Making a creative space

What should work look like? A convention still exists that work should look like work. Documentaries on the Industrial Revolution, showing images of vast factories with people working in long lines mass-producing every conceivable product, may seem chilling in the Western world, although such factories still exist in many parts of the globe.

The modern equivalent is the *open-plan office* with its blocks of shoulder-high cubicle walls, which has become the default mode of organisation for even moderately sized offices. But it doesn't have to be like that.

If you're serious about being creative, a good starting point is the place where you work or study. The best creative space for you is a place that reflects your unique personality. Start by reflecting on how you like to work creatively. Ask yourself:

- Do you prefer a conventional desk and chair, or are you a lounger?
- Do you like to hide in a confined space (like a cockpit), or do you prefer to spread out?
- Are you meticulous or messy?
- Do you like to create in silence, or are you a sound-lover?

There are no right or wrong, or good or bad answers here. You're only pleasing yourself. When you've decided how you like to work, fill in the rest of the picture by choosing the things that bring your workspace to life for you, things such as:

- ✔ The tools of your trade, such as paper and pens, and important technology
- ✔ Personal items that matter to you, such as mementoes and photos
- ✔ Stimulation in the form of whatever gives you inspiration – works of art, posters, and representations of heroes

Continue this process until you're happy with the result. And remember, when it comes to decoration, blue has proved to be the colour most conducive to creativity.

Expensive furnishings won't make you any more creative. The way to spend your money wisely is on personal items that you find stimulating. If, on the other hand, you have to make do and mend, that's no reason to compromise on your creative integrity. With a little imagination, you can transform even the humblest space into a haven conducive to creative thinking, with very little money. After all, you spend around a third of your waking week at work, so you may as well make the environment somewhere you want to be.

If you work with other people, engage the cooperation of your colleagues and the necessary permissions and try a new office or study arrangement for a month. First assess performance in current conditions and then compare output under the new arrangement. You may start a trend.

Living with the Difference between Innovation and Creativity

Being smarter about what you do is the defining characteristic of creative thinking. The vocabulary used to describe this concept isn't especially rich, and most discussions come back to familiar terms like *innovation* and *creativity*, especially in the context of business.

Defining the difference

If you're not on the front line of product development, the distinction between creativity and innovation may seem a bit arbitrary, with the two words being more or less interchangeable. And for once the *Oxford English*

Dictionary is not especially helpful, defining the verb *create* as 'To bring into existence', and *innovate* merely as 'To bring in something new' – definitions which are almost identical.

In practice, the debate concerning the distinction between creativity and innovation is intense, with both camps arguing strongly for their own stance.

In many businesses, *Innovation* (with the capital letter) has become a crucial mantra, generating action statements such as 'Innovate or die!' Advocates of innovation argue that it's the lifeblood of organisations, and without a constant flow the organisations will wither away. Many businesses build their organisations around the idea that they have to be continually smarter than the competition as well as delivering on their bright ideas.

Proponents of *Creativity* (again, with the capital letter) often have their roots in the classic creative industries and are protective of their role as keepers of the creative flame. (This was Charles Saatchi's personal job description by the way, as I explain in the upcoming section 'Making it happen at Saatchi & Saatchi'.)

For many, a real distinction exists between innovation and creativity. Perhaps the most acceptable definition to all parties is this: 'Creativity is what delivers innovation.' A business with a genuine investment in creativity at all levels of activity is likely to be capable of delivering consistent, high-quality innovation.

All of this concern with creativity and innovation, of course, is only meaningful if the business reflects its language in its behaviour. Creative departments where no one creates and innovation sections that never innovate still exist. In the final analysis, you know it when you see it.

Owning the creativity

If you want to know whether a business is committed to creativity, it's always good to ask 'Who *owns* the creativity?' This question isn't the same as discovering whether it has an innovation department or a creative director.

The issue here is about vision and the company's big picture. In some businesses, the creative force and the CEO are one and the same. This doesn't mean that the boss has all the best ideas, but that all the best ideas go through him.

In the best creative businesses, ownership of the creativity is in the fabric of the organisation, and the boss exemplifies those values.

Not waving but drowning

When Jacques Nasser was appointed to a new senior role in Ford, he immediately undertook a tour of the then-troubled European operation to root out the problems. Wherever he visited, he insisted on a thoroughly detailed and honest explanation of the problems.

At one site, after having endured endless self-serving presentations at other plants, Nasser was surprised to be taken to the company swimming pool, where the senior staff was assembled.

At a given signal, one of the team was nudged into the pool and began flailing his arms, crying 'I can't swim! I can't swim!' Nasser was horrified, but then the group yelled in chorus, 'He's drowning! Call McKinsey! Call McKinsey!'

A succinct demonstration of the disempowerment that management felt because all the main decisions were made outside the plant.

Making it happen at Saatchi & Saatchi

Many businesses attempt to incorporate creative thinking in their visions, but few have been as successful as Charles and Maurice Saatchi with their first advertising agency, Saatchi & Saatchi.

This section summarises the strategy created and applied by the Saatchi brothers to achieve the unprecedented growth of Saatchi & Saatchi from a two-man band (literally) to the pre-eminent force in the advertising industry in under a decade. This model is robust and has been proven to work not only for the Saatchis but also for other ambitious entrepreneurs. I believe it's one of the industry's best-kept secrets. Not all the lessons apply directly to every creative business, but all the principles repay close study.

Declare your manifesto and nail your colours to the mast

When they launched the agency, the Saatchi brothers took a full-page ad in *The Times* that laid out their manifesto, declaring themselves as a revolutionary force in a complacent industry. It declared their intention to bring a new vitality and sense of purpose on behalf of clients. This philosophy – essentially, 'Buy us, buy our values' – formed the core of all their (hugely successful) business pitches. It remains a very powerful message.

State your message clearly

The Times ad contained a key word, new to most readers. This word was *salience* (meaning prominence, jutting out). It was a promise that all Saatchi & Saatchi advertising would be outstanding (literally!), working as hard as possible on the client's behalf.

Use of the word 'salience' was an early example of Maurice's passionate belief in the power of language and the one-word brand. Essentially, his premise was that if you own the key word(s) in a market, then you own the market. Current examples are Google (it owns 'search') and Amazon (owner of 'sales online'). Being identified by key words is an argument for differentiation and keeping competitors out of your territory. Anyone trying to use Google's or Amazon's vocabulary is bound to come off second best.

By extension, salience is an argument for creating a unique language, as the Saatchis did. If you read Saatchi literature, you see very clear, simple text (in a pleasant, discreet font, by the way) with no hyperbole or florid language. It exudes quiet confidence and professionalism – and makes the competition look clumsy, brash and insincere. No wonder Maurice put such a premium on language – he knew how to use it.

Be your own best client

Looking at many businesses, the adage about the cobbler's children having no shoes comes to mind. In the communications industry, finding agencies that don't seem to know the first principles about marketing themselves is common. From the outset, the Saatchi brothers took a different tack. They explicitly decided to make Saatchi & Saatchi their own number one client, and all their efforts were directed towards the promulgation of the Saatchi brand. Doing so was Charles's domain.

The Saatchis single-mindedly pursued a strategy of raising their brand profile wherever they interfaced with existing or potential clients. Their relationship with the trade press is the stuff of legend. It was this relationship that allowed them on pitch lists for which they were totally unqualified at the time, many of which they won. (Maurice always believed that resources followed a win – mostly he was right.)

At any one time, only around a fifth of the Saatchis work was with the clients and campaigns that made them famous. The remainder was grunt work, which remained firmly unpublicised and provided the training ground for their in-house talent.

Be a faithful keeper of the creative flame

Charles Saatchi was notorious for never meeting clients. He assiduously cultivated an air of mystery, and few outsiders got to know him well. He still doesn't turn up to his own parties.

So what exactly was Charles Saatchi's contribution? Essentially, he had one of the best eyes in the industry. When he gradually reduced his role as an instigator, he still maintained a firm grip on every piece of work that left the agency. Famously, he was responsible for inserting the word 'favourite' instead of 'best' into the ground-breaking British Airways 'The World's Favourite Airline' campaign, and the stories about his creative interventions are legion.

In private, Charles Saatchi has a wicked sense of humour. Once, when asked about his role, he quipped: 'keeper of the creative flame'. Pompous from anyone but Charles Saatchi.

Pursue the prizes worth pursuing: clients, people, awards

The same single-mindedness applied to the notion of the advertising industry prizes. Unlike many of their competitors, who were grateful for any kind of gold star going, the Saatchis relentlessly sought only three very specific kinds of prize:

- ✔ **Clients:** They'd buy an agency just to capture one key client, which they did to obtain Tesco.

- ✔ **People:** They paid top dollar to poach key personnel, sometimes buying an agency to acquire a single key player, as they did to secure the creative guru Jeremy Seymour.

- ✔ **Awards:** Here, they were only interested in the industry's most prestigious awards. They'd create campaigns solely with an eye on the D&AD Award (the advertising industry's highest accolade), and they had no interest whatsoever in coming second.

Do what you do best

Coming as they did from a middle-Eastern merchant family, they placed great stock in the wise sayings of their father and his father before him. One of these was 'stick to the knitting', a call to stay focused, which they obeyed for many years. It was only when they drifted away from this precept that their model began to unravel.

Use innovative techniques to run the business

The brothers introduced many innovations to the running of the business:

- ✔ **Teams:** Whereas most traditional agencies tended to have departments, they introduced a team-based system that became deeply focused on the clients. ('Know the client better than he knows himself' was one of their mantras.)

- ✔ **Pairs:** Throughout the agency, everything was controlled by pairs: two managing directors, two account directors, two creatives, two planners, and so on. This approach ensured good chemistry with clients, a safety net because each watched the other's back, and constructive rivalry (which led to some interesting power struggles).

✔ **The pitch:** The main focus of the agency (despite the public manifesto) was the pitch. All the best resources were devoted to locating and delivering on the best pitches in town. Saatchi & Saatchi treated incumbents well, but treated hot prospects better.

The Saatchis created the new business model that has now become the industry standard. Previously, pitching had been somewhat random, even ramshackle (you win some, you lose some). The brothers thought this a most unsatisfactory way of doing business and initiated a systematic approach to identify, target and pursue key accounts until they won them.

✔ **Planning:** The planning function was an innovation in the advertising business, enthusiastically adopted and promoted by the brothers. It provided the agency with an intelligence resource, enabling it to improve the quality and depth of knowledge, not just about particular advertising campaigns but also about clients and their businesses, thereby increasing the indispensability of the agency.

Integrate everything in a matrix

This approach proved to be both the key to the brothers' rapid growth – and ultimately their failure. In order to control and direct the growth of the agency's empire, Maurice devised a matrix based on key business sectors and a hierarchy of players within each sector (including agencies, key clients and key personnel), along with an evolving global strategy. As the Saatchi brother focused on assimilating core businesses – advertising, marketing, PR, research, and the like – they ticked off the boxes and everything proceeded like clockwork for several years.

However, as the approach moved to more peripheral activities, represented by Hayes (management consultancy and personnel), things began to unravel. The USA (in the form of the Siegel & Gale acquisition) proved a bridge too far, and the final blow was a misconceived attempt to buy a bank (the Midland, as it then was). The Saatchis' father's advice proved prophetic: 'Stick to the knitting.'

Chapter 13

Embedding Creativity in Your Personal Life

*M*aking creativity and creative thinking part of your life can be very rewarding. Doing so doesn't necessarily mean you have to wear a beret and smock and go around painting everything you observe. Looking at the world through your hands like a film director framing a shot isn't necessary either – although you can if you want to.

Among the many benefits of living a creative life is having a richer view of the world and its possibilities. As your ability to think and view the world creatively grows, noticing the abundance of creative experience around you becomes second nature.

Integrating creativity into your daily life should be part of your natural interest in the world. As an adult, becoming blasé about what's around you is all too easy. Contrast that with the child's-eye view, which is full of wonder and curiosity about how things work and why things are the way they are.

At an active level, your ability to develop your creative powers is rooted in curiosity and active looking. Your brain is designed to filter out most incoming information – and that makes sense, because otherwise you'd be overwhelmed. However, there's nothing to prevent you turning the volume up a bit and recalibrating your perception. You can do many things to become more conscious in your engagement with creativity. Like most skills, the more you practise, the more proficient you become.

Passively embedding creativity is about noticing it wherever you see it, notably in the little things in daily life. How many times have you said to yourself: 'That's clever!' when you come across an ingenious product that solves a problem for you? The emphasis here is on embedding your experience of creativity in everyday life in order to become more continuously creative in your output.

Becoming Continuously Creative

One simple way to encourage development of your creative thinking is to consciously make small changes in your everyday behaviour. Life is full of moments of decision. Shall I take a break? What shall I have to drink? What shall I choose as my new computer password? Shall I pick up some shopping on the way home? Each of those choice points represents a moment when you can decide to do something differently.

Every day, you encounter creative thinking challenges big and small. Sometimes it's obvious that the challenges are about creative thinking, because they're flagged up that way. In your work or studies, you encounter situations defined officially as projects or ones built into the fabric of the work routine. Sometimes, creative thinking challenges are more subtle, but the more you look, the more you're likely to find.

Next time you take a break, use it in a way you've never done before. If you'd normally make a drink, don't. If you'd usually catch up on your emails or read a magazine, don't. Instead, draw a caricature of a colleague, just for fun. Examine your work area and move three items to new locations, or practise writing with your non-preferred hand.

Sometimes, doing things differently results in a 'so what?' response. But at other times you may surprise yourself, and one of these simple actions may create a knock-on effect, either in your behaviour or in the way you think about something. Don't try to predict your response or reject a choice out of hand. Make the effort, and from time to time you'll discover an unexpected outcome.

Changing the habits of a lifetime – or a minute

Because your brain is wired for patterns and programs, you live with many habits, both good and bad. Habits can be established quickly, and once in place they repeat every time they're triggered.

You notice habits at work if you change something. For example, if you store something in a different place, how many times do you find yourself going to the old location to retrieve it?

Habits serve a useful purpose, because without them you'd spend a disproportionate amount of time doing everything afresh. It takes only moments to embed a new pattern or habit. But breaking and changing habits takes a little longer.

Establishing habits quickly and easily

How do you develop a new habit? Extensive research into this aspect of behaviour demonstrates how quickly and unconsciously people acquire new habits of thought, and just how difficult these habits can be to change once installed.

One of the issues for people with memory problems is that many habit-based activities cease to operate, and the world becomes very bewildering. On a day-to-day level, you can get a glimpse of how frustrating this must be: 'Can't find my keys! But I *always* put them in the bowl by the door!'

One simple but effective example of how quickly new habits are formed is given by the Wisconsin card-sorting test:

1. **Take an ordinary pack of playing cards then shuffle it.**

2. **Deal the cards one by one, face up, into two piles – red and black. As you do, time yourself with a stopwatch.**

   This task is a simple one, so you're likely to accomplish it quickly and accurately.

3. **Shuffle the whole pack again and this time sort the cards into picture and number cards.**

   This task takes a noticeably longer time than when you sorted the cards into red and black.

The point of this test isn't primarily to compare your times, but to notice the pattern of your mistakes. In step 3, you're likely to assign some cards to the wrong pile at first, putting the same-colour cards in the same pile instead of sorting by type of card. You're also likely to become frustrated: 'Why did I do *that*?' But the errors don't stop.

Sorting the cards the first time establishes a pattern or habit, and the brain forms the association: red on red, black on black. When a new rule is introduced, the brain's programmed response is to apply the first rule. However, you don't realise at a conscious level how your brain is working, and are bewildered by getting such an apparently simple task wrong.

To test this, you can try the Wisconsin card-sorting test with several people and reverse the card groupings with each new volunteer. It doesn't matter whether you start with red/black or picture/number, the result is the same. And the test works with other similar choices: for example, if you have square and disc-shaped counters in two colours, you'll get the same result.

So, proof exists that habits can be instilled in the blink of an eye.

Current neurological thinking is that memories are stored in neural pathways. It seems that when you change a memory, you literally change the pathway.

Breaking habits 21 times

Although you can create a new habit in a matter of moments, it usually takes a little longer to change or break an old habit and replace it with a new one.

The rule of thumb in changing a habit is 21: experts commonly agree that it takes about 21 repetitions to instil a fresh habit in place of an old one.

The high number is due to the powerful resistance to set-shifting that almost everyone experiences, even in simple actions like sorting playing cards (see the preceding section).

So it's best not to assume that you can change a habit instantly, but instead to give it time and a little work. Performing 21 repetitions may sound a bit daunting, but if you think of it as seven lots of three, or three lots of seven, it becomes less of a mountain.

Perseverance versus perseveration

While perseverance is generally recommended as a method for diligently attacking problems, *perseveration* is the word for when you find yourself continuing a behaviour that's become outmoded.

For example, if you put something in a new location, such as when you find a new home for that item in your kitchen, notice how often you automatically look for the item in the old location. This is likely to happen even when it was your decision to move the item in the first place. This behaviour is another illustration of the strength of the brain's programs.

Appreciating Creativity and Culture

If you choose to make creative thinking part of your life, looking out for examples of creativity around you makes sense. While that may sound obvious, it's not something people tend to do naturally. Much of the time, the daily business of living occupies your full attention to the exclusion of everything else.

Culture, by definition, is the result of creative activity, so it's an excellent place to start looking if you want to embed creativity in your everyday life.

Culture should be what you enjoy. Just as some people live with the mistaken belief that they're not creative, many have the view that they don't have access to culture because they're not, as the characters in the film *Wayne's World* would say, worthy.

Hearing the term *elitist* associated with culture isn't uncommon, but nothing is further from the truth. True, some forms of culture only appeal to a small number of people, and some are expensive to experience. But limited appeal and high cost don't make them intrinsically elitist. While relatively few people actually go to the ballet or opera, both those art forms have huge appeal and have become universally popular. Think, for example, of the aria 'Nessun dorma' or the iconic images of *Swan Lake*.

Considering culture as a spectrum that you can select from according to mood makes sense. Creatively, great value exists in mixing experiences and enjoying the best from a wide variety of sources. Nothing prevents you from taking pleasure in manga and *Marvel* comics, reading both classic literature and crime fiction, or listening to traditional jazz and Toots and the Maytals as the mood takes you. You can play shoot 'em up video games and chess to sharpen your combat skills and strategic thinking. All these activities represent valid cultural experiences that can stretch your intellect and enhance the creative quality of your thinking.

The best way to develop a genuine interest in culture is to engage in it. Doing so doesn't mean you have to force yourself to tour endless art galleries, dig out your lorgnettes for the opera, or endure an evening of obscure modern dance. Culture begins with what turns you on.

Miners, fishermen, and other artists

As proof that culture isn't exclusively the province of an elite, it's interesting to note how often art of a very high standard flourishes in even the most adverse environments.

The 'pitmen painters', recently made famous through a National Theatre play about their work, were Northumberland miners who formed an art appreciation society in the 1930s and then took up painting. Despite never having painted before, they produced some exceptional work.

In a similar vein, when some English artists began to settle in St Ives, Cornwall, they were astonished to discover a thriving painting tradition among local fishermen, exemplified by Alfred Wallis, whose work became internationally celebrated. At the time, Wallis's style of painting was described as 'primitive', because it was untutored. But there's nothing primitive about the evocative images Wallis created.

Around the world, you can find numerous examples of artisans expressing themselves artistically through whatever media are available.

If you haven't yet allowed yourself to explore the riches that culture has to offer, here are two quick ways to kick-start your interest:

- ✔ The first is within yourself. You're creative, regardless of what you think and what others may have told you. Almost certainly some aesthetic experience has grabbed your attention or piqued your interest, even if only peripherally. That's a good place to start.

- ✔ The second is among your friends, family and colleagues. They can open doors to aspects of culture you may not have considered. If someone close to you acquires a painting, sculpture or new music that you weren't previously familiar with, take time to listen to the person's reasons for choosing it.

Try not to pre-judge a new cultural or artistic experience, and don't start from the position that you don't understand it. Instead, adopt an open attitude. Be curious about what attracted your friend to the form (after all, something did!). Give respect to the artist who created it. The finished product is a personal expression that the artist almost certainly gave a great deal of time and attention to. Above all, give it time. Most people can recall a song or product they disliked on first exposure and then later came to enjoy. The Mercedes bug-eye headlight design was panned when first launched, yet it now seems perfectly acceptable – as the designers predicted.

Asking what culture is

The *Oxford English Dictionary* defines *culture* as 'the arts and other manifestations of human intellectual achievement regarded collectively'. So culture is about achievement, and most people probably agree that they recognise high achievement when they see it. On a personal level, culture is something that catches your aesthetic eye. No arbitrary limits apply to what you can or should like, and it's best not to take notice of snobs who pick their culture from an approved list.

Setting your own cultural standards is constrained only by the limits of your curiosity. You choose your own cultural mix, and there's no referee to tell you what's acceptable and what's not.

Television and the Internet have opened a new world of culture in areas previously available to only a privileged few. In recent years, numerous experts and commentators have made it possible for everyone to access the best of the arts, and at the same time traditional boundaries have been eroded. You can enjoy Botticelli and Banksy side by side; you can switch between Hollywood and Bollywood; and you can experience Lady Gaga and La Scala at the flick of a switch. All these options provide a vast resource for creative thinking.

Pushing the culture button

The Internet makes it easy to explore every aspect of culture, from high to low brow and everywhere in between. Before the Internet, finding answers to questions about culture took some effort, which undoubtedly deterred some people. Now, however, the answer to even the most abstruse questions is a few key-strokes away. How many sonnets did Shakespeare write? What's a sonnet anyway? How many albums did Sid Vicious play on? And who else apart from him and Frank Sinatra recorded 'My Way'?

In terms of creative thinking, this kind of random walk through the highways and byways of the Internet can prove a productive stimulus for the imagination. Serendipity is a useful tool for creative thinkers. (Check out the www.stumbleupon.com website. Ideal for creative thinkers, this website encourages random browsing.)

Breaking the barrier – official creativity

So what does official creativity look like? On one level, you can say that something is creative because it says it is. For example, when the Dadaist artist Marcel Duchamp hung a ceramic urinal on a gallery wall in 1917 and declared it art (he entitled it *Fountain* and signed it R Mutt), he began a lively debate that continues to this day.

Creative output can also be awarded official status because of the context in which it appears. For example, prestigious art galleries like the Tate Modern in London have featured everything from toboggans and electric fly traps to tents and unmade beds, all of which were designated as art because of the location exhibiting them. This is why many people have a problem with modern conceptual art as exemplified every year by the Turner Prize. Sometimes, art just doesn't look especially creative. Piles of bricks and light switches make easy targets for those who like to denigrate art that doesn't conform to convention.

However, if you want to embed creativity in your daily life, suspending judgement, at least for a while, and considering the possible merits of even work that you dislike is a good strategy. People booed and walked out at the first performance of Stravinsky's 'Rite of Spring', which is now acknowledged as a masterpiece. And Bob Dylan evoked a similar response when he first went electric.

Celebrating everyday life

A major factor in embedding creativity is noticing clever thinking. As some astute observers have pointed out: *everything* is designed. Someone, somewhere, designed everything you encounter every day. Whether it's a sophisticated iPad or a humble garden gnome, it began with a plan which became a blueprint that went through tooling and manufacturing to produce the finished product.

To enhance your experience of everyday life, spend a little time examining familiar objects you come into contact with, by using fresh eyes. Simple objects are best; you can choose a light bulb, a Lego brick, a ballpoint pen, or any other object that catches your eye. Here are some points to consider as you examine your chosen objects:

✔ Think about life before the objects existed.

✔ Consider how you use them.

✔ Examine what they're made of.

✔ If the objects have several components, consider what materials the components are made from and how they join together.

✔ Identify one single feature you like.

✔ Consider how you would improve the objects.

As an additional exercise, consider the ways in which some simple objects have multiple applications. For example, a simple lens can appear in many guises: in spectacles, as a magnifying glass, as part of a telescope or binoculars, in a microscope, and so on. Then invent a new application; with a lens, you could light a fire, for example. Now apply the process to the electric motor, for example, and consider the number and variety of applications it has been put to.

Discovering Transferable Skills and Resources

Several of the skills and resources you acquire as you develop your creative thinking abilities are ones that you can apply in a wide range of situations. As you practise these skills, you discover that many of your old barriers to creative thinking begin to melt away.

Trying self-remembering

A resource that works well in a creative context and also has applications in many areas of daily life is self-remembering. Essentially, *self-remembering* is the art of noticing both yourself and your behaviour at any given moment. An important aspect of the consciousness-raising that's so conducive to thinking creatively, self-remembering is related to the practice of *mindfulness*, which is being present and aware in the moment. (This practice is explored in detail in the book *Mindfulness For Dummies* by Shamash Alidina (Wiley).)

Self-remembering is an exercise you can teach yourself to perform at any time. However, despite being easy to describe, it can be extremely difficult to execute successfully. When you first use the process I describe here, you're almost certain to find yourself becoming frustrated as your mind and body obstinately continue in their long-established patterns. But do persist, because the results get better and better.

Begin your self-remembering session when you're calm and relaxed without any pressing tasks to distract you. Follow these steps:

1. **Sit in a natural position and posture and do nothing for a few moments.**

   You're likely to notice that this quickly becomes hard to do. You'll probably start experiencing *self-talk* almost immediately (this is the mind's habit of providing you with a running commentary on everything going on around you, whether you want it or not). Exercises for switching off self-talk exist, but right now just acknowledge it and let it run.

2. **Assess everything about the here and now.**

   What happens now is a bit like the beginning of a meditation exercise, except that you're not going to get progressively more relaxed. Don't close your eyes as you would when meditating; keep them open while you perform this exercise.

   • Notice your posture, starting with your head. Notice the angle – where it is in relation to your body. Remember not to move it, even if you discover that you're not especially comfortable in this posture.

   • Progress down to your shoulders. Where are they? At what angle?

   • Where are your arms and your hands? Keep in mind that your aim is only to notice, not to move. (You may well feel a strong temptation to adjust your posture, but resist it.)

   • Continue down your trunk then your pelvis and legs. How are you sitting?

   • Where are your feet? Remember: don't wiggle your toes. Just notice where they are.

   • Finally, what are you seeing and hearing? As before, don't adjust anything, just notice.

3. **Analyse your experience.**

For most people, this process is unexpectedly difficult, especially the first time. The desire to adjust your posture can be almost irresistible. It's also likely that you'll find it hard to maintain your concentration, even for a short time.

Even though your first attempt may not seem very successful, you'll probably notice a general rise in your awareness of yourself and your surroundings. Do persist: continuing with this process is worthwhile, because it's a first step to the experience of living in the moment.

You can conduct this exercise before you embark on a creative thinking challenge in which you may have to concentrate on idea generation or problem-solving. You can try it in a different scenario related to a favourite cultural activity, which could be a visit to a gallery or to see a film, listening to music, or anything that stimulates your intellect.

Reaching resourceful states

A process less challenging than achieving self-remembering but with many beneficial effects is what neuro-linguistic programming (NLP) practitioners call the *resourceful state*. When you embark on any task, you naturally concentrate on what you're doing. You can take this to a higher level by focusing on yourself before you focus on the task. You remind yourself of your skills and abilities and your capability of tackling any situation successfully. Putting yourself in this resourceful state not only makes you feel good about yourself but also prepares you for the work to come.

When you next face a creative thinking challenge, take a few moments to settle yourself comfortably. Prepare the materials you need in advance so you can go straight into the task after this process. Now close your eyes and affirm your resourcefulness by saying to yourself:

'I have all the resources I need to perform this task.'

'I am ready and prepared for this task.'

'I know the outcome will be successful.'

Repeat these affirmations as often as you want – you'll know when you've done enough. You can then begin your task confident of the outcome.

Make these core affirmations your own by putting them in language you're comfortable with.

Using Your Creative Awareness

You can monitor your level of consciousness by using the three As to assess your awareness:

✔ **Acuity:** Sharpened vision, much like the hawk's ability to see its tiny prey from a great height.

Acuity can be characterised as a state of alertness, and you can develop this by making a point of noticing everything in your vicinity. The more you cultivate this habit, the easier it gets.

✔ **Adaptability:** The willingness to be flexible in the face of new information.

When you were a child, adapting was easy because you encountered new information all the time. So, adaptability is really the re-learning of an old skill.

✔ **Agility:** The ability to react rapidly and adjust to changing situations.

Along with adaptability, agility is an essential resource for when circumstances change. Quick reactions can prevent the kind of problems that often come from dithering.

Taken together, these three As contribute to your evolutionary thinking. They help generate a climate in which you can enhance your creative thinking abilities. As always, practice makes perfect!

Getting serious

Are you serious? This is something of a loaded question in the context of creative thinking. On one level, you're serious about developing and applying your creative thinking skills, and that's as it should be. Acquiring any skill takes time, effort and dedication, after all, so you'd expect to take the development of creative thinking skills as seriously as you would any other learning process.

But taking creative thinking seriously and *being* serious are very different. More than most subjects, this is an area in which you can enjoy the experience of learning.

Joining creative networks online

Now that the Internet gives immediate access to an infinite amount of information, bringing creativity into your daily life is easier than ever. Official and unofficial sources can provide a variety of perspectives for considering subjects that fascinate you. Whereas exploring a given subject used to involve time and effort, material is now available at your fingertips. The Internet has produced a massive change in the way you can explore topics of interest. And although there may be some negatives (for example, concern that students now find it easier to plagiarise material), the advantages are considerable.

Where creative thinking is concerned, whatever your interests, it's not difficult to connect to a virtual community of similarly minded individuals. Not only can you share your preoccupations, you can also broaden your horizons through the connections you establish. If you have a new favourite recording artist, for example, it's now simple to discover who wrote the songs, who else has covered the tracks, which other musicians played on the track, who the artist likes and admires (and who those people like and admire), when she's appearing live, and so on. Only a few years ago, finding all this information would've consumed hours of time and involved a lot of effort.

In addition, you can develop and hone your skills at every level. So if, for example, you've become interested in sculpture, you can visit many sites where you can share your fondness for a particular artist with like-minded people. And you can cultivate your knowledge through sites that explain techniques and give insights into the individual artist, style and period.

Being in touch with creativity around the world

One of the most productive ways to stay in touch with creativity is to develop methods for easy access. A few years ago, you would have needed contact with other creative individuals, perhaps through a college or professionals working in a creative field. If you didn't have the advantage of knowing creative people, your options were quite limited. In this traditional model, students learned their subject from lecturers who introduced them to established exponents in their chosen speciality.

Now it's possible to be much more eclectic, and you can pick 'n' mix in any direction that takes your attention. The world has changed. The Internet has enabled such easy access to the best of thinking from around the world that it's worth exploring some of the major sources and how you can use them in relation to your own creative thinking processes.

The rapid rise of the Internet, and the dot.com boom that flourished for a short but intense period, enabled the launch of many smart concepts that couldn't have existed in the pre-Internet world. For a while, creating new kinds of business was possible without having a conventional financial plan. Google and Facebook are both examples of ventures launched without clear projections about how they could ever earn money, let alone with any idea of how they would become so successful in such a short period.

Getting to know TED

One of the finest examples of creative thinking in recent times is the creation of TED (the letters stand for technology, entertainment and design). Founded in 1984, *TED* is an annual event based on the mission of 'fostering the spread of great ideas'. At TED, a wide cross-section of speakers present their thinking in short time slots. Everyone has the same constraints, regardless of eminence: just 18 minutes allotted to present their ideas, with the minimum visual aids (so no death by PowerPoint).

TED began in Monterey, California, in the heart of Silicon Valley, so the emphasis was originally on topics of interest to an audience with a technological bent. However, as it's grown, TED has widened its brief to include all kinds of speakers, from scientists to artists, and from poets to past presidents of the USA. Notable contributors include: physicist Stephen Hawking (see Chapter 15); Microsoft founder Bill Gates (see Chapter 15); *Blink* author, Malcolm Gladwell (I talk more about Gladwell's work in Chapters 3 and 16); and the founders of Google.

The TED concept has extended substantially over the years, and now includes TEDx, an international franchise that operates around the world to spread ideas in the TED ethos. A TEDWomen franchise also exists, and more recently TED Conversations – an interactive forum.

As it's grown, TED has expanded into publishing (short books designed to be read at a single sitting). It has ventured into the world of advertising, with specialist talks designed to raise standards in advertising. And TED has established fellowships, encouraging creative young people to share ideas that can change the world. The TED Prize is awarded annually for the development of ground-breaking or world-changing ideas. In 2010, for example, the internationally acclaimed chef Jamie Oliver won the prize for starting a movement to encourage people to cook and create healthy meals.

TED is an excellent example of applied creative thinking which has fostered the exchange of views and exposure to world-leading thinking, and which simply wouldn't have been possible without the Internet – certainly not on this scale.

If you're pursuing a line of thought – perhaps a creative problem you're wrestling with – TED can be a quick and effective way of exploring the issue, giving you opportunities to consider the perspectives of a variety of leading specialists.

Take a look at www.ted.com. Many of the TED talks are available on YouTube, as well, but beware – they're very addictive!

Getting inside your head

One example of the RSA's creative thinking applied intelligently is the film *The Divided Brain* (made by Andrew Park's Cognitive Media animation agency). The film features the very complicated subject of modern insights into how the human brain works, as explained by psychiatrist Iain McGilchrist, a leading expert on the subject. McGilchrist's book, *The Master and His Emissary*, on which this film is based, weighs in at more than 500 pages. Yet McGilchrist's highly articulate explanation supported by brilliant graphics makes this complex topic accessible to anyone in less than 12 minutes' viewing time.

Enlightenment from the RSA

Like many truly successful ideas, TED (see the preceding section) has encouraged others to create their own versions of the concept. One of the best examples originated at the Royal Society of Arts, or RSA (www.thersa.org), a UK charity dedicated to twenty-first century enlightenment. The RSA has taken up TED's baton with a superb series of animations on a variety of topics through its RSA Animate site (www.thersa.org/events/rsaanimate). This site uses a similar format to TED's – short films illustrating powerful ideas – but with the added twist of ingenious animation, which allows even the most complex concepts to be explained in ways anyone can grasp immediately.

RSA Animate is another fine example of bringing creative thinking into everyday life, and making the best creative thinking accessible to a wider public. Best of all, the animations are sharp and witty, which results in you absorbing the arguments almost without noticing.

You choose with YouTube

YouTube is another example of intelligent creative thinking emerging at the right time. Only a few years ago, YouTube's business model would probably have been strangled at birth. After all, what's the point of a site that lets anyone view clips on every subject under the sun – for free?

In the case of YouTube, the concept was probably helped by the fact that its founders migrated from PayPal, the online payment broker, and they apparently came up with the idea because they had difficulty sharing videos of a party some of them had attended. Even if this story is only partly factual (and it's disputed by one of the co-founders), it demonstrates that world-changing ideas can come from the most unexpected places.

Although much of its output is now in profitable fields like music and entertainment, YouTube still remains a primary means of free access to individuals sharing their ideas and views on their specialist topics. The work of both TED and the RSA is available on YouTube.

The YouTube format lends itself to open-ended exploration, so do make it an essential item in your creative toolbox. When you're considering a topic, remember that including YouTube as one of your sources can be helpful.

Working with Wikipedia

Since its launch in 2001, Wikipedia, the open-access online encyclopae-dia, has become the largest and most popular source of information in the world. Such is its dominance of the information market that *Encyclopaedia Britannica*, having experienced financial difficulties for several years, ceased publishing a printed product in 2012 after nearly 250 years as the undisputed reference work of choice.

If you enjoy playing with serendipity, Wikipedia is an ideal tool because you can drift from topic to topic as you like, following key words or ideas as they capture your attention. For the creative thinker, this tool is invaluable.

Many people just turn to Wikipedia when they have a specific search topic in mind. However, you don't have to be confine you use of Wikipedia to conven-tional reference searches. You can deploy Wikipedia in the same way you may use random thinking exercises: see where it takes you when you select some different key words related to your issue.

Maintaining a Creative State of Mind with Fun and Games

If you want to see the value of fun and games in creative thinking, watch children develop. In their earliest years, children experience a learning curve that would overwhelm most adults. From a standing start, they simultane-ously master complex co-ordination, social skills, language and many other capabilities as they grow into the world around them.

And because children are unable to use adult aids such as reading, writ-ing and abstract reasoning, they have to rely on other resources. These resources are mostly forms of play, as adults would describe it. When young children play, they provide an object lesson in the benefits of maintaining a positive and investigative state of mind. While many adults may assume they're just messing around in an aimless way, children are actually learn-ing through a combination of endless curiosity, mimicking, repetition and rehearsal.

Growing minds

In their early years, children live in a different level of consciousness from adults. Much time in early childhood is spent in delta and alpha brain states, unlike the dominant beta state of most waking adults. What this means in practice is that children oscillate between being in a light trance and a waking dream state similar to when you're dozing under a tree on a summer's day.

This curious state is well described by Lewis Carroll in *Alice in Wonderland,* when Alice sees the strange white rabbit for the first time – she doesn't know whether she's asleep or awake, and neither does the reader. As her adventures in Wonderland continue, it's obvious that Alice is dreaming, but Alice thinks she's wide awake throughout. This at least partly explains why children find it so easy to fantasise and can turn any situation into a scenario for play.

In these early stages, children absorb everything uncritically, with few filters. Anything they see, hear or experience is taken on board and stored to be used later in different contexts.

As soon as they're capable of doing so, young children translate their experiences into games, many of which are universal across all cultures. Two of the first games are peekaboo, and throwing things out of the pram to see what comes back. These very simple games rapidly evolve with toddlerhood into more structured activities.

Consider some of the typical games of young children and how they could work for you:

- **Let's pretend:** On one level, this universal game is a form of creative visualisation. At a stroke, any child can become a pirate, princess, superhero or pop star simply by saying so. Add a few props, and the scene is set for a thoroughly enjoyable play session.

  On the surface, let's pretend looks like play, but listen to the language and notice the play patterns, and you see that these scenarios are actually rehearsals for real life. Children incorporate the latest words and expressions they've heard and re-enact what they've seen the adults around them doing. Much of let's pretend is repetition, as children practise and perfect their recent learning.

As an adult, revisit the simple game of let's pretend and play out something you've recently learned. You can do this as part of a creative thinking session with colleagues, or if you're easily embarrassed, try it solo. Just take a problem or concept that's preoccupying you and don the superhero's cloak, or brandish your pirate's cutlass and slice through the problem! You may not solve your problem, but you'll certainly have fun trying!

✔ **Hide 'n' seek:** Another perennial children's game is hide 'n' seek. Part of the fascination is the hiding part, but a major element of the game is the countdown and the stirring call, 'Coming, ready or not!' Bring this feature to your problem. If you can let go of adult inhibitions, feel the energy of going hunting for your creative solution. It's worth a try.

✔ **Blind man's bluff:** You can use this traditional game alone or as part of a group exercise. Essentially, blind man's bluff is a basic form of sensory deprivation that helps heighten the remaining senses as compensation. Because sight is usually the dominant sense, eliminating it forces you to evaluate your environment by using your remaining faculties. You may be surprised at how different things seem when you rely on your other senses. (This idea has been taken to the extreme at a restaurant in London where blind waiters serve diners in a blacked-out dining room. Apparently it's very successful.)

You can play this game literally, by using blindfolds, which creates the most interesting and amusing results, but of course you can also do it without the blindfolds and simply imagine what it would be like to rely on the other senses. What if you couldn't see, or hear, or smell, or taste or touch – which senses would be the best substitutes? Either way, this process encourages you to adopt a different way of considering things.

Each of these children's activities tends to take place less as people age, and for much of adult life this is perfectly appropriate. It would, after all, be a little odd if your colleagues greeted you with the suggestion, 'Let's play hide 'n' seek!' However, creative thinking is, at its core, about attitude. Sometimes, introducing this playful note can help unblock even the most daunting situation, or it can at least provide a little light relief in an otherwise serious session.

Even if having fun during work or study time is frowned on, there's nothing to stop you putting the fun into your downtime. The only barriers to doing so are your own inhibitions.

Some creative businesses foster the best of both worlds by encouraging graffiti boards, contests to make the best paper planes, and indoor basketball. Of course, there's method in the apparent madness of these businesses, even if their clients can sometimes be taken aback by having to duck a paper aeroplane or join in an impromptu ball game.

What companies like these understand is that maintaining creative output relies on a combination of factors, several of them outside the conventions of the normal business world. This kind of organised anarchy can assist idea generation, and an atmosphere in which people feel comfortable with themselves is a great antidote to stress.

Playing games at work can provide a practical counterpoint to focused work. In short, when you've been switched on long enough, it can be good to switch off for a while.

Discovering an app for that

The invention of the app for smartphones and tablet computers has transformed the virtual landscape, placing a vast array of diversions at everyone's fingertips. Looking at the sales across categories, it's intriguing to see how many of the great successes are deliberately very trivial or silly. This reflects a universal need for fun and games and confirms how central these activities are.

The world of apps offers a vast range of choices for the creative thinker. One obvious starting point is the range that covers cognitive activities, from personal development to brain games. However, the panorama is much bigger than that, and going on a random browse through the app landscape can be fun.

Select a topic in which you don't have a personal interest, explore the apps on offer and then relate some of them back to the subject you're interested in. So if you're trying to develop a new product, select medical, for example, as your app subject. The apps in this category cover a huge range and may kick-start your thinking about different ways of considering your product. You may begin to think about the anatomy of your product. If it's not healthy (perhaps incomplete or imperfectly formed), how can you make it better? The medical instruments may encourage you to think about how to measure aspects of it or ways of conducting surgery on it. What's the prognosis? Do you know the history? And so on. If you find a promising line of thought, use the app and others related to it to burrow deeper into your topic, and extend the metaphors you're taking from the world of medicine to your own area of interest.

Here, you follow some of the tried and tested methods of creative thinking but incorporate new technologies to enrich and intensify the experience. You get the feeling that Edison would have loved access to the app store.

Dumbing down and smartening up

The pioneering days of the portable computer market saw some of the best and worst creative thinking in relation to product innovation and marketing. Two contrasting examples demonstrate the consequences of getting it wrong – and getting it right.

One of the first attempts at a portable computer was called the Osborne, which launched in 1981. It was the size of a small suitcase and had a carrying handle to show that it was truly portable. Unfortunately, in reality, putting a handle on this machine was like putting one on your car! It may have been a relatively small package, but it weighed a ton.

The advertising campaign for it was brilliant, showing a lithe young man (Osborne himself) breezing down the steps of a jet, lightly swinging his Osborne as he arrived for what would obviously be an important meeting. If that had been a real product, he would have wrenched his arm out of its socket, as early purchasers quickly discovered.

The company's history gave rise to what's become known as the Osborne effect because, apart from the computer's lack of genuine portability, the software alone cost almost as much again. Osborne himself talked publicly about the limited capabilities of the computer (and its lack

of expandability), and then suddenly launched a new version which left mountains of stock of the original. After a brief period of success, the company went bankrupt in 1983.

A classic example of finding better, smarter ways to do things in the history of the personal computer was Dell. As a bright 15-year-old, Michael Dell bought an Apple computer solely for the purpose of taking it apart to see how it worked. Looking at the PC market, he realised that parts were assembled from many sources, and so began making his own models in his bedroom. At first he customised versions to the specifications of fellow students, and then he began selling them to a rapidly growing national market. Dell soon became a Fortune 500 company, with Michael Dell himself its youngest CEO. The company is still a major player in a fiercely competitive market.

Both Osborne and Dell had great insights into gaps in the market and leapt on the opportunity. One failed to think through the concept, delivering a sub-standard product and making a series of elementary marketing errors along the way. The other, in contrast, tested his clever insight locally at first and then rapidly expanded, keeping to his original vision and outsmarting his competitors. Which was the creative thinker?

Simplifying

One important step on the path to embedding creativity in your daily life is to simplify both your physical environment and your mental space:

✔ **Physical environment:** A common problem is the accumulation of clutter. Collecting clutter wherever you work is very easy, because almost everything you do produces material. Much more difficult is disposing of it. Decide to be ruthless and immediately discard anything you don't need. After the initial pain, you can start to experience the benefits of your meaner, cleaner approach to life.

✔ **Mental space:** Harder to see but just as obstructive is mental clutter. Although you consciously organise and compartmentalise the information you handle every day, your brain doesn't quite work like that. You may try to focus on that important project but be easily distracted by thoughts like 'Should I buy those nice shoes I saw yesterday?' 'Did I remember to lock the front door?' 'Wasn't that news about the earthquake dreadful?' And so on. These intrusions happen because the unconscious parts of your brain store everything indiscriminately, not knowing what's important and what's not.

These different aspects of your brain have been described nicely as the *master* (your conscious self, which thinks it runs everything) and the *emissary* (whose role is to know everything that's really going on). If the master is in control, you feel you're in control too. When the emissary intrudes, your best-laid plans can go awry; that's why you can't help thinking about those shoes and the front door and the earthquake.

Although you can't switch off the emissary (and it does serve many useful functions), you can teach yourself to notice whenever your focus is drifting and gradually get better at 'parking' distractions.

A common misconception exists that a phenomenon called multi-tasking is possible. The brain isn't designed to multi-task, but it's quite good at switching rapidly from one mode to another, which produces the illusion of multi-tasking. While this rapid switching can work effectively for periods of time, ultimately it's stressful, which becomes counter-productive. A better strategy is to simplify your approach and consciously focus on one task at a time. Doing so pays dividends.

Noodling and doodling

Musicians have had to master their craft through many hours of arduous learning and practice. They have a great expression for those times when they're just sitting around playing odd random chords and runs alone or with other musicians. It's called *noodling* and is the musical equivalent of doodling. It's given the world some very memorable songs.

One of the reasons noodling works so well for so many musicians is that it's completely unstructured time, when musicians can release all their accumulated experience in a relaxed way. Here, a snatch of a melody, a certain chord sequence or an interesting time signature may begin to transform into something more substantial.

This unstructured approach can generate some unexpected and fascinating outcomes that may never have emerged through conventional rehearsal or composition. As with other people and their many creative high points, musicians have often commented that the idea 'just popped into my head'.

If you're not a musician but are in playful mode, doodling (described in more detail in Chapter 9) is a quick and effective way to ease yourself into a creative frame of mind. What you produce may start as nonsense, but it's likely to become a train of thought after only a few minutes.

Part V
The Part of Tens

The 5th Wave   By Rich Tennant

"Well, apparently this is a company that doesn't value someone who can look at familiar things in a new and creative way."

In this part...

*T*he Part of Tens is designed to deliver information in a quick and simple summary of some key topics. Here, you find a selection of top tips for getting creative. You discover ten acorns that some exceptionally creative thinkers grew into mighty oak trees, and ten or so essential books offering great insights into the creative process. As if that wasn't enough, you then get a peek into ten of the most inspirational creative businesses, and finally a look at ten people with an unusually creative streak.

Chapter 14

Ten Great Ways to Get Creative

Sometimes you *want* to get creative, and at other times you *need* to get creative. In the first scenario, it's usually you providing the motivation, and you're acting of your own volition. At such times, entering a creative space can be relatively easy. However, in situations where you need to get creative it can be because events – your boss, teacher, colleagues or the competition – demand it. Here, you may need a little assistance to get started.

This chapter offers a selection of reliable approaches that you can rely on to kick-start creative thinking when you're stuck or when you just fancy a different approach. I describe them all in greater detail in the main body of the book.

Seize the Moment

If you're in a resourceful state of mind, you'll know that your creativity is on tap. When that's the case, getting into a positive flow and generating abundant ideas is easy. However, like most people, you probably find that your creativity ebbs and flows. Sometimes you can be fortunate and find that feeling creative coincides with the need to be creative. But when it doesn't, you have to grab your creativity whenever you can.

If you've been considering a problem and an idea strikes you, record it immediately. Always keep a pad and pen or recording device handy. Creative thoughts can come out of nowhere, and they can disappear just as quickly, irrespective of how vibrant and clear they seem in the heat of the moment. This is especially true of the flashes of inspiration that wake you up in the middle of the night – by morning they may have evaporated, so keep a pad by your bed just in case.

Sometimes your creativity may require a little nudge, and you may need to use some of the techniques described in the chapters in Part III of this book.

Give Yourself Permission

A common block to creativity is your own inhibition. You may believe you aren't sufficiently creative or that you're not up to the task in hand. Such misgivings aren't uncommon, but don't let them hold you back. Jumping into creativity is like the moment before you dive into the water and think 'Will it be cold? Will I embarrass myself? Will I enjoy it?' Thoughts like these are only self-talk and they'll evaporate as soon as you take action.

Bear in mind that if you've ever been creative before (and you know you have), you can be creative again.

If you're hesitant, a little light meditation before you embark on the task can aid relaxation. Alternatively, you can ease into a creative frame of mind by doodling or visualising. Again, the chapters in Part III can help with techniques.

Make Time to Relax, Play and Have Fun

It's all too easy to spend your waking life being busy, busy, busy. If you're busy being busy, not only is it impossible to step back from the situation, but it can also be detrimental to productive work.

The brain, which runs so many of your daily life patterns, isn't tuned to prolonged periods of uninterrupted work. Studies have shown that a very effective work pattern is approximately 90 minutes of work followed by a 20-minute break. Depending on the intensity of a project, working for just 30 minutes followed by a short two-minute brain break can also be very effective.

And if you want to think creatively, the kind of serious focus appropriate for, say, financial calculation is likely to be counterproductive. Creativity flourishes in relaxed, happy and playful situations.

Immerse or Isolate Yourself

What are the best conditions for being creative? No single answer to this question exists, but it's worth considering two opposing approaches that work for a lot of creative individuals.

Immersion

The first option is total immersion. The working environment of the Rolling Stones during their most creative early years resembled a constant party. And Picasso surrounded himself with his favourite art and companions while painting.

If you're planning to be creative, try surrounding yourself with everything you find creatively stimulating. This can be music, films, books, art and treasured objects. Reminders of people you find inspirational may be valuable. You may want the company of creative friends. Depending on what you intend to create, you may need exposure to contemporary examples (many song-writers and film-makers, for example, want to experience everything in their genre when creating something new themselves). (Chapter 4 talks about building a creative space.)

Isolation

Exhausted by a whirlwind of song-writing and touring, Bob Dylan hid away in a remote log cabin in order, he hoped, to relax and write a book. After a while, the urge to write a song – an urge so overwhelming he couldn't resist it – seized him. That song was 'Like a Rolling Stone'. For some individuals, the environment most conducive to creativity is one that's stripped right back to basics with no distractions.

The approach that works best for you depends on a combination of your personality and circumstances. You may find that one of these options speaks to you while the other leaves you cold. Both are perfectly valid, so the choice is yours and yours alone.

Tolerate Ambiguity

Certainty is very comforting for most people. Much of daily life is built around habits and routines set in a predictable context: you know the train will come more or less on time, the post will arrive, and lunch will be at 1 p.m.

However, where creative thinking is concerned, that certainty may not be appropriate. In a work context, you may often be pressured to be focused and to drive towards solutions with a great deal of determination. However, the dynamics of creativity don't work like that, and you may find it beneficial to step into a different mindset where choices, options and ambiguities abound.

The simplest way to begin developing your tolerance of ambiguity is to work with 'on the one hand, on the other hand' propositions. Cultivating the technique of thinking in terms of *negative space*, whereby you deliberately consider what something is *not* as well as what it is, can also be useful.

Find Your Personal Centre

If you're planning to be creative, your mental state is very relevant. If you're feeling stressed or anxious, it can be next to impossible to have creative thoughts, because your focus will be on the immediate situation.

Finding ways to alleviate the pressures of daily life and find your centre makes sense. The two fastest ways to centre yourself are through two different forms of contemplation:

- ✔ **Meditation:** You can apply any of the simple techniques to enter a calm zone in a few minutes, and as you become familiar with meditation you'll soon find a method that suits you. (Check out *Meditation For Dummies* by Stephan Bodian (Wiley), and Chapter 3.)
- ✔ **Visualisation:** You can use visualisation techniques with affirmations to achieve a quiet focus deep inside. (Chapters 6 and 7 have tips on visualising.)

Whichever process you favour, centring is a quick and effective way to energise yourself and start the creative juices flowing.

Develop Endless Curiosity

At its best, creativity becomes a way of life and the habit of thinking creatively is second nature. To foster creativity, it pays to cultivate the habit of being curious. And not just being curious, but being curious about *everything*.

Curiosity involves three main elements:

- ✔ **Noticing:** Search for the detail, the unexpected, and anything you may have missed. The more you notice, the more your creativity benefits.

- ✔ **Questioning:** It pays to ask questions, even about things that seem obvious on the surface. Often this relentless interrogation can yield previously hidden insights.

- ✔ **A sense of wonder:** Children are gifted with this facility, and a sense of wonder makes the world a much more fascinating place. Trying not to lose this sense of wonder as an adult is a very good idea. Get into the habit of looking at things as if for the very first time. Look at every detail of a leaf, or consider how an ancient building was constructed without modern construction aids. When you take the time to look for it, you see wonder all around.

Make Things Bigger, Smaller, Distorted or Inverted

Part of the creative thinking process is intelligent imagination – being able to play with the possible rather than the actual. One of the most valuable questions is, 'What if . . .?'

When faced with a creative challenge, you can play with elements of techniques like SCAMPER (which I explain in Chapter 7), whereby you ask what would happen if things were different in various ways. Reconfigure every aspect of your challenge by changing the scale dramatically, stretching and bending it into different shapes. Transform it by turning it inside out and upside down. It doesn't matter whether you're toying with a tangible object or an abstract concept – the same principles apply.

Visualisation works best for this technique, so alternate between looking inwards (eyes closed, contemplative) and looking outwards (using pen and paper to sketch or mind map your ideas). During this activity you can capture ideas very effectively using mind mapping, which I describe in Chapter 6, and which you can also read about in the excellent *Mind Mapping For Dummies* by Florian Rustler (Wiley).

Organise a 'Creative Heroes' Dinner Party

You're never alone with a hero. If you want assistance in thinking creatively, a ready-made resource is to select a 'guest list' of your creative heroes. These are the individuals who inspire you, and who come to mind when you consider your personal creative *Who's Who*.

Cultivating these individuals and bringing them to life by imagining how they talk, their personalities and their sense of humour is a worthwhile exercise. How do they behave at your dinner party? What food do they like? How do they get on with the other guests? And most importantly, what do they think of your issue?

The more deeply you immerse yourself in this scenario, the more productive it can be for you. Most people find the dinner party a very enjoyable exercise, with their heroes being more fun than they'd anticipated.

And your heroes don't only have to turn up for dinner. As a contemplative activity, you can keep them on tap whenever you want to explore a line of thought. Having Leonardo da Vinci, Thomas Edison or Steve Jobs at your shoulder can be very useful indeed.

Indulge in Creative Sleep

So much of the mind's real work is done outside normal states of consciousness. If you allow it to, your unconscious can be a superb facilitator of your creative thinking. Each of these states provides a way of accessing the inner resources of your mind:

- **Daydreaming:** This is the mind in neutral. In this state, it becomes easy to tap in to the alpha state between waking and sleep, where all kinds of thoughts and images float into view. If you've been thinking about a problem, clues and even solutions can surface here.

- **Power napping:** This is intentional switching off. A few minutes of napping can prove remarkably effective in giving you fresh perspectives and renewed energy.

- **Meditating:** Although not a form of sleeping, strictly speaking, any kind of contemplation assists the creative process, and simple meditation techniques can contribute significantly to creativity.

- **Sleeping:** You can build sleep into your creative repertoire by developing the habit of thinking about a current problem before dropping off, and keeping a dream diary to record your recollections.

Chapter 15

Ten Acorns That Became Oak Trees: Great Ideas that Became Reality

. . . .

In This Chapter

▶ Juxtaposing ideas

▶ Daydreaming

▶ Persisting in the face of adversity

▶ Demonstrating true vision

. . . .

Anticipating there will be a need around 700 years in the future for something you've made takes a lot of foresight. New College Oxford was founded in 1379 (it was named New to distinguish it from Oriel, which dated from 1326). A few years ago, dry rot was discovered in the oak beams supporting the main hall, and the cost of replacement, even if possible, would've been astronomical. Then the university forester informed the administrators that when the main hall had been built, the architects had instructed that a grove of oak trees be planted and maintained so that when dry rot eventually set in, the beams could be replaced. And those oaks had once been acorns.

The great ideas in this chapter aren't all as tangible as those extra beams, but they've all proved their usefulness.

Gutenberg's Printing Press

Many truly innovative concepts are based on a combination of concepts that had never been put together before. Gutenberg's printing press is a unique example of the collision of ideas to produce a revolutionary solution.

Gutenberg brought together three essential ingredients – the agricultural press, moveable type, and oil-based ink – to make his world-changing printing press. Previously, books had been produced by the laborious process of hand-writing manuscripts or using primitive wood-block printing.

The revolution wasn't only technical, of course, and the capability of mass publishing introduced the world to the printed word. Gutenberg's personal crowning achievement was the Gutenberg Bible, which was praised for its aesthetic and technical virtuosity.

Legend has it that Gutenberg's idea of moveable type came to him 'like a ray of light' – another example of a eureka moment after a period of gestation.

Galileo's Understanding of Mankind's Place in the Universe

Creative thinking can be a risky – not to say life-threatening – activity, as the scientist Galileo found out. In Europe, in Galileo's lifetime, the central belief was that because humans were made in God's image, it followed that earth must be the centre of the universe. Various scriptures were cited to support this idea, so it had the firm backing of the Vatican.

Galileo developed his theory that the earth revolved round the sun (known as *heliocentrism*) based on the work of Copernicus. He was fascinated by the movement of tides, and although his early thinking was faulty, his persistence led to a sophisticated understanding of planetary circulation and its consequences for gravity.

Apparently Galileo's waspish tongue had got him into trouble since his student days, and in fighting superstition and petty politics, he made dangerous enemies. He was tried by the Catholic church, made to recant, and forced to spend the rest of his life under house arrest. There he wrote the works that changed the understanding of the solar system and earned him the soubriquet 'Father of Science'.

Newton's Insights into the Physical World

Newton was an alchemist who was fascinated by the transmutation of lead into gold. He also studied the occult. In fact, Newton wrote more on these two subjects than he did on science. That's probably not the Newton most people know, but those were his main preoccupations. There's no prescription for genius, and even the smartest minds sometimes explore offbeat avenues.

When he wasn't searching for the philosopher's stone, Isaac Newton made landmark contributions to mathematics and astronomy. Many consider his *Principia Mathematica* to be the most important book on the subject ever written. It defines gravity and includes the three laws of motion that governed science for the next three hundred years. And it confirmed Galileo's theories once and for all.

Newton also studied optics and extended his interests into geometry and physics. Cambridge University appointed Newton as Lucasian Professor, the post more recently held by Stephen Hawking, until 2009.

Henry Ford's Vision of Modern American Industry

Henry Ford's fascination with the internal combustion engine led to the Model T, the first mass-produced car. However, in many ways Ford's real legacy was his unique vision for the way people could work in the modern world.

Ford introduced the system he called *welfare capitalism*, paying his workers an unprecedented $5 a day (which forced his Detroit competitors to up their workers' wages). He was vehemently anti-union, believing that although the concept of unions had merit, in practice they led to poorer performance and served only the interests of union bosses.

Ford was also interested in the moral standards and personal quality of life of his employees, although he had to back-pedal when workers considered some of his investigations far too intrusive.

Ford's vision was of 'consumerism as the key to peace', and in pursuing this goal he created the pattern of much of modern American life.

Edison's Persistence and Inspiration

One of the most prolific inventors of all time, with over 1,000 US patents to his name, Thomas Alva Edison is famous for his claim that 'Genius is 1 per cent inspiration and 99 per cent perspiration,' which is also a good description of his temperament. His life was characterised by dogged determination.

At school, Edison displayed the classic creative thinker's trait of daydreaming, to the extent that his teacher called him 'addled' before expelling him. Subsequently, his mother educated him at home, which he declared was the making of him.

Edison's first job was in a telegraph office, where he found time to patent a ticker tape machine. He also invented the phonograph and an improved electricity generator as well as his most famous invention, the light bulb.

Edison's greatest invention, however, was the creation of the world's first laboratory workshop dedicated to new product development. His lab subsequently became General Electric, and GE is still one of America's largest and most innovative companies.

Tesla's Electric Inventions

Nikola Tesla had a turbulent life. He was born in a remote Serbian village, but when he arrived in America in 1884, he already had the reputation as a man to watch. Edison, never missing a trick, hastily employed him.

The relationship between the two geniuses disintegrated after Tesla said he could improve the electric motor Edison had devised. Edison offered Tesla $50,000 – an unheard-of sum – to prove it. Tesla duly did so and was surprised when Edison offered him a paltry $10 dollar increase on his wage, declaring Tesla didn't understand 'the American sense of humour'. This was the beginning of a feud that lasted both their lifetimes, to the detriment of the world at large.

The next stage of the feud involved the acrimonious battle over current – whether to supply electricity through alternating (AC) or direct (DC) current. Tesla favoured AC, but Edison was an advocate of DC. Tesla was indisputably right (a world of DC could never have been viable), but at the time vested interests sided with Edison, and it was touch and go for a while.

Tesla and Edison's very public dispute is said to be the reason neither won a Nobel Prize.

Among Tesla's seemingly endless patents for everything from radio to X-rays were working methods for conducting electricity without wires. Conspiracy theorists believe this threat to the burgeoning power industry was a step too far and triggered the start of a campaign to marginalise Tesla and write him out of history.

Tesla's legacy is a tribute to persistence in the face of adversity, and a truly original imagination, always ahead of its time.

Marconi's Radio

Whereas some creative individuals have led lives full of ideas, fizzing and buzzing with fresh thoughts, Marconi devoted his attention to the development and refinement of a single powerful concept that would change the world: communication.

One of Marconi's characteristics was eclecticism, and he was ready to beg, borrow or steal anything that would contribute to his vision. When Marconi demonstrated one of his radio inventions, Tesla complained that Marconi used '17 of my patents'. Indeed, much of Marconi's work was 'built on the shoulders of giants', to borrow Newton's phrase. But it was considered original enough to earn him the Nobel Prize.

Many individuals were working in the field of radio transmission at this time, but it was Marconi, still in his early twenties, who had the breakthroughs that allowed for long-distance transmission. Ignored in his native Italy, Marconi moved to England, and as a result the first wireless radio transmissions took place on Salisbury Plain and across the Bristol Channel.

Having spread radio across the world, the Marconi name has become synonymous with communication, as he would have wished.

Picasso's Works of Art

Summarising Picasso's life and work would be like summarising the history of twentieth-century art. Some anecdotes may provide insights into the uniquely creative man behind the myth:

✔ **Defining reality:** Picasso was on a train at about the time he was becoming famous. As usual, he was drawing in his journal, and a fellow passenger, intrigued at sharing the compartment with someone special, asked to see his work. It was one of Picasso's exploratory phases, and the sketches looked very unconventional. Picasso's companion could make neither head nor tail of them, so he asked, 'Will you draw me?'

'Sure,' said Picasso, and delivered a few strong strokes, showing the result to his new friend.

'Why – it looks nothing like me!' he protested.

'Hmm,' said the master. 'Do you have a photograph of your wife by any chance?' 'I certainly do,' said the man in a state of high dudgeon – this so-called artist was clearly a charlatan.

Picasso examined the tiny picture carefully. After a time he said, 'I'm sure you love her. But she's very *very* small. And she's black and white. And slightly out of focus.'

✔ **Knowing your value:** Picasso used to sketch compulsively on paper tablecloths as he hung around the bistros and bars of Paris. His charisma ensured an endless stream of female company. Some wanted attention, others more permanent proof of acquaintance with genius. One beautiful young woman observed his crayoning and asked if he would sell it to her. 'Certainly,' said Picasso. 'Let me give you ten francs,' she offered, thinking the price of a coffee would be a generous gesture to a struggling young artist. 'One million,' said Picasso quietly but firmly. 'One million?' she protested. 'Yes, ten for the coffee and the rest for my genius.'

✔ **Improving on the original:** At 17, Picasso failed to get into the Madrid Academy. His portfolio drawings still exist, and they're exquisite. The insurmountable problem is that they bear the marks of their creator. Even as a young student he couldn't restrain his desire to flourish in the face of great art. The Greeks and Romans, whose casts he was required to draw, did not represent the culmination of art – they were stepping stones in the process. The blinkered academics didn't understand that the original artists would have been delighted if someone had moved their ideas forwards, just as they had modelled their art on what had gone before.

✔ **Loving me, loving you:** Every time Picasso fell in love, he painted a beautifully realistic portrait of his new muse. These are the real markers of Picasso's evolution as a passionate individual. But they don't feature strongly in the canon of his work, because they don't fit with the mythology of the man who changed the way we see.

When he was painting *Guernica*, Picasso progressed through many arduous changes in his gargantuan work: this was destined to be the painting that transformed perceptions of war and its consequences. But, as often happens, real life intervened, and while he was creating the painting he was caught between two women who both loved him and demanded his undivided attention. The intimate facts aren't known, but the sequence of photographs in Dora Maar's book, and his portrayal by Anthony Hopkins in the film *Surviving Picasso*, give a mischievous notion of the dynamics of the situation. The defining moment is when Picasso, halfway up a stepladder, turns away from the screaming, scrapping, hair-pulling rivals and lets them sort it out for themselves. He has a date with history.

Alan Turing's Modern Computers

Alan Turing was the architect of the modern computer, and he made an invaluable contribution to the Allied victory in the Second World War as a cryptographer. In a cruel twist of fate, he was rewarded with chemical castration at the instigation of civil servants, because of his admitted homosexuality at a time when this was still a criminal offence. Turing blamed his chemical treatment for the diminution of his towering intellect, and this contributed directly to his depression and eventual suicide.

Before his tragic demise, Turing performed huge leaps of imagination over a sustained period to conceive, develop and deliver the world's first fully operational computer, and with it, the concept of artificial intelligence (AI).

The Turing test, which states that a human and a machine playing chess should be indistinguishable, not only captured the imagination of computer scientists (now IT specialists), but also gave rise to a whole genre of science fiction. It also inspired a generation of creative thinkers like Bill Gates, who co-founded Microsoft, Steve Jobs and Steve Wozniak, who founded Apple, and Bill Hewlett and Dave Packard, who founded HP, to bring computers into every home and office.

Turing was an extraordinary mathematician in a period of extraordinary mathematicians. The Second World War provided a unique springboard for a select elite at Bletchley Park, the location of the secret centre for cryptography. The team was charged with decoding enemy messages, notably those encrypted by the near-mythical Enigma machine, which were deemed unbreakable. Turing's eventual success (an astonishing feat of creative mathematical virtuosity) was achieved with his 'bombe', a valve-driven computing machine constructed with the invaluable help of Tommy Flowers, an unpretentious East End GPO (General Post Office) engineer with an exceptional gift for circuitry, and the only person who seemed to really understand Turing's mind. The pair also worked on Colossus, the next step in the evolution of the computer.

Turing conceived the idea of a 'universal machine' (later known as a Turing machine) which would be capable of 'computing anything that is computable'. His work in the 1930s was so far ahead of its time that few of Turing's contemporaries understood the implications, even though the concepts he explored are now the bedrock of modern computer science.

Turing retained his interest in the mathematics of computing science (which gained him much prestige on both sides of the Atlantic). He became fascinated by mathematical biology, specifically the principles of *morphogenesis* (essentially the patterns formed in nature). Anyone interested in the fascinating patterns of fractals, popularised by the French–American mathematician Mandelbrot, owes a huge debt to Turing's ground-breaking work.

Turing's epitaph, confusing to most of his contemporaries but instantly recognisable to any modern creative thinker, was 'From a contradiction you can deduce *everything*'.

Richard Feynman – Bongos and Atom Bombs

Richard Feynman had a remarkable mind and a personality to match. He got into Princeton University with a perfect score on his entrance examination, the first person ever to do so. When Feynman gave his first seminar there at the age of 23, Albert Einstein was among several leading physicists in his audience.

Feynman was contemptuous of everything he believed wasn't real science. He had an IQ of 125, bright but not exceptional, and thought that was proof that psychometric tests were rubbish. He was endlessly curious and an enthusiastic advocate for science, as his book *The Pleasure of Finding Things Out* testifies.

Feynman had an unusual facility for direct interrogation of both people and things, which made some nervous of him. But Niels Bohr, the Nobel Prize winning Danish physicist, sought him out for late night chats because he was the only individual at Los Alamos unafraid of arguing with the great man.

Feynman was a brilliant teacher, with a facility for finding simple explanations for the most complex problems. He came to national fame in later years when, as a member of the committee investigating the crash of the Challenger space shuttle, he demonstrated the cause of the disaster by simply dropping a piece of the faulty material into a glass of iced water and showing that it cracked.

He was also a skilled bongo player, having learned from the Native Americans in the desert around Los Alamos when working on the atom bomb. Known as 'Injun Joe', he loved jamming at jazz clubs, which was not considered proper behaviour for a Nobel Prize winner. He was also a prankster, and having learned to pick locks, he left cheeky notes in his colleagues' lockers to suggest that a spy was operating on campus. (Actually, there was a real spy, and Klaus Fuchs was later tried for treason.)

Feynman's love of frisbees – another unconventional hobby – led to a new branch of mathematics concerning spinning objects in space. This was typical of his ability to combine fun, creative imagination and clarity of thought in one topic. One of his books was called *Surely You're Joking, Mr. Feynman!* He was.

Chapter 16

Ten-Plus Essential Books

Creativity is a huge subject, and it's generated a substantial range of books on all aspects of the creative process. The list grows daily, because interest in creative thinking is now a major focus of business, education and scientific study. The books summarised here represent a cross-section of classics and current coverage, with an emphasis on practical issues.

The Act of Creation by Arthur Koestler

A classic work on creativity, *The Act of Creation* has stood the test of time (although not the vagaries of publishing, and is out of print). This comprehensive analysis attempts to crack the code of creativity and capture the birth of the creative spark. This absorbing book is full of rich anecdotes and stories of the creative process.

Koestler's *The Act of Creation* has two parts. The first explores creative processes in art and science. The best thing about this part is the author's insight into how creativity manifests itself. Koestler's interest is in the concept of juxtaposition – placing together different or directly opposing ideas. His insights chime with much current thinking around the nature of the creative process. Koestler suggests that juxtaposition is one of the roots of humour, and he provides an abundance of illustrations to demonstrate his argument.

The second part of the book builds a biological and psychological foundation for creation that focuses on the richness of human experience. Unusually for the time – the 1960s – Koestler explored the central role of play in the creative process. Dry academic behavioural studies dominated the psychology of the day, so Koestler represented a refreshing perspective.

Koestler made creativity a legitimate subject for study, provoking the debate between behaviourists and humanistic disciplines that continues to this day.

Hare Brain, Tortoise Mind by Guy Claxton

This book explores changing cognitive priorities in a changing world. Claxton's premise, neatly encapsulated in the title, is that the hare brain, tuned to fast reactions, quick decisions and certainty, is at home in an ordered and predictable world. However, the modern world is not at all like that, and the frenetic pace of change and unpredictability requires a different mindset. This is the tortoise mind, which is attuned to intuition and inspiration, and better able to appreciate the subtlety and complexity of today's world.

Professor Claxton is one of the leading authorities on how we think, and his book is an insightful and enlightening account of what works for today's intelligent creative thinker. As an advisor to the influential Mind Gym, which has established itself as one of the go-to companies for businesses seeking creative advantage, Claxton is in an excellent position to see his thinking applied in the real world of commerce.

Secret Knowledge by David Hockney

Secret Knowledge is an artist's insight into his own understanding of creative processes. David Hockney has produced several investigative books about how artists actually work on a day-by-day basis. *Secret Knowledge* is his exploration of the tools and techniques used by artists over the centuries.

Having made an intensive analysis of the works of the old masters, Hockney believes that the artists could not have achieved their understanding of perspective just by eye, and that optical instruments must have aided the process. This fascinating study, co-written with Charles M Falco, a physicist specialising in optics, reveals the detail of how past masterpieces were probably created using lenses, sophisticated mathematics, and even early forms of photography long before they were known to the wider world.

Not all art historians buy in to his theories, but Hockney has never minded controversy, and as well as taking the reader on a fascinating journey, the insights he gives, from an artist's perspective, are convincing.

The Power of Creative Intelligence by Tony Buzan

Best known as the inventor of mind mapping (which I look at in Chapter 6), Tony Buzan has spent his career as an advocate for opening the creative mind. *The Power of Creative Intelligence* is one of the best of his many books, taking the reader on a succinct tour of ten creative topics, including his mind maps, ways of expanding creative capability, and using the whole brain.

Buzan is a lucid writer and a strong advocate for creative intelligence. This book is a good starting point for exploring creativity on a practical level, and is likely to lead you to some of his other studies of creative thinking.

Thinkertoys by Michael Michalko

Lots of books on creativity and processes for thinking creatively are available. Among these, *Thinkertoys* by Michael Michalko remains the best single source of creative tips, tools and techniques. He uses an engaging format in which each process is explained lucidly with the aid of optical illusions, puzzles and real-life examples.

Thinkertoys is in three parts. The first offers dozens of simple but effective ways of kick-starting and developing the process of creative thinking. Many of these spring from variations on the SCAMPER model, which I talk about in Chapter 7. The second part focuses on deploying the power of the unconscious mind. The third part's unusual title is 'The Spirit of Koinonia' (koinonia is the ancient Greek term for fellowship), and argues the case for group dialogue and networking as an integral part of the creative process.

As a work of reference and a stimulus for thinking creatively, this is the definitive book to keep on your desk. And you also discover whether you're a kitten or a monkey.

The Creative Brain and The Whole Brain Business Book by Ned Herrmann

During prolonged recuperation from a life-threatening illness in the 1970s, Ned Herrmann, an executive at GE, began to daydream, and as a result he formulated a fresh view of how the brain works and also of how *we* work, individually and in teams. He created the system that became known as whole-brain thinking and ways of evaluating thinking, including the Herrmann Brain Dominance Instrument, or HBDI.

The Whole Brain Business Book and his workbook *The Creative Brain* detail Herrmann's model and are ideal for those who want to apply whole-brain thinking (which I look at in detail in Chapter 8) in their business and/or personal worlds. Having explained the concept, Herrmann demonstrates its application throughout organisations (many international companies use the model, so the book is rich in case material). He then discusses whole-brain leadership and offers his practical perspective on whole-brain creativity and innovation. Finally, Herrmann examines whole-brain personal development. All in all, this and the workbook together provide a comprehensive and practical guide to the practice of whole-brain thinking.

Blink by Malcolm Gladwell

Blink is one of a fascinating series of original and thought-provoking books by an individual with a uniquely inquiring mind. Gladwell's curiosity is boundless, and he has an engaging technique of picking apparently unpromising or obscure starting points (like contacting Fortune 500 companies to find out how tall their CEOs are), then weaving a compelling narrative full of nuggets of information. *Blink* takes its title from the phenomenon of *rapid cognition*, people's ability to assess situations in the blink of an eye, and Gladwell explores how it works, where it occurs and why it's important in creative thinking. His other books such as *The Tipping Point* and *Outliers* are equally fascinating reading.

How to Think Like Leonardo da Vinci by Michael Gelb

This is one of the best of the many books on Leonardo da Vinci.

As he tells it, Gelb was conducting a motivational session for an American corporation when he heard that its annual conference was scheduled for Florence and the organisers were looking for a guest speaker. Gelb is Italian–American, and Florence is his favourite city, so he devised a clever strategy and applied some creative visualisation: he dreamed that the CEO asked him what he'd do if invited to speak at this special event. Thanks to some creative dreaming, Gelb had the answer ready. Knowing that Leonardo da Vinci, the 'most creative man in history', grew up and worked in Florence, his pitch was that he would teach the audience how to think like Leonardo.

How to Think Like Leonardo da Vinci is the culmination of the journey that began with that event. Gelb was so inspired by what he discovered in his preparation for that seminal event that he decided to commit to several years of study, literally following in the master's footsteps as he journeyed around Italy, and applying the principles Leonardo lived by, as described eloquently in his extensive journals.

The outcome is a deep but very readable analysis of the seven principles Leonardo da Vinci lived by. It's an essential how-to book for anyone interested in cultivating a rounded creative lifestyle (even including mouthwatering advice on culinary pleasures), and in the hands of Michael Gelb is as relevant today as it was when Leonardo devised his principles half a millennium ago.

Strategies of Genius, Volume One by Robert Dilts

Many would agree that Steve Jobs, one of the founders of Apple, was one of the geniuses of the twentieth century, transforming technology into something both sexy and easy to use, and most of all, highly desirable. But who helped Jobs on his unique path to innovation? As one of the originators of neuro-linguistic programming (NLP), Robert Dilts spent time as a coach in Northern California, and legend has it that Steve Jobs, working out of his garage with Apple co-founder Steve Wozniak, was Robert's first coaching client. Certainly, expressions like Steve Jobs' often-quoted mantra about striving to be 'insanely great', which characterised Apple's phenomenal early growth, have the ring of Dilts about them.

The central argument of *Strategies of Genius* is that, if you understand precisely how someone performs, you can then use that knowledge to emulate them. Using this NLP technique (called *modelling*), Dilts describes the cognitive processes of several exceptionally gifted individuals then demonstrates how anyone can apply the methods of these people in their own lives. He models Aristotle and Albert Einstein, Nikola Tesla and Walt Disney, for example. In each case, he provides fascinating insights into their personalities and practices.

Lateral Thinking by Edward de Bono

Lateral thinking is one of those phrases that seems to have been around forever, and everyone has a rough idea of what it means. It's something to do with taking normal thinking and turning it on its side to get a fresh perspective, isn't it? That's a popular summary of the concept, and it's not inaccurate, as far as it goes. However, lateral thinking is certainly more than a sideways approach to problems.

Lateral Thinking is the definitive book on the subject from its inventor. Subtitled *A Textbook of Creativity*, it explains this popular concept and its applications and describes a number of related processes designed to enhance creative thinking ability. De Bono also introduces his approach to *provocative thinking* (he calls it *Po*), which is another essential tool for the creative thinker.

De Bono has been a prolific author, with more than 80 books to his credit. *Lateral Thinking* is an excellent introduction to his unique perspective.

The Art of Innovation by Tom Kelley

IDEO (a design and innovation consulting firm) is one of the longer-established specialists in creative thinking services for clients, and this book by one of its founders is an insight into how the firm does what it does.

Although a generation of successors has emulated and adapted its model, IDEO created many of the tools and techniques used to bring innovation to companies. This book is a guided tour through the processes IDEO uses to steer, stretch and provoke its clients into an innovative mindset.

A Technique for Producing Ideas by James Webb Young

Many professional creatives still consider this modest but hugely influential memo, first published in 2003, to be the best handbook on the creative process, and essential reading for anyone learning the skill.

The book identifies the five steps that typify idea generation and problem-solving, and offers practical advice on getting the best out of each stage. (Problem-solving is discussed in Chapter 8.)

Making by Thomas Heatherwick with Maisie Rowe

Thomas Heatherwick has been described by Sir Terence Conran as 'a Leonardo da Vinci of our times', and he's been responsible for some of the most exciting and imaginative architectural, engineering and design projects of recent years. Some of these, like his iconic cauldron for the 2012 London Olympics, are too recent to have been included in his book, *Making*. However, this substantial tome includes many of his finest works, detailing the creative processes involved in developing more than a hundred of his studio's projects.

For creative thinkers, *Making* is an excellent stimulus for the imagination. Each chapter title is a provocative question, like 'How do you design a building using an electron microscope?', 'How do you grow a meadow in the centre of a city?' and 'How do you make someone eat your business card?' *Making* then takes you on a journey of exploration as Heatherwick entertainingly describes the creative process involved in each project. Even the briefest description of some of the projects is intriguing: who wouldn't want to learn more about a roll-up bridge, a handbag made of zips or a 'seed cathedral'?

Chapter 17

Ten Inspirational Creative Businesses

In This Chapter

▶ Creating a great working environment

▶ Valuing the best people and their creative imaginations

▶ Having the best work ethos

Many businesses work in much the same way, and on the inside they're indistinguishable one from another. Visiting one of these companies can be like waking up in a chain hotel in a foreign city and not having a clue where you are. However, some businesses past and present have taken a radical path and gone to great lengths to create unique, inspirational work environments.

The ten companies I describe in this chapter are from different areas of business, and some have come and gone or mutated into other forms. What defines them is a clear ethos or set of principles at their foundation, and a strong belief in the creative intelligence and imagination of their employees.

Saatchi & Saatchi – Bringing World-Changing Creativity

When Maurice and Charles Saatchi completed their deal with the ailing Garland Compton advertising agency in the early 1970s, they took over Garland Compton's large nondescript offices in Charlotte Street in the less fashionable district north of London's Oxford Street. Estate agents called it Noho – North of Soho. Everyone else called it Nohope at the time. But the arrival of the Saatchi & Saatchi advertising agency changed the landscape.

When you arrived at the offices, two friendly, ultra-efficient receptionists, who seemed to have telepathic knowledge of your business and everyone you were due to meet, greeted you. Behind this smooth facade, however, things couldn't have been more different. Apart from the ground floor presentation room where all pitches took place, and the top floor, where the brothers had their private domain, the rest of the building was a permanent building site, unlike any other creative space in London at that time.

In line with the unique Saatchi ethos, this building was a cognitive, not a physical, space. Staff found themselves moved around frequently as offices were continually re-modelled to accommodate rapidly increasing staffing numbers and demand for meeting room space. Strangely, the constant hum of drilling and refurbishing lent a kind of energy to the environment, and few seemed to mind it. In some ways, it was symbolic of the relentless energy and drive that permeated the organisation. Whereas many other agencies continued life at a slow, dignified pace, with long leisurely client lunches, Saatchi people were always on a mission. The brothers set the tone by rarely lunching, instead snacking on sandwiches.

I describe the Saatchi paradigm in Chapter 12, and it was this unique management style, evolved by Maurice Saatchi, that helped Saatchi & Saatchi establish its unique reputation in the advertising industry. Saatchi & Saatchi is also where Martin Sorrell, now head of WPP, was finance director, and where Tim Bell conceived his public relations empire, not to mention being the seed bed for numerous other advertising and media ventures. The legacy of this venture is two major agencies both bearing the Saatchi name. Not a bad track record.

The Mind Gym – Instigating Intelligent Interaction

The founders of the Mind Gym conceived the company as a new kind of management consultancy during the build-up to the millennium, in the belief that, for business, the coming decade would be about the mind. They understood that the era of traditional management theory and practice was coming to an end, and that the turbulent conditions of the 2000s would require a radical approach. They rightly predicted that management would make fresh demands of employees. This new generation would need to be smart and agile in order to survive and thrive.

The Mind Gym has always adopted a workshop format, designed to facilitate rapid learning and transformation through interactive processes. The original model of 90-minute sharp, insightful workshops is still a central activity, and clients can now choose from a long list of themes that address all aspects of behaviour at work.

This foundation has now expanded in several directions, and the Mind Gym works intensively with its clients in extended interactive workshops designed to engineer change throughout organisations.

The original Kensington headquarters exudes a quiet hum of smart people being busy, and the model has now expanded to the USA with offices recently established in New York City.

Pixar – Creating an Ideas Playground

Any list of the best companies has to include animation studio Pixar, because it exemplifies so many of the features that distinguish the best from the rest.

Pixar seems to have learned from several other excellent California companies, and set out to establish a humane and slightly quirky physical space. This isn't surprising, given that the company was developed through an alliance between its founder John Lasseter, George Lucas of *Star Wars* fame, Steve Jobs of Apple, and the Disney company (Lasseter's ex-employer).

The interior of Pixar is a visual treat, as may be expected from a business dedicated to making ground-breaking animated films. Built in 2000, but designed to look like a much older factory, the huge interior space is divided into different areas for individual work (idiosyncratically reflecting the tastes of their occupants). Group work areas are another feature (like the storyboard workshops which are central to the way Pixar works, because everything is driven by the stories and the Disney-style storyboards used to develop them). And, of course, state-of-the-art technology for animation and production is evident in abundance.

In the central atrium is Café Luxo, complete with games facilities (table foosball is popular – and yes, it really is called foosball!). And this is really the key to the building, because it encourages everyone to socialise and interact freely.

Creating animations is very painstaking and labour-intensive, so the staff work long hours. Pixar wants its people to work hard but to play too. The philosophy is that the purpose of the organisation is to make the highest quality entertainment, so the people engaged in the process must not only be on top of their game but also must enjoy themselves while they work. As a result, the atmosphere is playful, with a lot of spontaneous humour pervading the building.

Apple – Sustaining an Atmosphere of Maverick Thinking

In Cupertino, California, Apple is housed in a circle of six low-rise buildings which form the hub of the business. In the middle of the complex, called the infinite loop, is the cafeteria, designed so everyone crosses everyone else's path every day.

The infinite loop is an excellent metaphor for the way Apple works, as the company operates an egalitarian structure with a loose arrangement of teams. Each team has a focus on its own project and also interacts with other teams as and when required. Apple is confident of the motivation of its people, and a hierarchical structure and traditional employee motivation schemes aren't needed.

Apple's bases its unique ethos on exclusively selecting what it calls A-team players – self-motivated, confident individuals working at the peak of their skills. As a result, there's no micro management; employees work to their own schedules (no clocking in or out), and the company expects them to pace themselves appropriately to meet individual and team goals.

This flat structure and fluid pattern of work foster an atmosphere in which each individual is valued both for personal and group performance. You can measure the success of this apparently relaxed approach by looking at Apple's phenomenal growth in the past decade.

And Apple isn't finished with the infinite loop. Plans are afoot to create a 3-million-square-foot glass doughnut-shaped headquarters. A doughnut shape is a torus, and *torus* is a mathematical term for – an infinite loop.

DPA – Thinking Space

However large and complex a company may be, sometimes space and time to think are invaluable, as is a guiding hand when navigating through turbulent waters. These activities are the special province of DPA, a unique management consultancy based in Godalming, Surrey.

One of the critical measures of a successful business is retention, and DPA scores highly both with clients, many of whom have been with the consultancy for more than a decade, and staff. Indeed, DPA is one of a handful of UK businesses to have earned the prestigious gold Investors in People award.

Working with an international client base of household-name clients, DPA predicates its unique ethos on doing worthwhile work for worthwhile people. DPA has a genuine and deep commitment to work exclusively with clients it respects, and this single-mindedness has brought deserved success.

LEGO – Building a Business Brick by Brick

A classic creative thinking question is, 'How many uses can you think of for a brick?' LEGO is one answer.

What are the odds of a small family business based on simple wooden toys surviving? What if that business is run by a carpenter living in a remote village during a recession, and his workshop has just burned down?

Ole Kirk Christiansen not only survived these inauspicious beginnings in 1912, but also the company that became LEGO has won many battles on the route to its current status as one of the world's best-loved and best-known brands.

In the early days, the area was so poor that Christiansen sometimes had to trade products for food. When the company decided to move into plastics in 1947, another factory fire nearly thwarted the plan. Moreover, potential customers and retailers were initially resistant to the idea of plastic.

Part of the LEGO story is one of persistence in the face of adversity. As a third-generation family business (one of the largest privately owned firms in the world), that backbone is still evident.

LEGO is a remarkable company by any standards. The small village of Billund in central Denmark, where LEGO began, now boasts an international airport capable of handling jumbo jets. The original Legoland Park adjacent to the headquarters handles more than a million visitors a year.

The company is characterised by careful planning, expanding only after thorough research and when conditions are right. LEGO has resisted many suitors wanting to take it in different directions. The result has been a track record of consistent growth, with only one blip in the 1990s, from which it rapidly recovered.

One step at a time, it has become involved in top-quality licensing in association with *Star Wars*, *Harry Potter*, and Disney's *Winnie the Pooh*, for example. It's also extended its franchise to younger children with Duplo, and older ones with Technic, which includes sophisticated robotics. In addition, LEGO has developed its interests in education and business, with products designed for each discipline.

If you visit LEGO at its headquarters in rural Denmark, it's striking that the site looks more like a university campus than a toy factory. On the campus are extensive research and development facilities and a substantial LEGO University designed for staff and visitors, creating a collegiate atmosphere. The innovation culture is deeply embedded, and staff are given ample space and time to let their work flourish.

All of this is rooted in an ethos based on the brick, which is both the product and the symbol for the way the company operates. If you meet a LEGO executive, you'll be given a business card which is a personalised LEGO figurine. One brick at a time, indeed.

Chiat\Day – Reinventing Creativity

From outside to inside, there was nothing conventional about the advertising agency Chiat\Day. The front entrance of the original building in Venice, California, was an enormous pair of binoculars designed by the sculptor Claes Oldenberg. The building itself was the work of the architect Frank Gehry. This assertive statement was a symbolic confirmation of a unique advertising agency described as daring, controversial and visionary.

Chiat\Day was created in 1962 with the merger between two small Los Angeles agencies seeking bigger clients. At every level, Chiat\Day set out to prove itself as the embodiment of creative imagination. The founder and CEO, Jay Chiat, worked on the principle that 'good enough is not good enough'. This single-minded vision permeated the agency and produced fiercely loyal staff who helped it win a string of major clients and industry awards.

This intense creative focus reached a peak in 1984 when Chiat\Day hired Ridley Scott to direct the world-famous hammer-thrower commercial for the launch of the Apple Macintosh computer. While Chiat\Day remained a great place to work, however, Jay Chiat's uncompromising personality led to the agency dropping clients who did not fit its demanding ethos, and it also lost several major accounts to bigger agencies that offered a more comprehensive (and well-behaved) service. The agency moved from its iconic offices and was taken over by the international group TBWA.

St Luke's – Redefining Creativity

St Luke's, a London advertising agency, had its roots in the California culture of Chiat Day. Under its CEO, Andy Law, it developed a uniquely British perspective on the business of creativity.

Through Law's stewardship, St Luke's became a magnet for young creative talent and the rare breed of clients who actively sought to break conventional boundaries and test the limits. The result was some extraordinarily original and memorable advertising that made an impact out of all proportion to the size of the agency at the time. If many of the commercials St Luke's produced look less original now, it's because many of the agency's innovations became part of the fabric of current creative thinking.

Not only was St Luke's an original creative environment, but also the company was deliberately a different kind of place to work. For example, it introduced stand-up meetings (always brief and to the point) and hot desking, in which many employees use the same workspace. And it placed clients in meeting rooms that looked nothing like conventional meeting rooms. Again, many of the practices that seemed outrageous at the time have now become accepted convention. The agency is still independent, both in spirit and ownership.

Caffeine – Stimulating Business

Caffeine Partnership is a UK specialist in business, branding and personal growth. Caffeine is unique because it doesn't exist, at least not in the conventional sense: whereas several of the businesses I mention in this chapter were or are based in the most sumptuous premises, the partners in Caffeine don't subscribe to traditional conventions about offices, and they operate in a virtual space.

The partners are seasoned professionals, well known and respected in their fields, who work closely with selected clients requiring advice at the highest level.

Caffeine predicates its ethos on a firm belief that clients are best engaged in their own environments, which is why traditional offices are unnecessary. The partners' innovative approach to management organisation extends to all levels of their client interactions. Partner Andy Milligan's provocative book *Bold* (Kogan Page) is a manifesto for Caffeine's commitment to making good businesses smarter throughout.

Jack Tinker – Achieving Creativity Heaven

The television series *Mad Men* was set in the post Second World War era of the great American recovery – the consumer boom when everything seemed possible and attainable. A central figure in this period of explosive growth was Marion Harper, who is remembered for two great achievements:

- ✔ Creating the world's first global advertising giant, Interpublic.
- ✔ Nurturing a tiny advertising agency that lasted only six years, Jack Tinker

What made Jack Tinker unique? The answer is: everything. Unlike other New York agencies, for which Madison Avenue was the centre of the universe, the Jack Tinker agency was housed in the penthouse suite of a discreet Manhattan hotel. This exotic location featured elaborate, sensuous décor, including a French-style zinc bar. Entrance, as in an exclusive club, was by invitation only, because Tinker didn't do pitches. It also employed women executives in a sexist industry, one of whom was Mary Wells, who went on to become a major force in the industry.

Jack Tinker was conceived as an elite think tank, the first of its kind, and employed only the top creative talent, making it the most desirable place to work in New York. It also made innovative use of psychologists and anthropologists to inform its thinking.

Another distinguishing feature was that the agency worked under conditions of total secrecy, with a small repertoire of hand-picked clients, lending it an air of mystery. For the first few years it worked solely for Harper's McCann-Erickson clients on special projects, before widening its horizons in the mid-1960s.

As Jack Tinker grew, it became a victim of its own success and was sold in 1966. For six brief years, it redefined the way a truly creative hothouse could inspire its clients, and it changed the face of Madison Avenue. Jack Tinker left a legacy that can be seen in some of the more original and imaginative agencies to this day.

Chapter 18

Ten Unusually Creative Individuals

Creativity doesn't happen on its own; it's always driven by individuals with vision, drive and determination to get their ideas across. Many of the best examples of creativity, taken for granted in today's culture, were once radical innovations. Some were ridiculed when first aired, others were ignored. Fortunately, others were received enthusiastically. You never can tell with creativity.

These are some of the individuals whose creative contributions have made a positive difference, whatever the odds.

Eric Clapton – Learning His Craft the Hard Way

John Mayall, the veteran English blues musician, spotted the talent of the young Eric Clapton and invited him to join his Bluesbreakers band (the home of many fine British musicians over Mayall's long career). Clapton has described himself during this period as something of a nerd, obsessively interested in the original blues artists, and learning their playing techniques by remorselessly listening to and copying each line of their songs, and working out by ear how they did what they did.

Any musician will tell you two things about this approach. First, it's a mind-numbingly tedious process to deconstruct how a song has been produced (especially when the source material is a poor vinyl recording from decades ago, originating from a single take in a tiny studio with bad acoustics). Second, working out the subtleties of fingering and chord shapes without the benefit of seeing the player in action is incredibly difficult. Mayall had an enormous record collection (said by blues aficionados to be the largest anywhere at that time), and allowed Eric free rein.

Like so many other dedicated creators, Clapton racked up substantially more than Gladwell's recommended 10,000 hours (see Chapter 5) as he perfected his art; he worked assiduously through his mentor's collection and became one of the world's greatest guitarists.

David Hockney – Working at Everyday Creativity

David Hockney has described how he painted and drew every day from early childhood. He made it a habit; 'like cleaning my teeth' is how he put it. Drawing inspiration from his daily life and surroundings, his early works abound with portraits, especially of his mother and father, and the bleak environment of the Bradford area. (Hockney wasn't alone in dramatising his industrial surroundings in stark black-and-white imagery. This was an era in which outsiders like 'angry young men' playwrights and novelists, and social-realism-style portrayals of the working-class domestic life of 'kitchen sink' drama, thrived as people came to terms with post-war austerity.)

Hockney's output has always been prolific, and he has rarely produced a work that doesn't meet his own high standards. I was privileged to have him as a visiting lecturer on several occasions during my fine art course, and when I plucked up the courage to ask how he maintained such consistent and regular output, his answer was characteristically down to earth. He said (with a wry smile) that he just got up in the morning and did it. The implication was that it didn't matter what mood he was in or whether he felt inspired, he just picked up his pencil or brush and began work. Often, he added, he surprised himself with the outcome.

A basic resource shared by many creative individuals is the ability to bring fresh eyes (and all the other senses) to even the most mundane situation. Hockney has now established himself in Bridlington, a classic Victorian resort town in the north of England surrounded by unspoiled countryside. In a remarkable demonstration of his unique and undiminished powers of concentration, he chose to paint the same location every day. Doing so has produced an intriguing insight into his perceptual and technical virtuosity, culminating in an enormous tour de force painting, *Bigger Trees Near Water*, exhibited at the Royal Academy Summer Show in 2009 and later donated to the Tate Gallery.

In this intensive work you can see a clue to Hockney's thinking: he has endless curiosity about the world around him. The site he chose for this epic venture is just a small lane off the main road; it's nothing special, the kind of track you'd drive by every day. It has no distinguishing features or landmarks whatsoever, but Hockney has made you look at it – to *really* see it for the first time, just as he does every day.

If you have a tablet computer, explore David Hockney's current interest. In a recent exhibition of his work (*The Bigger Picture,* at the Royal Academy in 2012) he revealed that his latest obsession is his iPad. Eternally fascinated by technology from Polaroids to lenses, Hockney has always been at the forefront of new methods of depiction. Nowadays, he explains, he begins the day iPad in hand, looking out of the window or drawing a vase of flowers or whatever catches his attention. (If you're interested in the technical details, he usually uses the *Brushes* app.)

Bob Dylan – Reaping the Rewards of Creative Persistence

When the youthful Robert Zimmerman was learning his craft on his journey to becoming Bob Dylan, he took every opportunity he could to play and to learn from his heroes. He grew up in Hibbing, Minnesota, but the city wasn't big enough for his ambition.

Moving to New York City, then the epicentre of the folk scene, Dylan played at every venue that would let him in Greenwich Village, while he was still wet behind the ears. Contemporaries have commented that in the early days his singing and guitar-playing left a lot to be desired, and he suffered a great deal of rejection by hard-nosed musicians. But he persisted and his passion and commitment got him on the stage, where he proved a quick learner.

On hearing that his hero Woody Guthrie was terminally ill, Dylan travelled to the hospital and stayed at Guthrie's bedside. There, Dylan listened to Guthrie's life story and shared his songs, as he kept Guthrie, his wife and son Arlo company – another example of his unswerving commitment.

Here again is a pattern, established very early, where the artist worked assiduously to develop his raw talent into a whole by unremitting work. He's still on his 'never-ending tour', as he calls it, playing an extraordinarily gruelling schedule of gigs every year, while at the same time exploring new musical avenues and proving himself an entertaining and knowledgeable DJ.

Brian Eno – Being Eclectic

From his early days as a highly creative art student, Eno became part of the band Roxy Music, contributing to its distinctive sound and appearance. He was an advocate of the collage technique – mixing a variety of styles in sound, words and image, and carried this passion through to his later work.

Although best known as a musician (having created and produced unique, innovative sounds for many major international performers, like David Bowie and U2), Eno has remained at heart an artist, and has many major works to his credit. One of the biggest – *77 Million Paintings* – involved the creation of a vast installation lighting the entire exterior of the Sydney Opera House. This show has since been repeated in other famous venues.

Eno is also responsible for the Microsoft theme – the distinctive burst of sound that announces the start-up on computers (which he wrote on an Apple Mac, because he doesn't like PCs and has never used one).

Like Leonardo da Vinci, Eno has always been a keen diarist and journal keeper, in line with his prodigious output and wide range of interests in music and the arts. Eno's work is characterised by a unique eclecticism, and he finds sources of inspiration everywhere and has constant curiosity about finding new and better techniques with sound and vision.

Vivienne Westwood & Malcolm McLaren – Producing Punk

Punk was a cultural explosion that took place in the 1970s, the impact of which is still being felt today in music, art and fashion. Vivienne Westwood, with her then partner Malcolm McLaren, can lay claim to having invented the genre. From a small boutique in London's King's Road, which underwent several name changes as the pair's thinking evolved, Westwood and McLaren created a series of innovative and controversial garments which grew into the now-familiar punk style. At the same time, McLaren entered the music business, creating and managing the Sex Pistols and cultivating other musicians in the punk idiom.

Westwood, as a self-taught fashion designer (she'd designed her own wedding dress), combined inspirations drawn from taboo and esoteric corners of culture such as bikers, bondage, fetishism and prostitution, with traditional fabrics and cutting techniques, resulting in outrageously original looks.

Just as punk has survived long beyond its predicted life, so has Westwood's unique vision. In the 1980s, she established herself in haute couture, where she remains a significant and influential force. Her work continues to be characterised by limitless curiosity and a willingness to stretch the boundaries of taste. Although many of her creations were mocked at the time of their launch, it remains fascinating to see how many of even her more outrageous ideas are quickly incorporated into mainstream design and celebrity culture.

As an inveterate radical, Westwood must be quietly amused not only to have been awarded a DBE (Dame of the British Empire), one of the ultimate establishment accolades, but also to have been the subject of a major retrospective at the Victoria and Albert Museum, a privilege granted to few living artists.

Benoit Mandelbrot – Fascinating Fractals

Just as many governments have a *minister without portfolio* (that is, a minister who doesn't head a particular ministry), some enlightened businesses reserve a similar role for special individuals. Benoît Mandelbrot was one of these. He had such a role at IBM's Thomas J Watson Research Center. Officially, Mandelbrot was a fellow, specialising in mathematical topics such as quantitative finance and mathematical physics, but he remained a classic example of the outsider throughout his long career. He spent much of his time on projects of his own devising, leaving others in the dark about what he was up to.

Despite his idiosyncratic way of working, Mandelbrot was a prolific publisher of work on a wide variety of subjects. The sheer scope of his output is impressive, ranging from original thinking about economic cycles through challenges to orthodox thinking on several fronts including information theory and fluid dynamics. He was also responsible for combining several mathematical topics which had previously been thought isolated from each other. His work may have been the product of a butterfly mind, but what a butterfly!

He is most famous for *fractal geometry*, a term he coined himself to describe the repeating patterns found in nature. As an inveterate observer, he studied all kinds of natural phenomena as he evolved his thinking on this topic, including plants (how leaves look like miniature trees), rivers and coastlines (how each rivulet resembles its larger source), and how mountains look like larger versions of hillocks. Similar observations extended into the human body (looking at blood vessels and lungs), and even into the galaxy. He summed up his view of the world with his succinct description of what he memorably called 'regular roughness':

> 'Clouds are not spheres, mountains are not cones, coastlines are not circles, and bark is not smooth, nor does lightning travel in a straight line.' (From Mandelbrot's book *The Fractal Geometry of Nature*.)

Mandelbrot's fascination with fractals, the subject he made his own, has not only cemented his reputation as an original mathematician and thinker, but also established his work as an element of popular culture, in the form of myriad designs that employ fractals.

Anita Roddick – Creating a Body of Work

When a brand dominates the high street, you might assume the brand has always been around. However, when Anita Roddick created The Body Shop, she not only started a new trend in cosmetics, she actually changed the retail environment. The Body Shop (so called because the first one was situated between two undertakers) began as a small enterprise selling ethical cosmetics, which was then a radical idea at the periphery of the market, untapped by the major brands.

However, Roddick had a much bigger vision, and when her husband Bernard returned from a sabbatical, they embarked on a plan for a highly original business which involved franchising the brand, working to a clearly defined ethical manifesto and distinctively branding the products. Along with these initiatives, unorthodox for the time, she retained a rigorously individual stance in all aspects of her business.

Roddick was a visionary thinker, not content with owning a business, but determined to make a difference and leave her mark on the world.

Malcolm Gladwell – Making New Sense

Creative thinking appears in many forms; and sometimes it's manifested by individuals who aren't artists in the conventional sense but who have a unique kind of curiosity and a different way of seeing the world. Malcolm Gladwell is one such one-off. Best known for his books and articles, he uses these as a vehicle for playing with ideas. He's also an engaging speaker, and you can find several examples of his talks on YouTube (www.youtube.com).

So what makes Gladwell stand out from the crowd? He'll often take unlikely starting points for his mental excursions, and many of his observations have entered the vocabulary: *tipping point* (meaning the moment when an idea or product enters public consciousness) is one typical example. He might start with an observation about a mundane product like cola or ketchup, and use it to explore a subtle theme that takes you on a journey of the imagination. His *associative thinking* – finding links where others may not spot them – is a hallmark of his writing. If you're stuck for an idea or searching for inspiration, a brief dip into Gladwell's world is a creative tonic.

Gladwell's unique insights have made him a popular reference point for creative thinkers, and his contributions are much in demand.

Ferran Adrià and El Bulli – Cooking Up Magic

Sometimes creative thinking happens in unlikely locations. While on holiday with his wife on the Costa Brava in Spain in 1961, a German tourist strolled along a remote sandy cove and had a vision. He decided he would build the world's finest restaurant from scratch there; by the time the restaurant closed in 2011, the man had attained his goal.

Another visionary, the chef Ferran Adrià, joined the restaurant in 1984 and then took it over, building it into El Bulli (named after the German's bulldogs). Over the next few years, this tiny place became the best and most sought-after restaurant in the world. Although it accommodated only 8,000 diners during the short season for which it was open each year, the restaurant received more than 2 million requests for bookings.

So what made this little venue so special? Well, the chef at its heart, Ferran Adrià, has been showered with accolades for his work, and has been described as 'the most imaginative generator of haute cuisine on the planet'. Adrià's creativity and passion for exceptional food and for the dining experience was manifested in the way he nurtured his team. He used regular workshops and deployed creative thinking tools like mind maps to encourage his people to think imaginatively about the whole culinary experience. In this idyllic setting, the team would dissect classic recipes and dream up new ones, exploring every nuance of every ingredient.

Nothing was too small or insignificant for their forensic analysis at El Bulli. The last course of the final meal in 2011 was a peach Melba, the original recipe for which was created by Adrià's hero, Escoffier, to honour Dame Nellie Melba, the Australian soprano. Starting from the notion that the original recipe could not be improved, the team decided instead to take it apart and play with the ingredients. The result is too exotic to describe in full, but one detail worth thinking about is that they even made an edible mould of the peach stone, filled with essence of the fruit. That's creative thinking!

Chefs and restaurants around the world have adopted Adrià's ideas, and his thinking has inspired top-rated chefs such as the UK's award-winning Heston Blumenthal. Philanthropic by nature, Adrià is planning a centre for creativity as his legacy, and there are rumours that El Bulli will reopen soon.

Richard Hamilton – Inspiring a Generation

Many artists have been described as influential, but in twentieth-century Britain, few have deserved this accolade more than Richard Hamilton.

Building on an early fascination for Dada, an avant-garde art movement, and the work of Marcel Duchamp in particular, Hamilton explored a number of themes associated with this revolutionary genre and incorporated them in his work. So many of his works combine political satire, fine draftsmanship (often used subversively) and collage. He reconstructed a major work by Marcel Duchamp – *The Large Glass* (also known as *The Bride Stripped Bare by her Bachelors, Even*) – which had been smashed in transit to the USA some years earlier. His major exhibition at the Tate Gallery in 1966 influenced a generation of artists and students, including David Hockney and Peter Blake, both of whom he'd championed at the Royal College of Art.

As an active and enthusiastic lecturer, Hamilton was a mentor to many students, including Bryan Ferry of the band Roxy Music. Many of Hamilton's ideas about art, especially about collage, are evident in Roxy Music's highly original output (their work has been described as 'sound paintings').

As a central figure in the art and culture of the 1960s, Hamilton is widely regarded as the originator of pop art – he was certainly one of the first to use that description – and has a reputation based on a prolific output of collage paintings and politically inspired satirical works. He was also an early adopter of computers and advocate for their use in art – just another little heresy in a career of individuality.

Index

• T •

About the Author

From his roots as a student of fine art, David graduated in psychology and became a clinical psychologist at Oxford before moving into the business world as a consultant to advertising agencies and their clients. Developing his early interest in the subject, David has become a leading global expert on creativity and innovation. In addition to his original background in fine art and clinical psychology, David is an elected Fellow of the Chartered Institute of Marketing and an NLP Practitioner, and has chaired and spoken at many international conferences and seminars.

Dedication

My thanks to Kerry Laundon for commissioning this book, and to all the friends, clients and mentors who have helped me.

Acknowledgements

To Sandi, my muse.

Publisher's Acknowledgements

We're proud of this book; please send us your comments at `http://dummies.custhelp.com`. For other comments, please contact our Customer Care Department within the U.S. at 877-762-2974, outside the U.S. at (001) 317-572-3993, or fax 317-572-4002.

Some of the people who helped bring this book to market include the following:

Acquisitions, Editorial, and Vertical Websites

Project Editor: Steve Edwards

Commissioning Editor: Kerry Laundon

Assistant Editor: Ben Kemble

Development Editor: Kathleen Dobie

Copy Editor: Kate O'Leary

Technical Editor: Gillian Burn

Proofreader: Mary White

Production Manager: Daniel Mersey

Publisher: Miles Kendall

Cover Photos: @ imacon/iStock

Cartoons: Rich Tennant, `www.the5thwave.com`

Composition Services

Project Coordinator: Kristie Rees

Layout and Graphics: Amy Hassos, Jennifer Henry

Indexer: Christine Karpeles

Special Help

Brand reviewer: Carrie Burchfield, Zoë Wykes

FOR DUMMIES®

Making Everything Easier!™

UK editions

BUSINESS

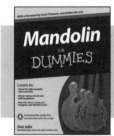

978-1-118-34689-1

978-1-118-44349-1

978-1-119-97527-4

MUSIC

978-1-119-94276-4

978-0-470-97799-6

978-0-470-66372-1

HOBBIES

978-1-118-41156-8

978-1-119-99417-6

978-1-119-97250-1

Asperger's Syndrome For Dummies
978-0-470-66087-4

Basic Maths For Dummies
978-1-119-97452-9

**Body Language For Dummies,
2nd Edition**
978-1-119-95351-7

Boosting Self-Esteem For Dummies
978-0-470-74193-1

Business Continuity For Dummies
978-1-118-32683-1

Cricket For Dummies
978-0-470-03454-5

Diabetes For Dummies, 3rd Edition
978-0-470-97711-8

eBay For Dummies, 3rd Edition
978-1-119-94122-4

English Grammar For Dummies
978-0-470-05752-0

Flirting For Dummies
978-0-470-74259-4

IBS For Dummies
978-0-470-51737-6

ITIL For Dummies
978-1-119-95013-4

**Management For Dummies,
2nd Edition**
978-0-470-97769-9

**Managing Anxiety with CBT
For Dummies**
978-1-118-36606-6

**Neuro-linguistic Programming
For Dummies, 2nd Edition**
978-0-470-66543-5

Nutrition For Dummies, 2nd Edition
978-0-470-97276-2

Organic Gardening For Dummies
978-1-119-97706-3

**Available wherever books are sold. For more information or to order direct go to
www.wiley.com or call +44 (0) 1243 843291**

FOR DUMMIES

Making Everything Easier! ™

UK editions

SELF-HELP

978-0-470-66541-1

978-1-119-99264-6

978-0-470-66086-7

LANGUAGES

978-0-470-68815-1

978-1-119-97959-3

978-0-470-69477-0

HISTORY

978-0-470-68792-5

978-0-470-74783-4

978-0-470-97819-1

Origami Kit For Dummies
978-0-470-75857-1

Overcoming Depression For Dummies
978-0-470-69430-5

Positive Psychology For Dummies
978-0-470-72136-0

PRINCE2 For Dummies, 2009 Edition
978-0-470-71025-8

Project Management For Dummies
978-0-470-71119-4

Psychology Statistics For Dummies
978-1-119-95287-9

Psychometric Tests For Dummies
978-0-470-75366-8

Renting Out Your Property For Dummies, 3rd Edition
978-1-119-97640-0

Rugby Union For Dummies, 3rd Edition
978-1-119-99092-5

Sage One For Dummies
978-1-119-95236-7

Self-Hypnosis For Dummies
978-0-470-66073-7

Storing and Preserving Garden Produce For Dummies
978-1-119-95156-8

Teaching English as a Foreign Language For Dummies
978-0-470-74576-2

Time Management For Dummies
978-0-470-77765-7

Training Your Brain For Dummies
978-0-470-97449-0

Voice and Speaking Skills For Dummies
978-1-119-94512-3

Work-Life Balance For Dummies
978-0-470-71380-8

Available wherever books are sold. For more information or to order direct go to www.wiley.com or call +44 (0) 1243 843291

FOR DUMMIES®

Making Everything Easier! ™

COMPUTER BASICS

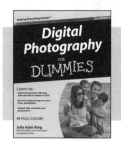

978-1-118-11533-6

978-0-470-61454-9

978-0-470-49743-2

DIGITAL PHOTOGRAPHY

978-1-118-09203-3

978-0-470-76878-5

978-1-118-00472-2

SCIENCE AND MATHS

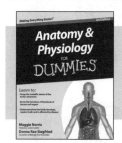

978-0-470-92326-9

978-0-470-55964-2

978-0-470-90324-7

Art For Dummies
978-0-7645-5104-8

Computers For Seniors For Dummies, 3rd Edition
978-1-118-11553-4

Criminology For Dummies
978-0-470-39696-4

Currency Trading For Dummies, 2nd Edition
978-0-470-01851-4

Drawing For Dummies, 2nd Edition
978-0-470-61842-4

Forensics For Dummies
978-0-7645-5580-0

French For Dummies, 2nd Edition
978-1-118-00464-7

Guitar For Dummies, 2nd Edition
978-0-7645-9904-0

Hinduism For Dummies
978-0-470-87858-3

Index Investing For Dummies
978-0-470-29406-2

Islamic Finance For Dummies
978-0-470-43069-9

Knitting For Dummies, 2nd Edition
978-0-470-28747-7

Music Theory For Dummies, 2nd Edition
978-1-118-09550-8

Office 2010 For Dummies
978-0-470-48998-7

Piano For Dummies, 2nd Edition
978-0-470-49644-2

Photoshop CS6 For Dummies
978-1-118-17457-9

Schizophrenia For Dummies
978-0-470-25927-6

WordPress For Dummies, 5th Edition
978-1-118-38318-6

Think you can't learn it in a day? Think again!

The *In a Day* e-book series from *For Dummies* gives you quick and eas
access to learn a new skill, brush up on a hobby, or enhance your
personal or professional life — all in a day. Easy!

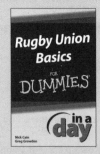

Available as
PDF, eMobi
and Kindle